EDWARD WINDSOR

ROYAL ENIGMA

EDWARD WINDSOR

Royal Enigma

THE TRUE STORY *of the*
SEVENTH IN LINE
to the BRITISH THRONE

WENDY LEIGH

POCKET BOOKS
New York London Toronto
Sydney Tokyo Singapore

To my parents, with love and thanks.

Contents

Author's Note

ON OCTOBER 8, 1998, AFTER MONTHS OF PRELIMINARY research, I wrote a letter to Geoffrey Crawford, press secretary to the Queen, informing him that I was writing a biography of Prince Edward and requesting a meeting with the prince.

I received no reply.

When I telephoned the palace press office, I was referred to David Tuck, assistant press secretary to the Queen. On December 3, 1998, I was invited to meet with him at Buckingham Palace. I was instructed to enter by the Privy Purse Door (which faces Pall Mall). As arranged, I arrived at Buckingham Palace at three. I gave the guard my name and was allowed to enter the vast iron gates into the palace courtyard. Just before I went into the palace itself, I turned for a moment and looked back at the forecourt, with Queen Victoria's statue in the center. I had never before viewed the statue from such a privileged vantage point. And as a British subject, born and bred, it was impossible not to feel a sense of wonder.

One of my earliest memories is of the coronation of Queen Elizabeth II. I was a very small child at the time, but I was permitted to watch the late-night fireworks. I remember the excitement, the grandeur, and my prized plastic replica of the Queen's coronation coach. The Queen was extremely pretty then, and the Duke of Edinburgh was debonair and handsome. They were revered by the entire nation.

Like most English children of my generation, I pored adoringly over respectful newspaper reports of the royal family and lovingly composed scrapbooks celebrating Princess Margaret's wedding to Antony Armstrong-Jones, and Katharine Worsley's to the Duke of Kent. I watched admiringly as Charles and Anne (who was exactly my age) grew up basking in the then gentle spotlight of public adulation. Strange as it may now appear, the royal children seemed to be connected to me and to all other British children.

When my stepsister, Madeleine, was fifteen, she was admitted to the National Heart Hospital for a painful, yet life-saving operation. While she was recovering, Princess Alexandra visited her ward. She spoke to Madeleine for a few moments, then posed for a picture with her. I was there when that photograph arrived in the mail. Madeleine was overjoyed, her suffering temporarily forgotten. At that moment, I understood the magical power of the British monarchy.

Through the years that followed, I watched as that magic diminished and the royals became mortal. As a journalist, I was often privy to the process. In the early eighties, I wrote about Diana and Fergie and their less-than-royal behavior for *New Woman*. For *US* magazine, I interviewed Prince Charles's valet, Stephen Barry, who accompanied the prince and Diana on their honeymoon. He confided to me various negative, intimate details about the private lives of the royal family.

It was clear then that the fairy tale in which I and the nation had once believed was coming to an end and that the fallout would irrevocably damage the British monarchy.

■   ■   ■

Once inside Buckingham Palace on December 3, 1998, I was introduced to David Tuck, a friendly, informal young man more like a kindly bank manager than someone representing the Queen of England. He showed me into an anteroom on the ground floor of the palace, and a valet brought coffee and chocolate biscuits.

Tuck asked me a few short questions about the book. Although he was consistently courteous, he made it clear that Prince Edward would not be granting me an interview and that if I had any questions, my best resource was the royal internet site.

I nibbled on a chocolate biscuit and realized that my visit to the palace had been relatively pointless.

In 1950 my aunt had tea at Buckingham Palace. She had been invited there by the Queen and Prince Philip because she had assisted in the delivery of Prince Charles and they were grateful.

In November 1948, my aunt was working as a nursing sister in London and was personally selected by the Queen's physician to assist in the delivery of her first child. The birth was expected to be difficult, and it was decided that the Queen should have a cesarean section.

On the evening of November 14, 1948, the Queen underwent a cesarean. Outside the operating room, Prince Philip paced the floor impatiently. Finally, unable to bear the tension, he opted to play squash on the palace courts with his private secretary, Lieutenant Commander Michael Parker. He had just finished his postgame swim, when Sir Alan "Tommy" Lascelles, King George VI's private secretary, arrived with the news that the Queen had given birth to a son. Without even waiting to dry his hair, Prince Philip dashed through the drawing room into a suite by the Buhl Room, which Queen Mary had transformed into a surgery many years before.

The Queen was still under the influence of the anesthetic. After Philip looked at his newborn son, he waited in an anteroom for the Queen to regain consciousness. Then he noticed my aunt.

She was twenty-five years old and indisputably beautiful. Statuesque, with lustrous long black hair and a shy smile, some said she reminded them of Ingrid Bergman. He perched on the arm of the couch on which she was sitting. He leaned towards her and stroked her hair. "You remind me of the girls from the Greek islands where I grew up," he said. Flustered, my aunt tried to make conversation and said, "It must be lovely living in Buckingham Palace." Prince Philip shook his head. "The palace is like a prison," he said wistfully.

His momentary flirtation did not go any further. Subsequently, my aunt was on standby to assist at Princess Anne's birth, should it be a cesarean. At the last minute, it was decided that the Queen deliver her second child without one, and my aunt was not called upon to assist. However, in September 1950, she was invited to Buckingham Palace for tea, at which she was served Lyons' Swiss Rolls, the British equivalent of Tootsie Rolls. Other than that, she received no letter of thanks from the palace, was not paid an honorarium, nor did she ask for one. When Princess Anne married Captain Mark Phillips, my aunt and uncle were invited to the wedding in recognition of her service to the crown in assisting at the delivery of Prince Charles.

On my aunt's seventieth birthday, she was a patient at the Royal Marsden Hospital in London, where she was being treated for cancer. My mother wrote to Prince Charles telling him of my aunt's illness, that she had been the first person to hold him after his birth, and that it would mean so much to her to receive birthday greetings from him. There was no reaction from Prince Charles or the palace. A year later, my aunt died in the Royal Marsden Hospital, of which the Queen is the patron.

The palace's inability to respond to the letter informing them of my aunt's terminal illness is indicative of the palace's bureaucratic inefficiency.

■   ■   ■

In April 1999, a full six months after my original letter to Geoffrey Crawford, I received a letter from Prince Edward's private secretary, Lieutenant Colonel Sean O'Dwyer. I had sent him a copy of my biography of John F. Kennedy Jr. and had requested an interview with him. He thanked me for the book, before stating that he and the prince had only recently heard about my new book. He went on to intimate that I had given the impression to others that this book had been authorized by Prince Edward. I wrote back telling him that I had never done so. I also pointed out that the palace had been officially informed of my book in October 1998 and that I had met with David Tuck on December 3, 1998.

I received no reply from the colonel.

Months before Lieutenant Colonel O'Dwyer wrote to me, it was obvious that Prince Edward was exercising his influence by conveying to potential sources that they should not talk to me. Film director Robin Bextor, who still works closely with Edward and has been characterized by those who know Edward well as being one of his best friends, initially refused my requests for an interview. Subsequently, we sat next to each other at a Christmas party held at Michel's restaurant in Chiswick, London, on December 14, 1998. Robin was charming, and the conversation centered around an upcoming Ardent production on Mick Jagger. After I told him that during my journalistic career I had interviewed Bianca Jagger, as well as other sources close to Mick, and offered to provide him with Jagger material, he agreed to talk to me about Edward. I telephoned him in January 1999 and invited him to have lunch with me on February 11 at Quo Vadis restaurant in Soho.

A few days before the lunch, Robin's personal assistant informed me that Robin would not be meeting me. Afterwards, he sent me a message via an intermediary that I had no right to put him in this book.

On March 16, 1999, Kay Jennings, assistant to Michael Mavor, Prince Edward's headmaster at Gordonstoun told me, "It is Prince

Edward's wish he doesn't speak to you. Mr. Mavor has to keep faith with Prince Edward." Prince Edward did, however, allow associate producer Christine Carter to write me a letter containing her memories of working with him. She sent him a copy of the letter for his approval, which he granted, without making any alterations.

Other potential interviewees prevaricated, with Edward's former comanaging director, Eben Foggit, discussing the possibility of talking to me, but then deciding not to. Nonetheless, countless sources close to Edward did, indeed, grant me interviews for the book. All interviews were taped, no interviewees were paid, and all of them were made aware of the fact that Prince Edward did not authorize this book.

I was afforded access to a number of libraries, including: BBC TV Archives; the British Film Institute; News International Library; Ealing Central Lending Library; the Electric Library; Associated Newspapers Library; Cambridge County Library; Celebrity Service; the Star, New York; Exeter Central Library; and Winchester Library.

I appreciate the generosity, time, and contributions to the book of Robert Lacey; Michael Cole; Roy Greenslade of the *Guardian*; James Whitaker, *Daily Mirror*; Sandy Williams; Noreen Taylor; Lady Colin Campbell; Steven Gaines; Jackie Holland, *Daily Express*; Gina Oates, Jason Deans, *Broadcast* magazine; Shan Lancaster, *Daily Telegraph*; Judy McGuire, editor, *Sunday* magazine; Erin Sullivan; Anne Adlington; Clare Vidal-Hall; Dame Barbara Cartland; Brenda Bland; Rose Tobias Shaw; Roger Penhale; Mark Nicholls; Elaine Simpson; Claudette Bryanston-Cross of the Cambridge Youth Theater; Ben Ronaldson; Terry Johnston; Sir Alan Cotterell; Lady Cotterell; Paul Daniels; Christine Carter; Paul Connew; Rosalind Clarke of McCann, Coiner, Clarke, Palm Beach; Desmond Wilcox; Sir David Attenborough; Russell Hayes, Top Gear; Sheila O'Brien; Sarah Boszormenyi; Vicki Mutehouse,

BBC Pebble Mill Press Office; Mauro Carraro; Derek Draper; James Campbell; David Tuck, assistant press secretary to Her Majesty the Queen at Buckingham Palace; Jayne Fincher; Steve Gruen; Alexander Slater; Madame Masson of La Grenouille; Carol White, Director of Premier Model Agency; Warris Hussein; Posh of Heart FM Radio; Richard Lay; Steve Poole; James Robinson; Sir Tim Rice; Ned Sherrin; Judy Ledger, Baby Lifeline; Vernon Lettingwell, *Hampshire Chronicle*; Paul Arengo Jones, international award secretary general of Duke of Edinburgh Award; Kate Haywood, Cambridge County Library; Daniel Bee; Howell James; Lord Andrew Lloyd Webber; John Whitney; Emma Wright, BBC Information and Archives; Tara Cole; Kristina Raven, Press Relations, Ritz Paris; Sarah Teal, Teal Productions, New York; Dr. Erika Padan Freeman; Esther Rantzen; Cornelia Guest; Laurence Kraches; Phillipe Goubert; Mark Andre Relave; Martin Sole; Liz O'Brien; Geraldine Aron; Simon Fanshawe; Muriel Britten, Jesus College, Cambridge; Lizzie Malick; Brigadier Robert Tailyour; Nora Veysey of the *Kent and Sussex Courier*; Mary Cavallero; Robin Peverett; Rebecca Michael; Margaret James; the Reverend Trevor Vickery; Harold Brooks-Baker of *Burke's Peerage*; Barry Turtle; Jim Bennett; Vicki Soole of Meridian Television; Dale Headington of *A Regal Reader*; Kathleen Dixon of BFI TV Archives; Stewart Dickson; Colonel Ewen Southby Tailyour; Richard Baker; Bryan Forbes; Nigel Dempster.

The book's unsung heroes and heroines are the confidential sources who took considerable risks in talking to me. These sources requested confidentiality for fear of repercussions if they spoke openly about Edward and Sophie. When a confidential source is cited in the text or notes, the source's relationship with Edward has been documented, the source's credibility is unimpeachable, and the interview is on tape.

Introduction

HIS BUSINESS CARD READS "EDWARD WINDSOR, Television Producer."

But the Queen of England's youngest child is no ordinary man. His mother is one of the wealthiest women in the universe; his ex-sister-in-law, Princess Diana, is an icon; his nephews, Prince William and Prince Harry, are doted on by much of the world; and his bride-to-be, Sophie Rhys-Jones, is a real-life Cinderella.

Until his engagement, in January 1999, Edward Windsor was relatively unknown. Despite his princely status, the spotlight had shone on him only sporadically. First, because he rebelled against the example set by his brothers, Charles and Andrew, and instead of embracing their role of royal action-men, Prince Edward quit the Marines for the theater. By working in the theater, he smashed another stereotype: throughout history, monarchs have tended to pluck their mistresses from the theater, giving rise to the Terence Rattigan play *The Prince and the Showgirl*. But because Edward followed his heart, in his particular case, the prince became the showboy.

When the media accused Edward of being a wimp, of being

gay, and of being arrogant and petulant, instead of following the example of Princess Diana and charming them, he instead embraced the example of his father, Prince Philip, and hit back. Stubborn and perhaps ill-advised, Edward berated the media whenever possible and fought them at every turn. Often, he would lose the battle but, forever dogged, would never capitulate totally and would continue to pursue his ambitions.

Born into astonishing wealth, luxuriating amid a fairy-tale lifestyle, pampered and privileged, Edward Antony Richard Louis Windsor decided he wanted more. The first of the Queen's children to form a business and take on the challenge of conquering the cutthroat television production world, Edward has become an expert in having it both ways.

While posing as an ordinary mortal, striving to make a buck, at thirty-five, Edward receives an annual £96,000 ($156,480) from his mother, has the financial backing of his father's close associates, and uses his royal connections as much as possible. In spite of debts that would sink the *Titanic*, Edward's television company, Ardent Productions, continues to stay afloat, while he claims that he is both a producer and a star.

And if his admiring public expect a prince of the realm to be above reproach, they will be disappointed. Taking a leaf out of the book of the legendary Al Jolson (who insisted that he be credited as cowriter on every song he introduced—but had not written—and that he be paid fifty percent of all royalties), Edward regularly demands credits when he has not fully earned them.

In that, he is no different from countless Hollywood moguls. He is battling to succeed in the only commercial arena open to him: making television documentaries primarily centering around his heritage and his family. And who would blame him? Fate has dealt him spectacularly good cards. He can but play them.

So that while Edward's brothers, Charles and Andrew, and his sister, Anne, focus their efforts on charitable causes, Edward (while doing some of the same) hankers to be a success in the real world. Not content to merely remain a steward of the royal fortune, in the best American tradition, he has set out to make his own fortune.

His rebellious, stubborn nature also asserted itself in his choice of a bride. Unlike his brother Charles before him, he refused to be prematurely pushed into marriage with an aristocrat. Instead, he bided his time and picked a commoner as his future wife. He has resolved to form a modern, working partnership with Sophie Rhys-Jones, who will continue working in public relations after she and Edward are married. By marrying a commoner, one who (unlike Sarah Ferguson, whose paternal grandfather was the first cousin of the third Viscount Hampton and whose paternal grandmother was a granddaughter of the sixth Duke of Buccleuch and a cousin of Prince Alice, Duchess of Gloucester) had no connection with the royal family, Edward is progressing even further towards becoming the People's Prince.

But unlike Princess Diana, Prince Edward lacks the common touch. When one thousand members of the staff at the royal residences (Windsor Castle, Buckingham Palace, Balmoral, and Sandringham), all of whom had catered to Edward for many years, were invited to contribute to his wedding present, only £200 ($326) was raised.

The staff had not forgiven or forgotten that the Prince had charged them each a £20 ($32.60) admission fee to attend a January 1999 party he had thrown for them. Many of the staff earn just £7,000 ($9,100) a year, and when they received a memo asking them for contributions for Edward's wedding present, they balked. "It's traditional for the staff to buy a dinner service for the royal couple and most people put a fiver in, but Prince Edward is very unpopular and it looks like it could be a couple of egg cups this time," a source confided to journalist Fiona Barton of the *Mail on Sunday.*

Unfortunately, Edward sometimes lapses into the petulant arrogance of a spoiled youngest son who also happens to be a prince of the realm. But marriage has softened many an arrogant young man, and may well do the same for Edward. However, Sophie Rhys-Jones, the commoner who has snared a prince, is probably far too enthralled by her good fortune in marrying him to rock the boat by attempting to tame him. Her attitude towards her impending nuptials is perhaps encapsulated by the following incident:

One Sunday evening at the end of September 1995, Prince Edward had a previous engagement, leaving Sophie at home. She whiled away the evening watching the BBC television dramatization of *Pride and Prejudice*, Jane Austen's fable of love and marriage. Millions of British television viewers also tuned in to watch, marveling at the romance between Austen's heroine, Elizabeth Bennet, and her masterful hero, Darcy. Darcy was played by Colin Firth, who won legions of fans with his brooding, sexually charged performance. And when Elizabeth—after a series of trials and tribulations—managed to marry Darcy and move into Pemberley, his palatial mansion, women all over Britain sighed and cheered the romantic conclusion of Austen's timeless love story.

The next day, Sophie lunched with a friend. She had one comment and one comment alone to make about *Pride and Prejudice*. "Oh," she gushed, "did you see that house?" Her companion nodded, slightly bemused. Sophie leaned closer. "You know," she declared, "that's what I want."

After she walks down the aisle of St. George's Chapel, Windsor, and marries her prince, Sophie Rhys-Jones will have it all: a prince, an £8 million ($13 million) home, and the applause of a nation. But as she recites her vows, one or two of the guests thronging the chapel may fancy that they hear the faint echo of shrill, mocking laughter: the distinctive laughter of Princess Diana. "If the ghost of Princess Diana is hovering over the wedding, she will laugh uproariously and say something like, 'Sophie Rhys-Jones! Who the hell is she? After all I've gone through—she's actually marrying into the same family? She must be insane,'" said a friend of Diana's.

"To Diana, Sophie was just a PR girlie on the make. She ignored her. Sophie is desperately trying to be what Diana already was—an aristocrat. Diana did not like Sophie's attitude, 'I'm Sophie Rhys-Jones, a member of the royal family and you will behave with respect in my company.' Diana was completely the opposite to that. If Diana came to your house, she just got down on the floor and played with the kids. Diana was more aristocratic than the Windsors. She did not feel in any way inferior to them. She stood up to them because she wasn't afraid of them. Whereas Sophie will look up to them. She will see them as aristocrats and better than she is. So she will toe the line and do exactly what she is told."

When Sophie marries Edward, she will, indeed, promise to obey him. In the process, she will also obey his family. For Sophie—to say the least, a smart cookie—is fully aware that she is not merely marrying a man, but an institution with magical, almost mystical powers. And while the years have served to tarnish some of the monarchy's magic and erode much of its powers, Sophie knows that she and Edward could prove to be the saving of it. For while their marriage is undoubtedly a love match, it is also the crystallization of a highly modern and attractive image: that of the working prince and his working bride, laboring together to create a brave new universe for themselves, their family, and their country. As such, Edward and Sophie will be in the forefront of leading the British royal family into the millennium.

EDWARD WINDSOR

ROYAL ENIGMA

1

CHILD OF THE
MODERN MONARCHY

*O*N JUNE 21, 1969, EXACTLY THIRTY YEARS, LESS TWO days, before the wedding of Edward Windsor and Sophie Rhys-Jones, Richard Cawston's documentary, *Royal Family*, was broadcast to forty million British viewers. The 105-minute film afforded a rapt audience their first ever glimpse of the Windsors' private lives. The resultant shock waves that shot through the British public can only be compared to those experienced by Americans when first lady Jacqueline Kennedy opened the White House to television cameras. Until the release of the film, the only television coverage of herself and her family that the Queen had permitted her adoring public was the broadcast of a select few ceremonial events, such as the State Opening of Parliament. Even then, the Queen sternly decreed that any close-ups of her were categorically forbidden.

The British monarchy dated back a thousand years and their private lives had always been shrouded in mystery. Rarely had the Queen been filmed without her crown or a formal hat, and never in relaxed, intimate circumstances. Nor had she ever been heard to speak, except when uttering scripted lines or elegantly crafted speeches. As far as the great British public were concerned, since time immemorial, the royal family were forever fixed in their imagination as smiling constantly, waving delicately, doing good works, and sailing through life with grace and fortitude, ever the perfect upper-class English family.

Two brilliantly gifted Australians were destined to shatter that image. In 1787, the British commenced the unjust practice of transporting convicts to Australia. There, they colonized the country, in the process founding a new nation. Kowtowing to the British royal family was not the birthright of Australians. In the second half of the twentieth century, Australians (unlike the British) were unaccustomed to worshipping the royal family uncritically. Moreover, many of them felt that the royal family needed to be brought down to earth and humanized. Thus it was that two Australians finally had the last laugh on the British establishment that had exiled many of their countrymen's forebears. Their names were Rupert Murdoch and William Heseltine. Murdoch, whose own story would play itself out in the years following the release of *Royal Family*, owned newspapers whose blunt reporting would ultimately cause the royal family's image to crack irrevocably.

But it was William Heseltine who, albeit unconscious of the long-term ramifications of his plan, unleashed the process of shattering, then re-forming the image of the Windsors. Heseltine, who in 1969 was appointed by the Queen as press secretary, had been privileged to see her privately in a more relaxed mode. He was charmed and resolved that the British public be afforded a similar view of the monarch—one that might reassure them that the royals were not gods, but more like the average family. At the time, he said of the Queen and her family, "No one knew them as people; we needed to make them more rounded and human for the general public." His solution was *Royal Family*, which was also conceived to coincide with Prince Charles's investiture as Prince of Wales.

Between June 8, 1968, and May 18, 1969, a film crew would

spend seventy-five days filming the royal family. Forty-three hours of film of the family in almost two hundred locations would be edited down to one hour and fifty minutes.

However, before Richard Cawston, head of BBC documentaries, embarked on the project, he enthusiastically informed David Attenborough, the controller of BBC 2, of his coup. Attenborough, a highly respected documentary maker, cautioned, "You're killing the monarchy, you know, with this film you're making. The whole institution depends on mystique and the tribal chief in his hut. If any member of the tribe ever sees inside the hut, then the whole system of tribal chiefdom is damaged and the tribe eventually disintegrates."

Thirty years later, Attenborough elaborated, "If you show that royalty is the same as we are, the consequence is that we no longer understand why we should invest royalty with all with which we do invest them. If you want to have symbols and images and you use a human being for that, you must cast that human being in a different role and remove him from everyday life."

As a child, the Queen studied *The English Constitution*, a classic work by Walter Bagehot, the respected Victorian economist and man of letters. Bagehot had written, "A family on the throne is an interesting idea also. It brings down the pride of sovereignty to the level of petty life. The influence of the Crown is not confined merely to political affairs. England is a domestic country. Here the home is revered and the hearth sacred. The nation is represented by a family—the Royal Family—and if that family is educated with a sense of responsibility and a sentiment of public duty, it is difficult to exaggerate the salutary influence they may exercise over a nation."

The Queen followed Bagehot's precepts in allowing her family to be perceived as an integral component of the monarchy. She had, however, ignored one of Bagehot's most famous conclusions: "We must not let in the daylight upon magic." It was a mistake, he believed, to dilute the royal family's mystique. In making *Royal Family*, the Queen and her family had submitted themselves to the spotlight in a hitherto unprecedented fashion.

Following the advice of William Heseltine, the Queen and her entire family participated of their own volition in affording the general public the first-ever peek into their private lives. The Queen colluded in the shredding of the seven veils that had once cloaked her mystique, and the cataclysmic consequences would echo down the years.

For Edward Windsor, specifically, those consequences would be multifaceted. "The documentary gave the public a glimpse of the royals' private lives," said *Guardian* newpaper media commentator Roy Greenslade. "The public cast off their postwar deference and decided they had to know more about the royal family." The palace had opened Pandora's box. The tabloids and the paparazzi would become insatiable in their hunger for royal scoops. Edward's life, and that of his siblings, would henceforth be dogged by a pitiless and relentless media.

At the time of the documentary, the palace, heartened by what it initially perceived as the success of *Royal Family*, started fancying itself to be grand masters of public relations. With *Royal Family*, Buckingham Palace began its love affair with the press. Until then, public relations executives were not considered acceptable by the British aristocracy. In the years that followed *Royal Family*, public relations gradually grew to become a respected profession. This shift in perception ultimately made it possible for Edward Windsor to select a public relations executive, Sophie Rhys-Jones, as his bride, without her profession being seen as a drawback or igniting society's scorn.

Royal Family was the genesis of everything Edward Windsor, embryonic actor turned television producer-presenter, would become. The documentary shows the strands that would one day weave Edward's nature and influence his destiny.

He was four years old in July 1968, when filming began, was winsome and cuddlesome, with long eyelashes more befitting a princess than a prince. Although in the future many would cast aspersions on his masculinity, in *Royal Family*, Edward is "all boy."

The documentary first depicts Edward with his mother in a shop in the village of Ballater, seven miles away from the royal castle, Balmoral, in Craithie, Scotland. The shop, George Strachan Ltd., bears the legend, "General Merchants by Appointment to Her Majesty the Queen." The Queen, dressed in a Scottish kilt, smiles radiantly as Edward says, "Mummy?" He clearly knows the routine and waits. After a pause, the Queen asks him what he wants, "Can I have an ice cream?" he replies. He does not add, "please," a word that most British children of his age, even today, are drilled to say as a matter of course. The lady shopkeeper smiles benevolently. "He always goes straight for the ice cream," she says, with well-placed deference. The Queen bends down and reminds her son, "The last time you were here, it was raining too." He takes the ice cream and says nothing, neither thanking the shopkeeper nor his mother, the Queen.

The next scene features the royal family having a barbecue by the shores of Loch Muick, an idyllic, if perhaps contrived scene. When the documentary was aired, television critic Milton Shulman commented, "Just as it was untrue that the royal family sat down to breakfast wearing coronets as they munched their cornflakes, so it is untrue that they now behave in their private moments like a middle-class family."

In the barbecue scene in particular, the royal family tries to convey that they are merely a nice middle-class family like any other. That they are "just plain folk." Surrounded by what appears to be every kind of dog ever bred, they prepare lunch in a cooperative fashion. Philip mans the barbecue, Charles makes the salad dressing, and the Queen oversees the entire operation, while Anne forecasts, "You realize this is going to be a failure."

It is Edward, however, who shines, projecting star quality in every frame. He is impish and charming, a royal precursor of the young Macaulay Culkin. While the rest of the family is preoccupied with the cooking, he clambers up on top of the Range Rover and yells gleefully, "I'm up on the roof!" Everyone ignores him. Unabashed, he shouts, "I'm on the roof, Papa! I'm waiting for my lunch!"

Charles is kind and gentle in dealing with him. Edward watches as he stirs the salad dressing. A dog edges towards them. Edward pushes him away. "What's. that stuff?" he asks Charles. Told it is cream, he inquires, "Do you put cream on it?" Then he marches towards his father, who is by the barbecue. "What's this for?" Edward demands. Philip ignores him, but Edward isn't deterred. "What's this for?" he persists. "For turning things over," Philip replies. Edward treats his father with extreme politeness, which may well indicate that he has respect for Prince Philip and that he is not afraid of him. "May I turn them over for you?" he asks. Then, overcome with curiosity, "What's this spoon for?" Prince Philip ignores him. "What's this spoon for?" he asks again. "There is not much use for anything here," Prince Philip explains gently. But Edward persists. "What's the *spoon* for?" he asks again.

The four-year-old Edward Windsor in the Balmoral barbecue scene is a child uncowed by his father, his mother, or his siblings. He is extremely strong-willed and determined—characteristics he would continue to display throughout his life. "Edward is the youngest child," observed Viennese-born New York psychoanalyst Dr. Erika Padan Freeman, who studied with Theodore Reik. "Most youngest children are pampered, cosseted, and adored. They are not accustomed to the word 'No.'"

Although he would later be dubbed by the acrimonious press as "The Weeping Wimp of Windsor," the child Edward was unequivocally self-confident, self-possessed, and not in the least bit wimpish.

In August 1982, the royal family was spending their annual vacation in Balmoral. They had always cherished Balmoral as their personal haven. Built over the seven years between 1852 and 1859, Balmoral Castle was originally commissioned by Queen Victoria and Prince Albert. Prince Albert, in particular, had become enamored of the serene Dee Valley, in Scotland, because it reminded him of his native Thuringia, in Germany. Above all, they relished their vacations there during the grouse shooting season, when the family would join forces and go shooting together.

Three photographers (whom some would label paparazzi) staked out the royals at Balmoral that summer of 1982. Mauro Carraro, Jim Bennett, and French photographer George De-Kerle stealthily tracked the royals through the moors up onto Delnadamph, 7,600 acres of good quality hill land and grouse moors situated on Upper Donside on the picturesque Cock Bridge to Tom Intoul Road, some sixteen miles north of Balmoral. The male royals normally leave for grouse shooting at around nine-fifteen in the morning. At around eleven-thirty, they are usually joined by the female royals, who spend an hour and a half with the men on the moors. All of them lunch in a forest lodge, and after lunch, the women sometimes do one more drive. The men usually continue shooting until five-thirty or six, then return to the castle.

On that particular day, the three photographers were resting in a hollow on the grouse moors. They had been staking out the royal party in the hope of capturing a shot of Prince Andrew with his latest romance. Up till then, they hadn't been fortunate enough to succeed. The temperature that day was in the eighties, a surprisingly hot day for Scotland, and the photographers were starting to dehydrate. They were in the midst of debating whether to stay on the moors in the hope of snatching a shot of the royals or to give up and leave, when they saw a convoy of three vehicles. Through their binoculars, they were able to identify the Queen's Land Rover, with its distinctive sparkling silver Labrador mascot on the front.

Now only about half a mile away from the photographers, the Queen climbed out of her Land Rover and trained her binoculars on them. Then she handed the binoculars to her detective. As the photographers had hidden their equipment in the hollow, the detective jumped to the conclusion they were simply three innocent ramblers who had lost their way. The Queen dispatched an aide in her vehicle up the hillside and instructed him to tell the "ramblers" that a shoot was in progress and their lives might be in danger.

When the hapless aide discovered that the "ramblers," were, in actual fact, photographers, he went deathly white and exclaimed, "F——hell," in a distinctly upper-class accent. He radioed down to the Queen's detective for guidance. After some consultation, the detective radioed back to the aide, instructing him to escort the photographers off the moors. The three photographers obediently climbed into the Queen's Land Rover, feeling almost relieved to escape the heat. The aide drove them down to the gates of the moors, while a backup vehicle driven by a Special Branch detective followed.

The aide left the photographers at the gate. From there, they walked about three quarters of a mile. Unexpectedly, on the right-hand side of the grouse moors, they caught sight of the royal shooting party, which included Diana and Charles, both clad in kilts. Delighted by this unexpected bonus, the photographers immediately began snapping away.

All of a sudden, Edward detached himself from the shooting party. Two of his Labradors followed him. Bristling with self-confidence and a touch of arrogance, the nineteen-year-old prince marched towards the three photographers. Without any preamble, he demanded, "What the f—— hell are you lot doing here? Get off our land!" His language was shocking for a prince of the realm.

George DeKerle, the French photographer, who clearly felt neither deference nor reverence for the British royals, turned on Edward and accused him of being very rude.

While Edward's father, Prince Philip, whose combative style of dealing with the media Edward was clearly attempting to emulate, might have sworn at the photographers and stormed off, Edward began debating with the French photographer as to who was ruder: the photographers for having trespassed on royal lands or Edward for swearing at them. It was a scene worthy of a *Monty Python* skit—replete with "you did that," and "you said this." The debate continued for a time, but neither the persistent prince nor the opinionated French photographer made much headway against the other. Finally, it was Edward who turned the tables by engaging the photographers with questions about their work and how they operated. Finally, they left.

Edward has always been unafraid of the media, instead doing his utmost to study them. "He asked a lot of questions," says Jim Bennett, one of the three photographers who were there that day. "We tried to explain the press 'rota' to him. In the end, he calmed down. We weren't that interested in him, but he was interested in us." And, striking the note that all who know Edward sound, "I've always found Edward pretty arrogant, but he isn't a wimp."

He may not be a wimp, but Edward was and is beguiled by limelight. His nascent exhibitionism, which would be demonstrated in later years during his acting performances, his television interviews, and when he presented programs, was already evident when he was four and being filmed for *Royal Family*.

In the documentary, he is adorable, even in moments of distress. Charles lovingly shows him how to tighten the string on his cello. There is a mishap when the string snaps against Edward's cheek. Charles had always treated him kindly, and the accident clearly shocked Edward. In a trembling voice, he asks Charles,

"Why did you have to?" Later, his equilibrium is restored in the classroom, when he reads out loud to his teacher. Painstakingly, he follows each word with a pencil. His teacher rewards him with, "Good boy!" Little Edward turns to the camera and smiles contentedly.

Throughout the documentary, Edward looks into the camera lens flirtatiously—perhaps far more flirtatiously than might the average four-year-old caught on camera. Critics remarked on Edward's talent "to steal the show."

Whatever its eventual repercussions, *Royal Family* was essentially a performance, heralding the royal family's unwitting show business debut. All of the royal family, even the media-shy Anne, spend much of Cawston's documentary with their faces wreathed in smiles—happy members of what appears to be the world's happiest of families. The possibility that this family might conceivably ever be touched by divorce, tarnished by scandal, or torn apart by death and deceit, seems unthinkable.

It is impossible not to feel nostalgia now for those far-off days when the royal family personified the ideal family: Charles, in his early twenties, kind, beloved by the public, the perfect son, is Prince Charming awaiting only his Princess. The Queen sparkles with warmth and confidence, forty-three and in her prime, glittering with allure. Prince Philip is by her side, handsome, with a sexual charisma somewhat enhanced by whispers of his manifold infidelities, whispered of but not yet published. For in those halcyon days, British journalists would sooner have filed their copy in Esperanto than cast aspersions on a member of the British royal family.

In the 1969 Cawston film, there is no Diana, no Fergie, no hint of scandal, no suspicion that the whole regal, yet now seemingly ordinary, facade, would one day virtually crumble. On the surface, the entire royal family gleams with promise, and despite his age and lowly position in the line of succession, Edward's promise shines more brightly than that of the rest. He is telegenic, strong-willed, and lovable, a charming child with every chance of growing up to lead an exquisitely charmed life.

Edward was born at 8:20 P.M. on March 10, 1964, in the bathroom of the Belgian Suite on the ground floor of Buckingham Palace. The Queen was attended by her family doctor, Dr. Ronald Boldey Scott, Sir John Weir, Dr. Vernon Hall, John Brudenell, as well as two midwives, Sister Helen Rowe and Sister Annette Wilson. The duke was with her as she gave birth.

At the time of Edward's birth, the Queen was thirty-seven, and the birth was rendered less painful by the relaxation techniques of Betty Parsons, who advised women on childbirth. The Queen did not rely solely on natural childbirth, but also on gas, oxygen, and a painkiller.

As soon as she was able to gaze at her delicate (5 lb. 7 oz.) son, one of the first things that struck her was the extraordinary length of his eyelashes. Two months after Edward's birth, the celebrated photographer Cecil Beaton came to the palace to take the baby prince's official photographs, and the Queen reiterated her amazement at her youngest son's eyelashes. "It's most unfortunate that all my sons have such long eyelashes while my daughter hasn't any at all," she said.

Sixteen years separated the birth of Charles and the birth of Edward. In a later speech, Prince Philip said candidly, "People want their first child very much when they marry. They want the second child almost as much. If a third comes along, they accept it as natural—but they haven't gone out of their way to get it. When the fourth child comes along, in most cases it's unintentional."

The birth of Edward, the monarch's fourth child, delighted the British public. When Charles was born in 1948, England was austere and grim, still in the throes of rationing—with the average baby subsisting on powdered milk because the real thing was unavailable. Now, however, it was the swinging sixties, and with the advent of Twiggy, Mary Quant, and the Beatles, Britain appeared to have emerged from the postwar doldrums with its glory burnished anew.

Edward, gurgling, quiet, and cherubic, seemed to symbolize some of that glory. Cities throughout the Commonwealth heralded the news of his birth with twenty-one-gun salutes. The Archbishop of Canterbury greeted Edward's birth with joy, using it as an illustration of the perfect family: "There was around the throne a Christian family united," he said. "Happy and setting to all an example of what the words 'home and family' most truly meant."

Prince Charles was elated at Edward's birth. Soon after, he wrote to the Queen's lady-in-waiting, Lady Susan Hussey, "It's so wonderful having babies in the house again, isn't it? The only trouble is they grow up so quickly." A few weeks after he first saw the new baby, Charles went back to Gordonstoun, where he was at school. From there, he wrote in his diary, "It will be wonderful to see everyone and to see Edward again. Mummy says he's great fun and laughs and turns over." Charles was scheduled to go to Australia. He wrote wistfully in his diary of how much he would miss Edward and his nanny, Mabel Anderson, "I shall hate leaving everyone for so long, especially Edward and Mabel. I hope he isn't too big when I get back."

The royal baby's first unofficial outing took place on April 4, 1964, when the Queen drove him and Princess Anne to Windsor Castle. Although the sky was stormy and grim, the Queen and Anne were both in sunny moods, waving and smiling at the crowds. Beside them in the car, Edward slept peacefully.

On May 2, 1964, in Windsor Castle's private chapel, the dean of Windsor, Robert Woods, christened him Edward Antony Richard Louis. His lace christening robes dated back to 1841, when they had been fashioned for Queen Victoria's daughter Princess Victoria. Looking at her youngest son, beatific in his christening robes, the Queen was content.

When Edward was three months old, she swept onto the balcony of Buckingham Palace and proudly displayed him to the crowds below. They cheered enthusiastically. The palace staff, too, warmed to the new royal child. His nanny found him undemanding and happy, despite the fact that his serenity was often disturbed by his mischievous elder brother Andrew's boisterousness.

During his childhood, little Edward led an ordered life in the nursery. Situated on the second floor of the palace, the nursery (which Edward shared with Andrew) looked out on the forecourt, affording him a prime view of the daily Changing of the Guard ceremony. With two bedrooms, a sitting room, a bathroom, and a kitchen, the children spent their days in the sitting room with green walls, a fireplace, and a chintz-covered couch. Two large cupboards with glass doors held Charles and Anne's old books and toys. The Queen's old rocking horse was in one corner.

Edward's day began each morning at eight. At eight-fifteen, he ate the classic British breakfast of eggs, bacon, and sausage. At nine-thirty, the nanny carried him to the elevator, which took them down to the Queen and Prince Philip's private apartments. The baby would be left there to play with his parents for half an hour; then the nanny took him upstairs again. Sometimes, Edward wouldn't see his parents until four in the afternoon, when they had tea together in the nursery.

"A child wants a mother to be emotional, hugged, kissed—and that's not what the Queen's good at. She's tough, totally unsentimental," a confidential source told biographer Ben Pimlott, author of *The Queen.* "She was a less natural mother with Charles and Anne, whereas she was much more the besotted parent with Andrew and Edward," a member of the royal staff confided to Pimlott.

On a few special occasions, Edward was permitted to visit the

Queen in her study, where she would invariably be working on her state papers. He was alert and curious, but not noisy or destructive, so that sometimes the Queen would relinquish protocol and relax as he crawled around the floor.

The Queen did her part in educating her youngest son. When he was two, she had a blackboard erected in her sitting room. She taught Edward the alphabet, numbers, and how to read the time, demonstrating with a clock. Eventually, she taught him to ride horses and gave him a pony of his own, named Flame.

From the first, Edward's father was an important presence in his life. Contrary to his often negatively slanted press coverage, Prince Philip was and is a consistently loving father to Edward. In her book, nanny Mabel Anderson praised Prince Philip for his nurturing qualities as a father. She wrote that Philip would "always set aside time to read to them or help them put together his little model toys." The prince also taught Edward to swim and, when he was old enough, to drive. While Philip's relationship with Charles gradually disintegrated through the years to the point where the duke and his heir rarely communicated on any level, Philip and Edward were always close. Prince Philip never called Charles "Chuck" or "Charlie," but early on he took to calling Edward by the affectionate nickname "Ed."

The palace staff, however, did not treat Edward with informality, nor did they dare to call him "Ed." The Queen ruled that until Edward reached the age of eighteen, the staff should address him as "sir." She decreed that upon Edward's eighteenth birthday the staff address him by his title, "Your Royal Highness."

In September 1968, when he was four and a half years old, Edward began the first stage of his formal education. For two months, he was taught by Miss Adelaide Grigg, who had been recommended by the Queen's lady-in-waiting, Lady Susan Hussey.

Adelaide was governess to Lady Susan's four-year-old daughter, Katharine. Classes were held at Lady Susan's house in Chelsea.

After Christmas, Edward's permanent governess, Miss Lavinia Keppel, took up her post at Buckingham Palace. Miss Keppel was a distant relative of Alice Keppel, Edward VII's mistress, and she also was related to Camilla Shand, who eventually became Camilla Parker Bowles and Charles's mistress. At forty, Lavinia Keppel was an experienced teacher who had taught for fifteen years at the Lady Eden School in Kensington.

The schoolroom, which overlooked the sweeping Mall thoroughfare, along which the ceremonial coaches travel to the palace, was bright, airy, and sufficiently big to accommodate Edward and his aristocratic schoolmates: Sarah Armstrong-Jones, Princess Margaret's daughter; James Ogilvy, son of Princess Alexandra and her husband, Angus Ogilvy; and Princess Tanya of Hanover, the granddaughter of Prince Philip's sister. They all took classes in the palace schoolroom together.

The day generally began with a Bible story, followed by simple geography, arithmetic, reading, and writing lessons. At around eleven, the children were served milk and biscuits. In the afternoon, they either played games or went on field trips to art galleries.

A great deal of history was taught in the palace schoolroom, so much so that at four, Edward already knew who Queen Victoria was. He was also privileged by birth and consequently able to experience history at firsthand. When he was five, he was witness to one of the most glittering royal ceremonies ever held in Great Britain and which evoked the past more vividly than did any number of history books: Prince Charles's investiture as Prince of Wales took place at Caernarvon Castle, which dated back over seven hundred years. Captured in 1282 by the English, the castle was the location at which King Edward I declared his English son to be the Prince of Wales. Now Charles would be accorded that same title.

Edward traveled to Wales with the family on the royal train. The spectacular investiture ceremony cost £500,000 ($815,000). Although it overshadowed all the rest of the pageantry Edward would see during his childhood, there would be many other events that emphasized to him the majesty of his status and that of his family.

He had already seen his mother, resplendent on her horse, during the traditional Trooping the Color ceremony. By the age of six, he would cruise to Norway on the Royal yacht *Britannia*. There, the royal party was joined by King Olav of Norway on his own yacht *The Norge*. There had also been a visit to the Braemar Highland Games, for which Edward appropriately wore a kilt.

Edward would be no stranger to cheering crowds. Even in the palace he was rarely alone. His brother Andrew was always a rival and at times a bully. Sometimes Edward would be blamed for his brother's misdemeanors. Andrew enjoyed nothing better than to disturb Edward's reading by initiating a prank or by teasing or taunting him. As he grew older, he would face the taunting of others, in particular the media. He would have to call on all his early training to remain cool, poised, and in control. Sometimes he would succeed, and sometimes he would fail and be humiliated.

2
A LIFE WITH A BLUEPRINT

*P*RINCESS MARGARET NEVER FORGAVE PRINCE PHILIP for his fierce opposition to her romantic liaison with the divorced group captain Peter Townsend. She used to mock the prince's role in the Queen's life by calling him, "Con-sort." Philip, always quick to avenge an insult, retaliated whenever the opportunity arose. On one occasion, when Princess Margaret's then-husband, Lord Snowdon, arrived at Windsor Castle for tea bringing with him an extremely distinguished guest, Prince Philip glanced up at Lord Snowdon from his newspaper and said laconically, "Good god! Look what the cat has dragged in."

But even Lord Snowdon and Princess Margaret couldn't deny the prince's influence on the British monarchy. In past generations, children of the Windsors (and those of all previous British monarchs) were, without exception, educated by private tutors or governesses. Philip introduced into the Windsor dynasty the daring idea that his children be educated in schools, along with other children.

Like his siblings before him, Edward was dispatched out into the great wide world. In September 1971, he was sent to the Gibbs School, in Collingham Gardens, Kensington, along with ninety other boys whose parents had paid £100 ($210) a term for the privilege. Along with Edward was his cousin James Ogilvy. His brother Andrew had preceded them at Gibbs, and Andrew had already gained a reputation as a sociable, friendly boy.

Edward, in contrast, was more solitary, preferring to return home to his mother at the palace, just ten minutes' drive away, rather than join in after-school activities with the rest of the boys. In theory, he was just another Gibbs pupil, but his status was never forgotten. His bodyguard was ever present. Thirty-three-year old Andrew Merrylees, a six-foot tall Scotsman, would guard Edward until the prince was twenty-six. Even when Edward played happily with the other boys during break, Merrylees, who was armed, kept a watchful eye on him. Edward tried to be like his school friends, but he unwittingly revealed his difference. When he and the rest of the class were asked to draw a picture of a house, Edward drew *his* house, Buckingham Palace.

Edward's exalted status was underscored just two months after he started at Gibbs. In December 1971, a select committee, which had been established in 1970 to examine the royal family's finances, announced their findings. Those findings resulted in the doubling of the royal family's Civil List Allowance, an annual "salary" paid to the royal family by the government. Edward would benefit from the committee's largesse at the age of eighteen, when his yearly allowance would start at £20,000 ($32,600).

On September 15, 1972, Edward's childhood universe expanded yet further when he arrived at Heatherdown Preparatory School, seven miles from Windsor Castle, where he spent the next five years. The school, set in thirty acres of land, had its own rugby and soccer grounds, cricket pitch, and swimming pool. Unlike Gibbs, Heatherdown was a boarding school, and it is a tradition among the British upper classes to send their children to boarding school. Edward was permitted to go home for three weekends a term and during Easter, Christmas, and summer holidays, but apart from that, he had to spend the rest of the time at school.

At first, he was desperately homesick. He was made to share a room with two other boys in a house known as Heatherlea, a hundred yards from the red brick Victorian building where the main school was housed. Like the other boys, he was permitted to bring his teddy bear to bed with him each night, and in the morning he donned his school uniform like everyone else, a black blazer edged with red. Each day, like everyone else he followed the school's strict routine. He did not enjoy it. Edward admitted, years after he left Heatherdown, "A school is a school. I don't agree that school days are the happiest days of your life."

His day began at seven-fifteen when he and the other boys were awakened, not by a royal valet calling him "Sir," but by the clang of a loud bell. After breakfast, Edward went to class, studying French, Latin, music, woodwork, history, geography, the Bible, biology, English, and physics.

It is the pattern in most British boarding schools for every afternoon to be devoted to sports. At Heatherdown, Edward learned and grew to love tennis, and he played cricket, of which he was fond, and football (of which he was not).

Supper was served at six, then the boys studied for an hour and went to bed at eight. Television was banned, except for a few select programs, picked for their suitability by the school headmaster, James Edwards.

The headmaster was impressed by Edward's good manners, his self-control, and his desire to do what was expected of him. His fellow pupils soon got over their awe at his status, even making fun of it by nicknaming him EARL, after the initials of his name (Edward Antony Richard Louis).

Eventually, Edward's fellow pupils reached the stage where they virtually obliterated his princely status from their minds altogether. One school friend, Jonathan Holms Smith, was playing rugby with the prince. "There was a ruck going on, the ball flew up and I ran towards it. A little blond boy was lying on his back clutching it, and as I ran at him, I got him in the neck with my knee. He started crying his eyes out. The game stopped. Everyone gathered around, and when he was all right, they all clapped him for being brave and said, 'Well played, the Prince.' I hadn't realized until then it was Edward."

On November 14, 1973, the nine-year-old Edward was in the limelight once more. His sister, Princess Anne, chose him to be a page at her wedding to Captain Mark Phillips. Although his nature was far more sensitive than that of the brusque, tomboyish Anne, he always loved and respected her. Throughout his school days, she wrote to him regularly. At times, it seemed that she was virtually a second mother to him. As he grew older, he often took refuge in her home, Gatcombe Park. They both shared a passionate love for horses, and both of them were good riders. Anne, who disguised her deep affection for him by calling him by the somewhat ambiguous name of nig-nog, kept a pony there for him. Their affinity was such that, in a crisis, Edward often turned to his sister for guidance. She had common sense and a certain amount of guile, and he knew that she would never lead him astray. In times of trouble, he felt he could always escape to Gatcombe, where Anne had reserved a small bedroom just for him.

Before the wedding, Edward took great pains to practice his role as page. The Heatherdown headmaster prepared him for his walk down the aisle. Edward was excited and, on the day, acquitted himself well. He stood still throughout the wedding service, didn't fidget, and, in his Scottish Highland tartan outfit, he looked the perfect page.

Edward was growing up. That same year, the Queen judged that he was ready for the ski slopes. Accompanied by a group of Heatherdown pupils and the ever-present Merrylees, Edward traveled to Austria under the alias of Edward Bishop. His surname was well chosen, for within the tightly knit circles of Heatherdown, Edward was known as a goody-goody. On the strength of his exemplary behavior, he became first dormitory captain (supervising the boys with whom he shared his living quarters), then house captain, and then joint senior school captain. Edward was also above average academically, and he passed the entrance exam that would enable him to gain admission to almost any top school he would like. But Edward had no choice in the matter. Prince Philip had formulated a blueprint for the education of his sons, and there was no possibility that Edward would deviate from it. That blueprint would become both the bane and the backbone of his future.

Prince Philip believed passionately that the Gordonstoun School had been the making of him. Gordonstoun stood on three hundred acres, near Elgin, on the Moray Firth, in Scotland, and it was founded in 1934 by Dr. Kurt Hahn. Prince Philip was one of the school's first pupils. He had originally attended Salem, based in a castle/monastery on the north shore of Lake Constance, in the south of Germany, a coeducational boarding school founded in 1920 by Dr. Hahn with Prince Max of Baden. Dr. Hahn, who was Jewish and a committed anti-Nazi, was arrested but later released, after which he fled to Scotland and founded Gordonstoun.

The school opened in the summer of 1934 and Prince Philip joined twenty-nine other boys there. Gordonstoun had a lifelong impact on Philip, who believed strongly in Hahn's precepts. Those precepts could be classified as somewhat left-leaning in that Hahn believed that "wealthy children needed to experience the moral equivalent of war. With privilege comes duty." In a wider sense, he believed that "any nation is a slovenly guardian of its own interests if it does not do all it can to make the individual citizen discover his or her own powers: and further, that the individual becomes a

cripple from his or her own point of view if he or she is not qualified by education to serve the community."

The motto of the school, *Plus est en vous* ("There is more in
you"), was based on Kurt Hahn's belief that "by lighting fires in the
hearts and minds of boys and girls and by challenging them to
appreciate that there is more in them than they think, they will be
prepared for citizenship and for life." The goal of the school was to
foster in young people qualities of skill, compassion, honesty, initiative, adventure, and service to their fellow beings. It was and is a
rigorous environment.

When a boy arrived at Gordonstoun, he was given a personal
training plan aimed at improving his physical fitness and mental
self-discipline. Each boy was also given a chart to fill in each
evening during his time at the school, recording whether certain
duties have been done or rules kept. The chart was sporadically
inspected by the housemaster.

Life at Gordonstoun was extremely spartan. Boys lived in dor-
mitories with bare walls and uncarpeted floors. They slept on
wooden beds, windows were kept open all night, despite below-
freezing temperatures outside. The boys were awakened at seven
sharp each morning. No matter how freezing the temperature,
each boy was compelled to take a cold shower, then go on a run
(even in the dead of winter) dressed only in vest and shorts. After
breakfast, each boy was required to make his own bed, clean his
own shoes, and empty the garbage.

Great physical endurance was mandatory at Gordonstoun. Boys
ran, threw javelins, hiked, climbed rope, and did community service. At different times, they were sent on arduous land, sea, or
mountain expeditions. They also, during various periods of their
education, manned a coast guard station, took part in mountain
rescue, and worked with the local fire-fighting force.

■   ■   ■

Prince Philip, hardy, macho, and an independent spirit, thrived at Gordonstoun. After Hahn's death in 1974, the Queen, aware of the debt her husband felt he owed Hahn, paid Hahn the handsome tribute of traveling to Gordonstoun and unveiling a plaque in his memory. The plaque was engraved with the words "No man with his wisdom could have done more. No man with his wisdom should have done less."

When Charles was born, Philip decided that he, too, would attend Gordonstoun. Charles was the first heir to the throne to attend school outside of the palace. Far more sensitive and shy than his blustering, ultramasculine father, Charles was desperately miserable at Gordonstoun. He later recorded in his diary, "The people in my dormitory are foul. They throw slippers all night long or hit me with pillows." Charles was bullied at Gordonstoun, but he was not the only one. Bullying was a way of life there, and Edward, too, would bear the brunt of it.

Neither his father nor his brothers had prepared him for what lay ahead for him at Gordonstoun. "My brothers told me nothing," Edward confided to journalist Julian Pettifer. "The Prince of Wales hated his time so he never talked about it. I arrived here with absolutely no previous knowledge at all. I had no idea what was going to happen."

Perhaps he had a premonition of what lay ahead for him. Before his first term at Gordonstoun, Edward spent the summer at Balmoral. The night before he left to start school, he cried on the Queen Mother's shoulder, telling her he didn't want to leave home. The party line perpetrated by the royals was that part of the benefit of attending Gordonstoun was its proximity to Balmoral. Mollified at the promised prospect of repeated family visits, Edward squared his shoulders and braced himself to take on Gordonstoun.

Unlike Charles, with whom his fellow pupils were afraid to be friends, Edward fitted into the fabric of the school fairly well. "It wasn't very easy to begin with at all," he said in a rare moment of candor. "But it got easier with a little help from my friends. I don't think anybody enjoys their school days. It's only in retrospect, because you only remember the good times. But I don't think Gordonstoun is as tough as it used to be."

"He was a very gregarious youngster who got on well with pretty well everyone," said his chemistry teacher, James Thomas. Edward was wearing braces, and soon he was dubbed with the nickname Jaws.

He won his schoolmates' respect, if not their affection, through his skill at sport, sailing, hunting, riding, and at breaking some of the school rules. He rarely got caught breaking those rules. With a degree of smugness, Edward later boasted to Julian Pettifer, "It's always the sign of a good criminal. If you can get away with it and don't have to do the punishment. Everybody thinks I was a goody-goody. They don't know. Just because I didn't appear in the punishment book very many times doesn't mean I was always on the straight and narrow."

John Staunton, who attended Gordonstoun with him, corroborates Edward's account of himself. He recalls that at Gordonstoun, there were four cardinal sins: drinking, drug taking, smoking, and having sex. The rumors of Edward's supposed homosexuality were still ahead of Edward. At Gordonstoun, at fifteen, he was fast gaining a reputation as a lothario. Apart from clandestine drinking sessions with a clique of other boys, Staunton claims, sex was Edward's deadliest of sins. "We all knew that he and the most beautiful girl in the school were having a thing. It would be ungallant to name her, but she had the longest, loveliest legs I've ever seen. And she flaunted them in the miniest of miniskirts! All the boys lusted after her—but Edward was the one she bestowed her favors on," says Staunton.

However much he endeavored to be a macho member of the

school and one of the guys, the other boys still turned on him, exercising their malice and perhaps their jealousy. "Some other boys used to fill plastic spoons with saliva and flick it on his back in class," said a source who was at school with him. "Edward didn't say anything at the time."

Years later, a contemporary, who grew up to flourish in shipping, recalled the worst incidence of bullying suffered by Prince Edward. Some of his so-called friends approached him in a spirit of bonhomie and offered him some wine. Disarmed by their inexplicable generosity, Edward gladly accepted. One of his "friends" produced a bottle of white wine and proceeded to pour the prince a glass. Edward thanked him and took a sip. "He spat out what he could," said Edward's contemporary. Edward's "glass of wine" was, in fact, urine. "Some of the others had filled the bottle, then chilled it."

"As one birthday treat," recalled John Staunton, "Edward suffered the indignity of being stripped and thrown out of the ground-floor window of the dorm—straight into a snowdrift."

On another occasion, Edward's schoolmates devised an even more unique way to humiliate him: "They put Super Glue all over the bench just as Edward and the prefects came in for a service," confided John Staunton. "The look on his face was a joy to behold as the royal bottom met the bench. He realized instantly he was in a fix, tried to stand up, and half the seat of his pants ripped away! There was an uproar of amusement. But Edward didn't see the joke, and neither did the headmaster. He demanded the culprits own up, but nobody did."

Edward would, in time, get his revenge. In his last term, he became school guardian (or head boy) and slid into the role of disciplinarian extremely easily. Caning, the classic British public school punishment, was permitted at Gordonstoun, and Edward believed firmly in it. "I think corporal punishment is extremely valuable in any school," he said piously to Julian Pettifer. "If people decide to break the rules, they've got to run the gauntlet of punishment. Corporal punishment is the last resort. A beating or thrashing if used in the right context is, I think, very valuable, because it always shows people you've come to the end of your tether and that's where you draw the line."

Although Edward's power as school guardian did not extend to administering corporal punishment, his inability to maintain the common touch and his insistence on pulling rank often alienated his Gordonstoun contemporaries. He appeared to take delight in informing on them. "You could never expect Edward to look the other way if he caught you breaking the school rules," complained one of his disgruntled classmates. "Even before he became head boy, he would consider it his moral duty to inform your house captain if he caught you out."

Edward snitched on boys he found smoking and drinking in the woods. Unmoved by their pleas, he insisted on reporting them to the school authorities, even though he knew that their transgressions could lead to expulsion. His authoritarian attitude would be matched once he joined the Marines, but it would never win Edward much popularity.

He did relatively well academically. The British education system, in Edward's day, was divided into Ordinary level ("O level") examinations and Advanced level ("A level") examinations. Each level is divided into subjects. Students who wish to apply to university need to obtain a minimum of six O levels and two A levels. When Edward left Gordonstoun in 1982, he had gained seven O levels—in English language, French, math, physics, biology, history, and Latin—and three A levels—in English literature, history, politics, and economics. He had acquitted himself well, and his headmaster, Mr. Michael Mavor, said approvingly, "He has had a very successful school career, and we are all proud to have had him here."

■   ■   ■

In the years that Edward spent at Gordonstoun, three new elements entered his life. The first, and perhaps most enduring, was the birth of his lifelong interest in acting. The British monarchy, whose traditional pageantry surpasses anything Hollywood portrays, has always been drawn to the theater.

Henry VIII composed and played songs. Charles II, with his actress mistress, former orange seller Nell Gwyn, performed lustily in Jacobean masques. Edward VII, Prince of Wales, once made a surprise appearance in *Fedora* on the Paris professional stage, playing opposite one of his most flamboyant lovers, the actress Sarah Bernhardt. Even Queen Victoria showed herself capable of being amused by the theater and loved to sing the songs of Gilbert and Sullivan.

Acting had always been in the blood of the Windsors, whose entire dynasty, some said, was predicated on each and every member's ability to put on a theatrical performance, resplendent with glory and the trappings of pomp and circumstance. While the greatest role played by the leading members of the royal family nowadays is clearly that of themselves, all of them possess a degree of theatrical talent.

The Queen Mother excels at playing the game of charades, in which she acts in a variety of skits with gusto. The Queen took part in a 1943 family production of *Aladdin*, exhibiting such theatrical flair that her governess, Marion Crawford, exclaimed, "There was a sparkle about her none of us had ever seen before."

Prince Philip first acted in a play at Gordonstoun, where he had the role of Lord Donalbain in *Macbeth*. His sister-in-law, Princess Margaret, to this day, still prides herself on her ability to entertain cabaret style. Her imitation of Sophie Tucker is legendary in royal circles, as is her personal weakness for romantic liaisons with actors. The late Peter Sellers and Warren Beatty were both said to have caught the princess's fancy.

The Windsors' fascination with the theater extended to the next generation. Prince Charles showed a strong inclination for playing the clown while at Cambridge. He formed a strong friendship with a celebrated cluster of English comedians who performed on radio as *The Goons,* including Peter Sellers. *The Goons* were the precursors to *Monty Python,* and Charles developed an abiding passion for such quirky humor. He also acted in a variety of plays at Cambridge and appeared to thoroughly enjoy himself. Princess Anne, despite her gruff exterior, was not immune to the smell of greasepaint. She appeared in school plays and starred as Cinderella in a Buckingham Palace production of the pantomime.

Edward's theatrical debut launched him on a passion for the theater. "I found the best fun ever was working with other people on stage," he enthused, before becoming introspective. "Life is one big act for me and, I am sure, for a lot of other people."

His first role was in the Gordonstoun production, *Black Comedy,* by Peter Shaffer. "It's great getting people to roll about the floor with laughter, and crying," he said, remembering his Gordonstoun stage debut. "That's what we managed to do in *Black Comedy,* and I always remember that." The Queen and Prince Philip attended the performance, although they were not seen to roll about the floor with laughter. Subsequently, he also appeared in *Romeo and Juliet,* playing Paris, and later in *Hay Fever,* the Noël Coward comedy. He reveled in each of his onstage experiences. "Edward lived for acting," said his acting coach, John Lofthouse. Asked to define the high point of his time at Gordonstoun, Edward's unhesitating answer was, "As far as the good times are concerned, I think I'll remember the theater."

Years later, Edward revealed that his most cherished career ambition had been to act. That ambition, born at Gordonstoun, tells us much about the real Edward Windsor.

During his years at Gordonstoun, Edward first became involved in the Duke of Edinburgh Award Scheme, an organization that today still remains close to his heart. The award scheme, created by Prince Philip, was inspired by the ideals of Dr. Kurt Hahn, who had pioneered the Moray Badge, which he awarded to young people for personal achievement in extracurricular activities. Those activities might include mountain rescue, ocean rescue, fire fighting, or guarding the coast. Prince Philip himself won the Moray Badge and went on to formulate the award scheme, which he later defined in the following terms: "It is designed as an introduction to leisure-time activities, a challenge to the individual to personal achievement, and as a guide to those people and organizations who are concerned about the development of our future citizens."

Prince Edward characterized the award as "character building." "When someone says they have earned the Duke of Edinburgh Award," he said, "you'll very quickly find what makes that person tick; what motivates them. The program gives young people self-confidence, and that is very important in this world."

In 1988, when Prince Philip became sixty-seven, Edward joined the Duke of Edinburgh Award board. "He was the only one in the royal family still in the age group for the award," said Sir Michael Hobbs, chairman of the award scheme. "He could go around and talk on equal terms to the young people doing it and find out what they thought and what needed doing. The prince is so different from his public image. It always saddens and infuriates me that he is seen as someone who is not interested in performing any public service. . . . We know how wrong that is."

Today Prince Edward is trustee of the Duke of Edinburgh Award in the United Kingdom and also a trustee of the International Awards and chairman of the International Council. His role includes fund-raising, as well as managing the program worldwide. "He puts in an amazing amount of time. I get the feeling that working for the Duke of Edinburgh Award is something that Prince Edward is genuinely involved in," says Paul Arengo Jones, secretary general for the International Duke of Edinburgh Awards.

"He is genuinely concerned about making life better for young people worldwide. You only have to see the way he walks into a room when there's a bunch of young people there to see that he's got a very good communication with them. And I think he is genuinely concerned about what faces young people in the future. I think he sees that, through the award, he has a possibility of making a difference. And he throws himself into it wholeheartedly. He puts more time in than I've any right to expect from him."

There are those who dwell under the misconception that Princess Diana was the first royal to dedicate herself to charity work and public service. However, nothing could be further from the truth. The Windsors have always selflessly devoted themselves to serving the public and to helping those less fortunate than themselves. However, unlike Diana, they have assiduously avoided publicizing their good deeds. In that, Edward is the same as the rest of his family. He works diligently and passionately for the awards, without seeking personal publicity.

His involvement in the awards also carries with it another, deeper, more personal resonance. "The fact that Edward took over the Duke of Edinburgh Award," says well-known former royal correspondent, Michael Cole, "indicates something about Edward's closeness to his father."

The third new factor introduced into Edward's life during his time at Gordonstoun was his new sister-in-law, Diana, Princess of Wales. When they first met, Lady Diana Spencer was the little girl next door, whose father, Earl Spencer, had rented Park House on the Sandringham estate from the Queen. Diana often came to Sandringham to have tea with the prince and his brothers. When he was twenty, Charles wrote a story for his siblings, "The Old Man of Lochnagar," and thoughtfully sent a copy to Diana.

As the world knows, romance between the prince and his fairy-tale princess-to-be blossomed, so that by August 1980, Diana was

Charles's guest at the Cowes Regatta in the Isle of Wight. Edward was sixteen at the time and sailing at Cowes too when he met Diana. She was two and a half years older than Edward, and she found his bright sense of humor endearing.

Edward, however, was not particularly enamored of Diana. According to a former palace staffer, the relationship between Diana and Edward appeared to cool considerably once she became engaged to Charles and moved into Buckingham Palace. Her rooms were situated on the same corridor as Edward's own. "Whenever Edward came home from Gordonstoun, he found that Diana was now the center of attention," said the palace staffer. "Whenever one of the valets did something for the new princess-to-be, Edward obviously didn't like the attention she was getting. There was a distinct chill in the air. Diana had stolen the limelight from Edward, and he was jealous."

Diana was probably never aware of Edward's jealousy. "She liked him," says Lady Colin Campbell. As Diana's relationship with Charles progressed, she spent many vacations at Sandringham and Balmoral with the royal family. In retrospect, the happy ambience of those vacations was part of the lure that led her into what she would later view as the trap of life with the Windsors. "She came from a close family and believed that the royals are close," a royal courtier told Lady Colin Campbell. "You can see how she made that mistake. Up to that time, all her experience of them had been on holidays. At Sandringham, at Cowes, at Balmoral, when they're all together. But you know as well as I do that they're only ever together for set pieces, and otherwise they see next to nothing of each other. It was quite a common occurrence for the Queen, the Prince of Wales, and Princess Anne to all be in the palace together, each of them having their dinner off a tray in their own rooms. They can all go for weeks, sometimes even months, without ever seeing each other. It would never occur to them to drop in, or to be companionable together."

Talking about Diana in the months after she married Charles, the courtier recalled, "Diana had more cordial relations with Prince Andrew and Prince Edward, but at the time they were both away, one in the Navy, the other at university, if memory serves me correctly. I think Diana thought that things would look up when they returned home, so to speak. Edward and Diana used to be quite friendly. He used to stay at Highgrove with her."

Diana was fond enough of Edward to travel with Charles to Gordonstoun to see his performance in *Hotel Paradiso*, the French farce by Georges Feydeau. Diana heartily applauded Edward's performance, but clearly was not particularly inspired by Gordonstoun. When selecting a school for her own sons, she flatly refused to consider sending them to Gordonstoun and enrolled them at Eton instead.

In time, Edward grew fond enough of Diana to pick a girlfriend, Sophie Rhys-Jones, who resembled her. Nonetheless, the example of Diana's abortive union with his brother terrified him. As he watched their love affair unravel and their marriage shatter, he resolved to learn from Charles's and Diana's mistakes.

3

THE VIRGIN PRINCE

*I*N JULY 1982, EDWARD TOOK A THREE-WEEK FLYING course at RAF Cranwell, an air force base in Lincolnshire. Classes entailed flying a Bulldog two-seater piston-engined trainer. At the end of the course, he received his first solo certificate from the training school's commanding officer, Group Captain Dick Joyce, and qualified for his private pilot's license.

By August 10, when the royal family made their annual pilgrimage to Balmoral, Britain was in the throes of the hottest summer the country had experienced in years. Edward was eighteen years old, he had his own private annual income—the £20,000 ($32,600) afforded him from the Civil List—and he was no longer a schoolboy. He reveled in his newly won freedom. As the sweltering temperatures escalated, so did his exhilaration.

Until now, Edward had only experienced puppy love. In 1981, at a party at Princess Anne's Gatcombe estate, just before Charles and Diana's wedding, Edward encountered one of Princess Anne's girl grooms, Shelley Whitborn. They danced to John Lennon's "Woman"; then he invited her to accompany him to the new James Bond film *For Your Eyes Only,* in London's Leicester Square.

A few days later, he also invited Shelley to dinner at Buckingham Palace. Although they were alone for much of the evening, he was shy, polite, and did not attempt a seduction. Shelley was shown into her bedroom next door to Edward's and spent a peaceful night there alone. Edward was young and inexperienced, and only a woman of the world would be capable of stripping away his inhibitions.

During the summer of 1983, in Balmoral, he found one—or, rather, she found him.

She was a housemaid, twenty-two, perky, and voluptuous. He was nineteen and a prince of the realm. What transpired between them, as told to *Sunday People*, was redolent of *Upstairs, Downstairs*. It was also straight out of an ancient British tradition whereby the lord of the manor routinely had his way with a luscious, compliant serving wench.

Michelle Riles, a Yorkshire lass, was considered a competent maid by the Buckingham Palace staffers. She had been working in the palace for just a few months and had already been deemed sufficiently diligent to accompany the royals to Balmoral.

When Edward arrived in Balmoral at the start of the vacation, Michelle was assigned to unpack his suitcase. Edward had been away at Gordonstoun all year, so Michelle had never met him before. She was just in the process of unfolding his clothes when Edward appeared at the bedroom door. He smiled at her warmly, asked her name, then disappeared again. "My heart was pounding," Michelle said afterwards to the *Sunday People*. "I had spoken to Edward for the first time and fallen for him."

Within fifteen minutes, he was back again. Michelle was in the midst of ironing his shirts. Seeing him, she stopped and began flirting with him. He did not discourage her. Emboldened, she complimented him upon his blue eyes. Amused, Edward informed her that the corner of one of them was actually green. She examined him closely and saw that the prince did, indeed, have a splash of green in his left eye.

For a week, they flirted, teased, and led each other on. Michelle was brazen in her pursuit of the prince. She left a love note under his pillow. He reciprocated by playing hide-and-seek with her along the winding, wood-paneled corridors of Balmoral.

Then Michelle made a decisive move. She approached the prince and asked for his advice. She said she very much wanted to take a stroll in the grounds of the castle, but was afraid of getting lost. Obligingly, the prince offered to write her some directions. She could, he suggested, pick them up from his room that very evening.

Despite the fact that she was terrified of being spied by the security guards who prowl the corridors of Balmoral, Michelle was brave enough not only to don a green miniskirt and glamorous matching blouse, but also to go braless. Then she tiptoed to Edward's room.

True to his word, the prince was at his desk, still clad in his kilt. He was painstakingly drawing Michelle a map of the Balmoral grounds. He handed it to her. Simulating shyness, she asked if she should leave. He said she should stay. He put his arm around her waist, his head on her shoulder, and began to slide a gold chain down her cleavage.

"You know that if you drop that, it will fall through because I am not wearing a bra," she said, giggling. In answer, he kissed her. Michelle, clearly a well-seasoned seductress, inquired whether it was true what they said about kilts. "Do you wear anything underneath?" Now completely caught up in the mood of the moment, Edward challenged her. "That's for you to find out," he said.

Michelle didn't need any more encouragement. She slid her hands under Edward's kilt, to discover that he was naked. For a moment, he stopped kissing her. "We shouldn't be doing this, should we?" he asked. "No, not really," she conceded. Then, afraid that he would change his mind, she said quickly, "We may as well get undressed now."

Edward needed no further encouragement. He stripped naked, as did Michelle, kissed her again, then asked her if she was on the pill. She told him she was and lay down in bed. Mollified, he climbed on top of her.

"The sex was a bit disappointing," she said. "It wasn't the greatest sex I've ever had. It was all over rather quickly."

She did not, however, allow sexual disappointment to eclipse her euphoria at having captivated a prince. "It was a thrill," she said later, "to think I had made love to a prince."

After sex, Edward, ever the English gentleman, did not dispatch Michelle back to her room. Instead, he hugged her and they fell asleep in each other's arms.

They slept until two, when reality intruded into "romance." Michelle had to go to the bathroom. Afraid of being caught by a security man leaving the prince's room, she woke Edward and asked him to accompany her. Astonishingly, they both ran naked to the bathroom past the room where Diana and Charles were sleeping.

Still sustaining his gentlemanly manners, Edward did not ask Michelle to return to her own room. Instead, the two of them went back to his room together and slept till nearly six in the morning, when Michelle's duties began. She kissed him good-bye and left.

They met again at a staff disco a week later. Michelle took Edward aside and whispered that she wanted to see him again. He concurred, and they agreed to meet in his room a short while later. There, Michelle gave the prince a massage, and again they had sex.

Afterwards, she asked him what he thought would happen if his mother or father caught him making love to her. Instead of answering, he fell asleep. The next morning, Michelle bounced into the kitchen and confided to a footman that she had been the proud recipient of Prince Edward's virginity.

Despite Michelle's indiscretion, the liaison between the prince and the palace maid ended without either the Queen or the Duke of Edinburgh discovering the truth. A month after he first dallied with Michelle, Edward departed for New Zealand, where he spent a year as a junior teacher, and Michelle left Balmoral for Buckingham Palace. On the coach back to London, she wept pitifully, having left Balmoral without saying good-bye to Edward. She was heartbroken. But she clung desperately to a glimmer of hope. He had left her his address in New Zealand, and she was convinced that their love story was not yet over.

In 1983, Michelle Riles attempted to sell a British newspaper the saga of her sex romps with Prince Edward. Attorney General Lord Havers applied for an injunction on behalf of the Queen against Michelle Riles. The injunction was granted. Nonetheless, on February 18, 1996, *Sunday People* published a full and lurid account of Michelle's story, all in her own words.

Today, her sister, Gina Oates, casts doubts on Michelle's story: "She does live in a fantasy world. She was working in Buckingham Palace, but I never saw any proof that she had a relationship with the prince. She did tell me about it, but I took it with a pinch of salt. Sometimes she fantasizes a lot."

But Edward's subsequent reaction to Michelle's story appears to substantiate it, so the sister was probably prompted by embarrassment to deny the episode. "We're not happy with what she's done," she said.

In February 1992, Michelle wrote to Edward's secretary, telling Edward of her problems, her current lack of a job, and her desire to see him. A few days later, the phone rang. "A man said, 'Do you know who it is?' I said no. He said, 'It's Prince Edward.' I couldn't believe it. I had really poured out my troubles to him in my letter, and he said he felt sorry. I was in such a state. We spoke about his family and the problems Charles and Diana were having. We

spoke about the most intimate details of my personal life," a bedaz-
zled Michelle confessed later to the press.

Edward phoned her repeatedly. His reasons for responding
to Michelle's letter have never been clarified, but, given what
followed, his calls were clearly prompted by fear rather than
lust.

On April 30, 1993, he called and arranged for her to visit him at
Buckingham Palace to see him. A green Rover was dispatched to
pick her up. She was taken to the palace and into Edward's private
quarters. They hadn't seen one another in over ten years. Edward
was tense and didn't touch her.

Attempting to lighten the mood, he suggested she remove her
shoes. She did. She then curled up on a sofa, delighted by his
informality. "I wanted to be closer to him and felt he wanted to be
closer to me," she later reported. After a time, she got up from the
couch, took an orange from the sideboard, and began to peel it.

Michelle's sister, Gina Oates, has since said, "Michelle is a
dreamer, and I doubt if what she said really happened." And if her
story is at all suspect, it is in the following detail, which is totally at
variance with Edward's somber mood that day.

"I had my back to him and was bending over," Michelle claims.
"He walked towards me and gave me a playful slap on the bottom
and laughed. That slap aroused me. I thought I was in with a
chance. I must admit I wanted sex with him."

Edward patently did not want to have sex with Michelle, but
merely wanted to neutralize her. He gave her a gentle kiss; then
the telephone rang. When the call was over, he told Michelle that
he was going out for the evening. She asked whether she could go
with him. Edward said no, then got to the point of the meeting.

"He asked me what I wanted from him," said Michelle. "I said,
'I know I can't be your lover, but can we talk on the phone occasionally?' He agreed."

Whether the two of them ever met again is not on record. Michelle continued to claim that she loved the prince, then gave an indication of her true emotions by saying, "I could have been Princess Michelle in my wildest dreams." Instead of being Princess Michelle, though, she did make an attempt to be the prince's rescuer. When the stories about Prince Edward's alleged gay life emerged, Michelle Riles rushed to his defense. "It was a ludicrous suggestion," she said. "Nothing could be further from the truth."

In September 1982, Edward escaped both Michelle and the vestiges of Britain's long, hot summer. He had been appointed junior house tutor at one of New Zealand's leading boys' schools, Wanganui Collegiate, 122 miles northwest of Wellington, the country's capital.

The imposing brick Anglican school was founded in the mid nineteenth century, and, at the time of Edward's appointment, had 525 pupils, mostly from wealthy sheep-farming families. School fees were £2,000 ($3,260) a year, and the school was close to the little town of Wanganui (population 40,000), which boasted two cinemas, a small opera house, an art gallery, and a museum featuring Maori artifacts.

There was great excitement at Wanganui on hearing of the prince's appointment. "There's no chance of the Prince feeling homesick," said the headmaster's mother-in-law, Janette Budd. "There's a very family atmosphere here. My daughter, Jennifer, who is very calm and gracious is always entertaining. So I am sure he will be invited to dinner a lot."

If Edward's heart was not melted by the promise of the McKinnons' hospitality, then perhaps headmaster Ian McKinnon's pledge that "I want the prince to be treated the same as other members of staff" caused him to hope that he might have a fairly decent chance of leading a relatively normal life at Wanganui.

However, the fact that he continued to be accompanied by

three bodyguards—and that a house was built at Wanganui specially for them—did not bode altogether well for his New Zealand interlude. When he arrived at the college, he found it difficult at first to fit in, as he always has in every new situation where he attempts to be like everyone else.

"At the start he was unsure of himself. He was lonely, reserved, and hesitant," said the Reverend Andrew Sangster, Wanganui's vicar. But the headmaster did his utmost to help the prince feel at home. He suggested that the boys in his class write the prince a letter, telling him about their life. "You know about me," explained Edward, "but I know nothing about you."

The ploy worked. Soon after, McKinnon confirmed, "The prince is settling in very well indeed. The boys think highly of him. He has successfully begun teaching a third form class of thirteen-year-olds. He teaches English grammar and literature. This is our cross-country season. He goes out with the boys three or four miles a day. It can be tough going."

It may have been tough, but Edward adapted well to school life. While at Wanganui, he coached one of the college's hockey teams and took parties of thirty boys on weekend camping trips to the local hills, where he organized campfire games of charades.

His attempt to live a normal, relatively anonymous life was momentarily halted when, without a previous appointment, an enterprising *Daily Mirror* reporter named Bryan Rostron called him from Britain. On receiving the call, Edward was extremely irate. "You've got a right nerve," he snapped. "What on earth gives you the right to call me?" The reporter tried to explain in a polite manner, but Edward refused to be soft-soaped. "Your curiosity just killed you. Something rude will happen to you," he threatened. Edward was clearly aping his father's abrasive response to the press. Sadly for him, he did not possess Prince Philip's wit or charm. Bryan dismissed Edward as "arrogant, juvenile, and extremely slow witted. He just came across as a rather callow young man, and one whose life has been protected so much that he doesn't know how to talk to people." The call was unexpected, unwelcome, and, cutting as it did into his New Zealand idyll, almost menacing, but unfortunately for Edward, Bryan Rostron's negative response to him would be the first of many he would elicit from the British press.

At the end of April 1983, Prince Charles and Princess Diana visited Edward in Wanganui. He had been made the honorary chieftain of a Maori tribe and greeted his illustrious visitors clad in a ceremonial Maori cloak. Charles was highly amused by the spectacle of his brother covered in kiwi feathers. "Good Lord! It must be a fancy dress party. What have you come as? It looks like a blanket," said Charles, laughing.

But the highlight of Edward's time at Wanganui was his appearance in the farce *Charley's Aunt*, by Brandon Thomas. He took the cross-dressing part of Charley, the English aristocrat who dresses up as his own aunt. Edward threw himself into the part with gusto. The first night audience later praised his performance as "witty, gifted, and professional," and Edward was elated by his reception.

Edward's love affair with the arts didn't end with acting. While at Wanagnui, he wrote and published, under the nom de plume of Fenton Ryder, a thinly disguised account of life at the school, *Full Marks for Trying*. The book was published in New Zealand and all twelve thousand copies sold out overnight.

One enthusiastic purchaser of Edward's effort was John Tanner, a third form student at Wanganui when Edward was there. He had seen the prince's tour de force in *Charley's Aunt*, and admired it. "Both John and I were impressed by Prince Edward's performance in the play. John liked the fact that the prince had opted for a career in theater," said a Wanganui student.

Edward left a few broken hearts behind at Wanganui. A sixteen-year-old girl named Alison Bell costarred with him in *Charley's*

Aunt and was smitten by him. They went out on a few dates, but unlike Michelle Riles, Alison did not confide in anyone. "I don't want to say how our relationship developed after that," she said firmly.

In May 1983, Edward returned from New Zealand, his time at Wanganui over. In retrospect, he said, "I regard this as part of my educational process. After all, we go on learning till death. You can never know everything."

He sounded confident, and perhaps he was. At least, about his education. About women, he was still shy and inexperienced. Michelle Riles had been a momentary roll in the hay. Now he was nineteen, primed to go to college, and ready for real romance.

Her name was Romy Adlington; she was seventeen years old and a fashion model. "She was a very nice, well-educated, happy sort of person," recalled her agent, Carol White, of Premier Models.

The prince and the five-foot-ten brunette met in August 1983 in the most glamorous of circumstances—at the Royal Yacht Squadron Ball during Cowes Week Regatta on the Isle of Wight. Romy was voluptuous and sultry, with cascades of chestnut hair, and resembled the flamboyant girls hitherto favored by Edward's brother Andrew. Edward was instantly attracted to the statuesque model. The daughter of a wine importer and his wife, Anne, who owned a store selling party balloons, Romy was far more sophisticated than the brazen Michelle Riles.

Romy later remembered her first meeting with Edward extremely tenderly. "He was polite and charming, but also very shy," she said. His shyness, however, was only momentary. A few days later they met once more at the Royal London Yacht Club. Edward found Romy surprisingly easy to talk to and, within weeks, wrote to her and invited her to come to Balmoral with him for a two-week vacation.

The invitation took Romy unawares, and not quite believing her good fortune, she was stunned when he phoned to confirm it. "I was halfway through Sunday lunch with my mother," she remembered. "He said, 'Hello, it's Edward here. I wonder if you had thought about Balmoral?' I told him I would love to come."

Before leaving for Balmoral, they met at Buckingham Palace. Edward and Romy dined by candlelight in his private rooms. A liveried retainer served the couple beef in cream sauce and fresh vegetables, accompanied by wine and fruit juice. They dallied over dinner; then a butler removed the dishes and silver tureens. "Edward and I were allowed to be by ourselves. We stayed up until the early hours chatting about music and things in front of the fire before going to bed," recalled Romy. "Edward needed lots of hugs and cuddles. He was very anxious to prove that he was a red-blooded male."

His drive to prove himself sexually was so strong that once they were up at Balmoral, Edward did not allow the Queen's close proximity to inhibit him from making love to Romy. "I was lying in bed at midnight when there was a knock on my door. It was Edward. He was only wearing a dressing gown and seemed in a bit of a state."

They talked for a while. Edward attempted to seduce her. But Romy was utterly overawed by the fact that the Queen was just a few doors away. "I thought trying it on at Balmoral with the Queen so near was a bit much," she said. She told Edward so and asked him to go back to his room. Reluctantly, he agreed.

A few days later, Romy succumbed to Edward's advances. "I think he felt quite proud that he could get a girlfriend to stay the night with him, right under his mother's nose," she said afterwards.

They spent two weeks in Balmoral together, riding, fishing, and going on picnics. Nonetheless, Edward still clung to some of his inbred formality. With hindsight, Romy understood the reasons. "If he seems awkward at times, it is because of the emotionally inhibited way he had been brought up," she said. At dinner, Romy sat close to the Queen. "You never heard Edward or Charles call her 'mother,' " Romy observed. "At the end of the meal, there would be a toast to the Queen and people could smoke. You obviously had to be on good behavior, but generally all the royal family were relaxed. The Queen was just as I imagined her but less formal and more smiley than at public engagements.

"At Balmoral, Edward could really unwind. Far from being the tense and stressed boy at public functions, he was able to smile and be normal. Edward seemed happy and far less tense than I had seen him before."

Romy felt a certain amount of tension regarding the rigidity of the Balmoral regime. Each day began at seven-thirty A.M. with bagpipers playing the Highland reveille. At nine, a complete English breakfast was served, consisting of porridge, bacon, kippers, and eggs. Then the royals either went fishing, riding, stalking, walking, or shooting. Sometimes, the Queen would drive them through the fifty-thousand-acre estate in her Land Rover, always driving at high speed along the winding mountain roads.

Although Romy admits that she probably unwittingly breached royal protocol on many occasions, the family seemed relatively receptive to her playing a part in Edward's life. When she and the prince returned to London, their fledgling teenage romance continued apace. Yet despite the couple's compatibility, Edward was not yet prepared to make their relationship public.

"Edward was paranoid about being spotted out on the town with me. Because of this, I hit on the idea of him dressing up in disguise," Romy remembered.

She was a resourceful lady with a rich sense of humor, so she enlisted the help of a makeup artist whom she trusted to create a disguise for her princely lover. "We built up his nose, greased his hair back, added sideburns, and gave him a wonderful mustache, stuck on with glue," said Romy, laughing.

Emboldened by his new identity, Edward took Romy to an elegant London restaurant. His appearance was decidedly odd, and waiters looked at him askance. Edward couldn't contain his laughter. But the meal passed without incident—until coffee, that is. At that point, he reached across the table towards Romy, and his false mustache caught fire on a candle. The couple beat a hasty retreat.

Romy's mother, Anne Adlington, met Edward on many occasions and remembers him with great fondness. "He's absolutely charming," she says today. "Very kind, artistic, and a very good friend. When he was younger, he was quite shy. He's a very kind, gentle person. By gentle, I don't mean weak. He has his own strength of character. He was never pompous, but just very nice."

Yet despite Anne Adlington's enthusiasm for Edward, the relationship between Romy and Edward eventually faded. "Edward and I had a lot of fun together," Romy mused in retrospect. "But it was a teenage romance. I was just seventeen and he was twenty. Eventually, our lives became very different and we just drifted apart."

The relationship's downward spiral began during a weekend the two of them spent at Sandringham, the royal residence in Norfolk. Romy adored Wood Farm, where they spent the weekend on the estate. She was prepared for a classic royal vacation of duck shooting, riding, and fishing, so she had brought her rubber boots and raincoat.

They took one more romantic trip to Balmoral in the summer of 1985, but Romy knew that their affair was over. "He was looking for a really committed relationship—more of a commitment than I could give him at the time," she said. "I know he was very upset, but I tried to explain that I wasn't ready to settle down."

She may not have been ready to settle down with the prince, but she seems to have been ready to settle down with someone else. The previous year, she had moved into a flat with import-export manager Nick Hooper, who lived in the City of London. By the time she broke up with Edward, she had replaced Hooper with another boyfriend, Nic Sunnucks, a fashion buyer. Soon after she and Edward broke up, Romy became pregnant by Nic and later gave birth to his child, a daughter.

Edward continued to telephone her during the years that followed; their romance was over. He would turn to Romy again when he faced the worst crisis of his life.

4.

THE STUDENT
PRINCELING

*H*E WAS THE SON OF ONE OF THE WORLD'S WEALTHI-
est women, the brother-in-law of the world's favorite fairy princess,
and the brother of the heir to the throne of England. But Edward
wasn't always automatically welcome wherever he chose to go.
The University of Cambridge was a case in point.

After he left Gordonstoun, he had applied for admission to
Cambridge University, England's equivalent to Harvard. He was
duly invited to visit a number of colleges there. His brother
Charles had attended Trinity College, Cambridge, but Edward did
not want to follow in his brother's footsteps in every aspect. So he
selected Jesus College, the alma mater of the poet Samuel Taylor
Coleridge and the British broadcaster Alistair Cooke, known in the
United States as the host of *Masterpiece Theater* on PBS.

Jesus College was one of Cambridge's oldest colleges. In 1496,
Bishop Alcock established a College for a Master, six Fellows,
and "a certain number of boys." His coat of arms (three roosters)
became the coat of arms of Jesus College. The college chapel,
which dates back to 1140, still stands today and is the oldest college building in Cambridge. The serenity of the college was
reflected in a comment made by King James I: "Were I to

choose, I would pray at King's, dine at Trinity, and study and sleep at Jesus."

The British university is a far different institution than its American counterpart. In medieval times, the university itself was only an examining and degree-giving body and all the teaching was done separately by the colleges. When they judged that the students had achieved the right degree of academic excellence, they submitted them to the university for examination leading to a degree. That system is still in place in Cambridge today, with the college being responsible for a student's education, providing the student with a residence, tutors, and directors of study. While the university still offers lectures in all fields of study and laboratories in which to study science, the direct responsibility for the education of each student belongs with the individual college.

In early 1981, Sir Alan Cotterell, the master of Jesus College, was informed that Prince Edward was selecting a Cambridge college. When Edward arrived at Jesus College on February 6, 1981, for his interview with him, Sir Alan asked three undergraduates to invite Edward to lunch and spend a few hours with him. This was different from standard college interview procedures of meeting the prince and introducing him to senior college staff. "I think he was rather taken by that and by meeting people of his own kind," said Sir Alan.

Edward selected Jesus College and was slated to start his studies there in October, 1983. However, in November 1982, thirty-eight percent of Jesus's undergraduates rose up in protest against his admission. For the first time in his life, Edward met with wholesale rejection.

A 150-signature petition, signed by Jesus undergraduates, protested against Edward's admission to the college, on the grounds that his O- and A-level grades were far too low to merit a place there. While Edward never commented publicly on the movement to bar him from Jesus, it must have rankled with him that while his three A level grades were a mere two D's and a C, one of the undergraduate leaders of the movement, Richard Parker, a history student, had obtained four A levels, three at grade A and one at B.

The petition listed Edward's low A-level grades and observed, "Privilege should not be a passport to a university education." Richard Parker explained, "This is certainly not in any way an attack on the monarch, but solely an attack on privilege."

The National Union of Students weighed in against Edward's admission, with spokesman Alan Hiscock declaring, "It would be appalling if Prince Edward was made a special case. There can be no justification in setting one standard for a member of the royal family and another for the rest of the country. It makes a mockery of the procedure. The first-year entry requirement for degree courses at our universities is now a minimum of two B's and a C."

Edward's academic fate rested in the hands of Sir Alan Cotterell. Luckily for Edward, Sir Alan had no intention of allowing a minority of students to deprive Jesus College of the prestige of having Prince Edward as one of its alumni, which the *Varsity Handbook* (written for students by students) described as being "a mix of fervent Left-Wingers and drunken boaties who spend their time bellowing in the college bar, imbibing, vomiting, letting off fire extinguishers, and molesting female students." Sir Alan made the decision to admit Edward to Jesus. After all, as a fellow student later commented, "Which university in the world wouldn't want the son of a sovereign?"

As at Gordonstoun, Edward overcame the initial hurdle. The next was his personal security. The Irish Republican Army had only recently launched a bombing attack on the British people. In 1979, Edward's own great-uncle Lord Mountbatten had been a victim. So the young prince's safety was of paramount concern to the college.

Four private detectives were assigned to occupy the same floor as Edward in 7, North Court, a three-story sterile block built in 1965, housing seventy-three students. Before the building was deemed safe for Edward, a team of security men moved in and strengthened all the windows, replaced the door locks, and erected special security curtains to cover the windowpanes, which had been fitted with bulletproof glass.

Other than that, Edward's bedroom was identical to that of every other undergraduate and was furnished with a standard single bed, armchairs, and a big desk. He had a small kitchen with a two-ring electric stove and facilities for making tea or coffee. Edward brought his own coffee machine with him to Cambridge, along with a box of spaghetti. On his first morning at the college, he didn't attend the early service at Jesus College Chapel, nor did he eat the vast English breakfast on offer of kippers, eggs, bacon, sausage, and spaghetti, but instead remained in his room playing pop music, including the very apropos hit by Paul Young, "Wherever I Lay My Hat, That's My Home."

He was not always so reclusive and eventually even progressed to doing his own laundry. As a fellow student later commented, "He is often seen waddling off to the college launderette laden with dirty washing and a pocket full of 10p pieces. He doesn't get it picked up and done for him."

His rooms were supervised by a sixty-two-year old woman named Florence Moore, who had the quaintly named post of "bedder." She had been Charles's bedder at Trinity College fifteen years before and would perform the identical services for Edward. When asked by prying press what exactly those services would be, Mrs. Moore smiled and said, "Exactly what your wife does for you. Apart from the obvious thing." She would become Edward's cleaner, his bed-maker, and, judging by her relationship with Charles (who invited her to his wedding), ultimately his friend.

Edward would need all the friends he could make at Cambridge. From the first, the press was in hot pursuit of him. "We knew there would be problems, but we never dreamed it would be like this. What shocked us was the harassment and the lies," said Edward's tutor, sociologist Dr. Gavin Mackenzie.

In Edward's very first week at Cambridge, the London *Evening Standard* dispatched letters to all first-year female Jesus students inquiring of them what it was like to be at college with Prince Edward. Later, when he was appearing in *The Crucible*, Edward's leading lady, Corinne Taylor, was devastated by the treatment meted out to her by ruthless reporters. "Life was hell for three days," she complained. "They tried to bully me with threats." She was staked out by reporters and photographers, who kept a constant vigil outside the front door of her house. One reporter spent hours perched on top of a multistory garage in the hope of trying to snatch a picture of her through his long-range lens. Corinne ended up entering her house by climbing over the back fence of her garden.

The press was so aggressive in stalking Prince Edward that they even managed to recruit spies inside the college to report on him. "It is common knowledge in Fleet Street," reported the local Cambridge paper *Stop Press*, "that at least two Jesus undergraduates are on retainers from national dailies to relay gossip both about the prince and about anybody he might be linked with."

During Edward's three years at Cambridge, press pursuit of him became so virulent that Sir Alan Cotterell twice complained to the Press Council (the governing body overseeing press ethics in Britain) regarding the behavior of journalists. "They hounded Edward, but he is practiced at handling that. He expected it. It was that they hounded anyone who was remotely likely to have been in touch with him. For example, a charming little Indian girl lived on the same staircase as Edward. The press drove the girl to tears. We had to move her to another room. And head porter John Haycock was tricked into giving the papers a quote. He thought he was going to lose his job as a result. He was almost suicidal."

The British press had become far more intrusive since the days when Charles was at Cambridge. Edward suffered from their enhanced aggression. But it was only the beginning. It was to get worse. But who was to lambaste the press for their voracious appetite for Edward-at-Cambridge stories? After all, in the words of Harold Brooks-Baker of *Burke's Peerage*, "This is the first group of royals really to work, to study at university, to be people in their own right. In the past, the brothers and sisters of whoever was on the throne and their children were never visible to the outside world. They tended not to be well-educated and lived in a cloistered world. This is the first time in history that royals are becoming normal rich people not locked away in the tower. They're leading an upper-class existence, working, having affairs, going skiing, and surfing."

Edward's degree subjects were archaeology and anthropology (described by students as "arch and ant"). While all his tutors judiciously avoided raising the sensitive subject of his bad grades, there was an awareness among the staff that Edward was not a candidate for academic glory. "If he fails his degree, I'm going to have egg on my face," admitted Dr. Mackenzie. And although he maintains a loyal discretion, years after Edward first arrived at Cambridge, Sir Alan Cotterell conceded, "Gordonstoun is a sort of an Outward Bound place"—a school that stresses physical excellence above all else—"and so he had a bit of catching up to do in his first year."

His most immediate task was overcoming the initial hostility of his fellow students. "After all, there can't be many students who arrive at their college having already been pilloried by fellow students for not being bright enough," pointed out Cambridge reporter Peter Aspden, who went on to say, "The truth is, Edward's A-level results are well below average for a Cambridge undergraduate." But there was a certain amount of hope, as Aspden went on to point out: "The same applied to his brother Charles, who nevertheless emerged with a good honors degree."

Like Charles, Edward quickly overcame past opposition to his admission. Sir Alan Cotterell maintains, "As soon as Prince Edward came up to Cambridge, the other undergraduates were charmed by him. They found him such a pleasant person, and he mixed in well with them. He became a normal undergraduate."

He was, of course, far from normal, and his life at Cambridge did little to negate his status or diminish the aura of privilege surrounding him. He was accompanied at all times by his longtime personal detective, Andrew Merrylees, and also by Inspector Richard Griffin, a sharpshooter who even attended lectures with him. The palace offered neither advice nor guidance regarding how the university should treat Edward, so that everyone addressed him as "Edward." "He was used to dealing with people of his own class," remarked Lady Cotterell, who also noted his ease in dealing with his bedder, his porter, and the rest of the college staff. He would chat to them informally, sometimes spending more time with them than with other students. He was accustomed to dealing with palace staff, and at times, it appeared that he was more comfortable with the Cambridge domestic staff than with his fellow undergraduates. "When I am here, I try my hardest to be an undergraduate and do the things undergraduates do," he said. "When I am away from here, I do the things a prince does. I try to keep the two things separate."

He was always alert, watchful, and took great pains never to compromise himself or his status. "He was capable of handling all the scrutiny. He was very firm in how he was going to behave. He was mature for his age," recalled Sir Alan. "He did his best not to cause embarrassment to the royal family." According to a fellow undergraduate, "He'll pop into a party and say hello, but generally he doesn't mix. He never stays that long and is usually one of the first to leave. He doesn't really like late nights."

He did not hesitate, though, to brave the odd late night when it came to taking part in plays. He was aware that, by selecting Cambridge, he was following in the dramatic footsteps of previous famous undergraduates like Emma Thompson, John Cleese, and Stephen Fry, all of whom had taken part in amateur dramatics at Cambridge. He was set on making the most of any acting opportunities open to him at Cambridge.

Almost as soon as he arrived at Jesus, in October 1983, Edward auditioned for the part of Deputy-Governor Danforth in Arthur Miller's play *The Crucible*. "He simply turned up to an open audition and showed himself to be a very talented actor. He was an obvious choice," said Nick Walmsley, the play's director.

There was a certain amount of grumbling among the students that Edward had not been picked for the part because of his thespian talents but merely because of his crowd-pulling potential. Nick Walmsley agreed that, "We know that on our first night we will be packed out with people wanting to see the prince, but that is not why he was chosen. He was the best actor that we saw, and any worries I have about the production do not concern Prince Edward's acting ability."

Walmsley's faith in Edward was justified by the praise of critics reviewing his performance. "He rapped out his lines with all the swagger and arrogance of a brash, young Army officer," wrote one critic. "Rarely can a student have looked so comfortable in a position of authority and gave a thoroughly professional display," wrote another critic.

After the first night, Edward granted a press interview in which he bared his feelings about acting. "Life is one big act," he said, revealingly. "You may be nervous, but you don't show it." At the time, he said he was tentative about appearing in any more Cambridge plays. "In some ways, I feel it's not fair on the other people involved. As much as I want to lead the life of a normal undergraduate, I cannot because of who I am. It's a paradox, really. I would like to do more plays because I really enjoy them, but I don't see many other chances to do it. This term has had ups and downs, but I have thoroughly enjoyed doing the play. It has been fun."

Sadly for Edward, the fun didn't last long. In December 1983, his acting career was temporarily derailed when he contracted infectious mononucleosis. The illness lingered into March and prevented him from directing the University Rag Revue as planned. But nothing, not even illness, could keep Edward away from his beloved theater.

Although Edward couldn't appear in the revue, one of his detectives took part in it, and also acted as deputy stage manager as well. Instead, Edward busied himself with raising cash for the annual charity event. He puzzled for a time on how to promote Rag Week, a five-week event of singing, dancing, and gags. "We've got to try to find the money for the show. We have to pay for light and props," he confided to Radio 1 disc jockey Peter Powell. "My job is to try to get as much money as possible—so there's a bit of bartering going on as well." A few days later, his solution for raising money was made public. London cabdriver Maurice Hamilton was approached by his sister, Doreen Sass, to help out with a charity show. "I had no idea what it was about except that they wanted a London cab," said the bemused cab driver. "When I got to Cambridge, I found myself shaking hands with the prince. He gave me a glass of champagne. I was dumbstruck. He was a proper gentleman and very concerned about me and that there should be no damage to the cab."

Edward's scheme for promoting the charity was to take two fellow students, Vicki Thaxted and Dave Howard, to a local Cambridge shopping mall, tie dozens of balloons to the London cab, then hoist them onto the cab roof. Vicki, clad in a sexy white dress, then did the Charleston with great verve. Edward defined the event as "a crowd-stopper," and it was. Tickets were sold to the review, and Edward gained a reputation among his peers as a good organizer.

Edward's university rugby career was not so successful. He made his debut during his first few weeks at Cambridge, playing wing forward on the college's second team. He tried hard to play well, but referee Don Taylor noticed that he was continually offside, "He needs to sort out his binding, as he will always be in trouble with referees," warned Taylor.

He clearly was also already in trouble with his opponents. Some of his fellow students took malicious delight in tackling the Queen's son, rubbing his face in the mud, and, in general, roughing him up considerably. "He played rugger for the college in his first year," said Sir Alan. "He gave it up then because I think he found it pretty hard going. People went for him. Rugger is a tough game. The individuals who play it are pretty beefy. He didn't have the beefiness of some of the other players. I think he is a bit small for the game." A close friend afterwards confirmed, "His pals would cover up for him. They'd say it was unfair the way he was singled out for a showdown because of who he was. It was a great chance for ordinary people to give the son of the Queen of England a bad time."

Edward gave up rugby, initially citing mononucleosis as a reason. Later he admitted, "I gave up the game because I was getting fed up with being a target."

At the end of Edward's first year at Cambridge, he took exams in archaeology and anthropology and gained a 2.2—an average grade. "More undergraduates at Cambridge get a 2.2 than any other grade, and this is a very respectable result," said his senior tutor, Dr. Gavin Mackenzie. He went on to summarize Edward's first year in extremely favorable terms. "Prince Edward has played rugby, taken part in drama, Rag Week, and had glandular fever to boot. I think you could say he has had a well-rounded year."

In spring 1985, he received the accolade of being appointed to organize the annual May Ball. Like the rest of the royal family, Edward was always intrigued by magicians. So he decided to hire Paul Daniels, Britain's leading practitioner of the art, to entertain at the May Ball.

"The phone rang and I said, "Yup!" remembers Paul Daniels with amusement. "A voice said, 'Could I speak to Mr. Daniels?' I asked who was calling. He said, 'Prince Edward.' I said, 'Very funny!' and put the phone down. He really didn't have any trace of the royal voice. He really has a middle-of-the-road voice. He phoned back. He convinced me he was who he said he was. I said, 'I am sorry, Your Royal Highness; a lot of people in our business clown around.' He asked if we could meet on Monday. I asked him where, and he said, 'Have you ever heard of a place called Buckingham Palace?' "

Despite the initial confusion, Edward hired Daniels to perform magic tricks at the show. He also hired glam rock singer Gary Glitter to perform at the ball, negotiating his £3,000 ($4,890) fee himself. As it turned out, Gary Glitter's music was far too loud, and the neighbors complained bitterly. Edward requested that the rock singer turn down the volume, but Glitter flatly refused. Edward, far too busy running security, keeping in touch with fellow officials via walkie-talkie, and stamping guests' hands, chose not to argue with him.

At the end of March 1985, he was onstage again. Acting with the Cambridge University Light Entertainment Society, he appeared in *Catch My Foot*, playing a cleaner, a civil servant, and a spy chief. His fellow undergraduate and friend Lady Sophie Birdwood saw his performance and said, "Edward loves acting, that's for sure. He's very amusing onstage. He is a very charming, bubbly, and funny person who is also sensible and straightforward." Gary Ernest, manager of the university ADC theater agreed. "He seems a bit shy, but when he gets onstage, he likes a good fling."

Acting came to be his escape from playing the arduous role of himself, Prince Edward. "Edward puts on the greasepaint and becomes a different person," said a friend who was at Cambridge with him at the time. "It is as if he gets away from the demanding role of being a royal."

It was at Cambridge that Edward first became fully aware of his commercial value. British and foreign newspaper photographers jostled to get photographs of him in the review. The realization struck him that he was a commodity. So instead of acceding to photographers' requests, he began demanding a £500 ($815) fee for the pictures—that fee to go to charity. Although the end result of his haggling with the media was that a worthy cause benefited, Edward's negotiations set the tone for the future. In years to come, he would be first of the Queen's children to turn his royal status into a business.

Towards the end of his time at university, Edward became patron of the Cambridge Youth Theatre, an organization for underprivileged teenagers aged from thirteen to eighteen. The theater was funded by the Cambridge City Council and had the same ethos as the Duke of Edinburgh Award. "It is allowing and enabling young people to take some sense of responsibility for their own lives," explained cofounder Claudette Bryanston-Cross. "Prince Edward has been very supportive of our organization."

The Cambridge Youth Theatre was the first university organization for which Edward agreed to be patron. The Queen was alarmed by his decision and went so far as to write a letter to Claudette Bryanston-Cross, who revealed later that the Queen, ever protective of her youngest son, had admonished, "'Study comes first and the prince is in Cambridge to work.' The letter we have from the prince's private secretary says that the Queen has made it clear that she does not want this to open the door to other organizations for similar requests. What the Queen is anxious about is that he does not get inundated by various organizations until he is finished at Cambridge."

In the summer of 1985, Edward became involved with yet another theatrical venture, this time more for his own pleasure than for charity. Haddo House is an iconoclastic British theatrical institution run by June Gordon, Marchioness of Aberdeen Temair in Scotland. For the past forty years, the marchioness, a keen thespian and a professional orchestra conductor, had persuaded a dazzling group of professional and amateur musicians, singers, and actors to perform in the theater on the grounds of her home at Haddo, a mansion about forty miles north of Aberdeen, Scotland.

The Marquis of Aberdeen, to whom the marchioness had been married, was, for a period, the governor general of Canada. After his tenure there, he was given a huge log house and he had it shipped back to his home in Scotland. There, he transformed it into a theater-barn, complete with dressing rooms and seats for over three hundred sixty people. That became the site of the Haddo Amateur Dramatic and Operatic Society.

For most of the year, Haddo is open to the public. But in the summer, the marchioness holds a big house party before the opening of the season's major dramatic production. The Haddo atmosphere was both artistic and congenial. "Old friends, food, drink, a marvelous country house, ambience, camaraderie. We just pick up where we all left off last year," said Christopher Harley, assistant curator with the National Trust for Scotland.

Haddo is an hour and a half drive from Balmoral, and Edward had become a great friend of the marchioness and her family. A guest at the 1985 Haddo house party remembers Edward well: "All the guests spent time in the main drawing room of the main house, where we would light a fire and play and talk. Edward was hugely amusing. He did an absolutely wonderful imitation of Madame Vacani, who taught all the royal family boys how to dance. In a stern, female voice, he imitated her, saying things like, 'Now, then, Andrew, hold your brother closer.' He was a wonderful mimic."

The day began at Haddo with breakfast served in the kitchen. "There was a huge pan of cement-thick Scottish porridge," the guest said, "a large industrial-size toaster, some eggs, and some boiling water. The guests made themselves breakfast, and the cast came to breakfast in their theatrical costumes. Some of the guests brought their children to Haddo House, and as they stood in line for porridge and toast, they were stunned to see the Queen's son dressed in full costume, complete with pink tights. Edward was utterly unself-conscious. He was very charming to the children, winning their hearts with his relaxed, informal warmth."

That summer of 1985, Edward was appearing in the Haddo House production of *The Taming of the Shrew* with British newscaster Richard Baker. The production would run for three nights. Edward and the cast rehearsed around the clock until the first night, August 28. Dick Griffin, Edward's personal detective, played the part of an officer so that he could protect his royal charge by being as close to him as possible. He wore pink tights, frilly Shakespearean knickers, and, sticking out of the belt of his costume, a gun. "The audience were very amused at the spectacle," says a source who saw it.

"I played the part of an old gentleman called Vincentio and Prince Edward was the rascally servant, Biondello," recalled Richard Baker. "At one point I had to chase him round the stage with a big stick, which seemed a disrespectful way to behave to a prince of the blood. Prince Edward was friendly and pleasant at all times, and came to rehearsals very well prepared. He knew his lines a lot better than some of us, and played the role very well."

He would take part in the Haddo House festivities many times through the years. At times, members of the audience were less than kind regarding his performance. World-renowned international casting director Rose Tobias Shaw—who was Lew Grade's head of casting for seven years, worked with Grace Kelly, James Dean, and John Houston, and cast a large number of ABC, CBS, and NBC miniseries—went to see Edward play Prince Florizel in *The Winter's Tale* in 1987. "I thought he was embarrassing. He came over like a cipher. Everybody wants to be in show business because they think it is so easy. But Edward wouldn't have been successful in the theater. I have the feeling that he's a person with no energy and no attack," she said.

Those who acted with Edward at Haddo were generally kinder in their assessment of his acting ability.

"The thing that struck me was how hard-working he was. Always willing to rehearse yet again or try yet again to get it right. He's quite a perfectionist and is willing to drive himself very hard. He's determined to be taken seriously. He wasn't just playing at it. He wanted to prove that he was taking it seriously, and so he wanted to be taken seriously," said Charles Barron, the artistic director at Haddo House.

"People thought he wouldn't be any good as an actor just because he's a royal. He had a lot of theatrical knowledge and wasn't slow to get his hands dirty either by moving scenery. I had the impression that acting was his great love, and that no matter how small the part, he just loves acting."

Charles Barron had a great many opportunities to observe Edward closely. "He could never have an entirely normal life when there's a policeman within a few feet of him twenty-four-hours a day. The protection officer is always there. Edward could never completely let his guard down. I am sure it is always in his mind that somebody might be lurking round the corner waiting for that shot that would make the front pages tomorrow morning and embarrass him."

It was only when he was engaged in leisure pursuits that

Edward could really relax. Barron observed, "He doesn't mind embarrassing himself in things like games or sport or in a part he plays. He has a schoolboyish sense of humor and particularly enjoys practical jokes. He's a good comic actor, particularly in the sort of knockabout roles. Not quite so good in the straight drama, although he makes a good shot at it. There is that sense of fun in everything he does, and that gives him strength as a comic actor. He is likable onstage, and his great success was in parts where he had some communication with the audience."

Barron felt that Edward was far less at ease offstage. "He is understandably cautious and guarded. I wondered just how much he lets his guard down in terms of being able to relax with people he knows or works with. He comes across as a very sensitive man."

From an early age, Edward had been drilled in manners and the British art of keeping a stiff upper lip. "I was always impressed by the public control he was able to show," observed Barron. "He's very self-contained. I don't ever remember seeing him angry. That is unusual in the theater with all the short rehearsal times we have and everybody's working in a stressed kind of way. I never saw him angry or showing impatience with someone—although it was quite obvious that sometimes he must have been feeling it inside.

"He could make people feel at ease however nervous they were at first about working with him. And obviously, in many of the roles he played he had close contact with people on the stage. He always managed to break down their silence or their reserve with a joke and just by being relaxed about it himself."

His sensitivity was apparent that summer of 1985 at Haddo. "The play was an amateur production of professional standards, beautifully costumed, and well-directed," remembers a confidential source who was there during the week in which Edward was appearing in *The Taming of the Shrew*.

"Edward rehearsed like mad. It was clear to all of us that

Edward would have loved the Queen and Prince Philip come to see him in the play. He'd put a lot into rehearsing.

"Night after night, special elegantly upholstered chairs were put in the front row of the audience for the Queen, Prince Philip, and the rest of the royal family. On the first night, they remained empty. On the second night, they were empty again. On the last night of the play, a buzz went round the theater that the Queen and Prince Philip were about to arrive to see the play. But they didn't. Instead, the Balmoral butler and some of the staff came in their stead. Edward said of his parents' failure to come to the play, 'Well, they are busy. They've got a house party and can't abandon their houseguests.' He was very well brought up, so he said those things. But the disappointment on his face was transparent."

Edward managed to stay out of the British tabloid press headlines for most of his time at Cambridge. Romy Adlington was no longer a part of his life but, for a brief spell, he was linked with Georgia May, a girl whom Edward called "George" and her friends had dubbed "Girl George," in parody of the singer Boy George.

They first saw each other at the same Royal Yacht Squadron Club where Edward first met Romy Adlington, and which must have evoked strong romantic memories in him. Unlike Romy, Georgia was passionate about sailing. Her father, David May, was the millionaire owner of the Bethon Boat Company in Lymington, Hampshire. For a short while, Georgia also appeared to be passionate about Edward as well. She was twenty years old and had the confident veneer that came from being a millionaire's daughter. Consequently, she was unfazed by Edward's invitation to Sandringham. Georgia was bold, down-to-earth, and straightforward, and very taken with Edward. "Edward is very humorous and kind," she said. "He can be rather shy at first, but once you get to know him he's great company."

But the relationship ended when her former boyfriend, New Zealand yachtsman Ed Danby, returned to England, demanding to marry Georgia. Despite her sophistication, Georgia found it difficult to cope with the press scrutiny. "All this attention is terrifying me," she said. During an interview with BBC Radio Cambridgeshire, Edward commented on the stifling attention the press imposed upon his girlfriends. "If I talk to a girl more than three times a week, then we're likely to end up in the gossip columns," he said. "The problem about that is not going to affect me at all because my anonymity has gone and I accept that. The problem is that if I meet anyone else they [the press] want to go and dig up their past and get photos of them splashed across the papers—and their anonymity goes. I cannot have a normal relationship with just about anybody, but that's the way it goes. You become very conscious of the feeling that if you do try to get to know anybody, they are going to suffer a stigma for the rest of their lives."

Despite his misapprehensions, Edward nonetheless risked having relationships with several women during his Cambridge years. Eleanor Weightman, who was studying history at Newnham College, Cambridge, was to become a girlfriend whom he liked and respected. She was from Cheshire, in the North of England, was sporty, vivacious, and academically brighter than Edward. She was exactly one year and one day younger than Edward. She was also tiny—only five feet tall—and Edward took to teasingly call her "Munchkin," after the Munchkins who danced up the yellow brick road with Judy Garland in *The Wizard of Oz*.

They admired each other's sporting triumphs, with Edward cheering Eleanor on at ice hockey and Eleanor watching him play rugby, but their relationship was more friendly than romantic. "I sometimes pop into his room for tea after I've been rowing," said Eleanor. "Our friendship is neither new nor romantic. We share a lot of interests."

Edward went so far as to spend a vacation with Eleanor at her parents' home in Cheshire, and also in Balmoral, but the friendship never escalated into a full-blown romance. And Eleanor was not the only woman in his life. "During his time at Jesus, to my amusement, there were at least two attachments with female students that the press never found out about," claimed one of his tutors.

Dr. Gavin Mackenzie, his senior tutor, bolstered the image of Edward, the Cambridge Casanova by claiming, "I had to send him several rude warning letters for having girlfriends in his room after midnight." And a fellow student claimed, "Edward got away with blue murder. All his girlfriends were pretty, but from normal backgrounds. He is very discreet."

One of Edward's friends, Professor Jonathan Howell, who arranged matches in the ancient sport of Real Tennis for Edward, encapsulated Edward's attitude towards women during his Cambridge years, "He's warm and delightful to women without getting deeply involved. He thinks about marriage very deeply, and when he does it, he will get it right. He's very good with children."

That was the first clue that, unlike his brother Charles, Edward would not allow himself to be pushed into marriage until he was good and ready.

Until his graduation from Cambridge, in June 1986, Edward devoted himself to his twin passions: raising money for charity and acting in the theater. At a ball in aid of the Save the Children Fund (of which Princess Anne is president), Edward danced happily with a number of girls, many of whom had lined up for the pleasure. "I thought he would be a bit of a Wally. But actually he's a smashing little mover," gushed Elsa Lifac, a bubbly brunette who was introduced to the prince by her sister, the chairman of the organizing committee of the ball. "A real sweetie, too."

He also got into the spirit of Rag Week once more. In a slapstick stunt, Andrea Vidler, a twenty-one-year-old student, pushed a custard pie straight into the prince's face. But Edward remained cool. "I learned how to do this in student shows," he said, calmly. "The secret of slapstick is to keep a straight face."

In April 1986, the Queen was sixty years old. Andrew Lloyd Webber and Tim Rice wrote a special minimusical, entitled *Cricket*, specially for the occasion. Edward played the part of a corpse in the musical. "He was good, though," said Tim. "He turned up, which is all you have to do in life. I am a great fan."

He also appeared at Haddo again, starring in Sir Arthur Wing Pinero's farce *The Magistrate*. Afterwards, the *Daily Express* afforded him a fairly barbed review: "The role taken by the Prince has little depth to it, and he summons up the necessary shallowness. He seemed eager and enthusiastic, and on the opening night only fell over himself when it was desired."

Negative reviews never dampened his enthusiasm for acting. After he left Jesus College, he paid tribute to his theatrical career there: "It initially helped me overcome shyness and gave me the ability to stand up in front of people." Acting had also helped him to blend in with the other students, and he was grateful. He said, "We get a new influx of students each autumn and it's 'Spot the Prince' time. But after that, they very quickly come to realize I am almost exactly the same as everybody else. I have two legs and two arms, and I talk in almost the same way and act and think as everybody else."

Edward graduated from Cambridge with a fairly average 2.2 degree. But he was not dismayed. "These have been three of the best years of my life that I am likely to spend," Edward said. "Everybody says that about school, but I don't think I ever enjoyed school as much as I enjoyed university. There's a wonderful mix of people, and I am never likely to mix so informally with such a wide range of people." Dr. Gavin Mackenzie echoed Edward's sentiments: "Every year there are a handful of undergraduates that one knows have derived absolute maximum. This year Edward is one of that handful. He has proved he is a good student."

Edward had completed his degree and emerged from Cambridge unsullied by scandal or ignominy. His next challenge was to transport him from the artistic world of Cambridge theatrics to the macho world of the Royal Marines. Edward had selected that challenge himself, unaware that it was a challenge that would result in public humiliation and that he would escape once more into the safety of the footlights.

5

TELL IT TO THE MARINES

$\mathscr{I}$N OCTOBER 1998, A SIXTEEN-YEAR-OLD ROYAL MARINE recruit, Nathaniel Burton, was drowned during the Marines' thirty-week commando training course based at Lympstone, near Exmouth. Before the exercise, the recruits, who were carrying their fifty-five-pound Bergen rucksacks fully loaded for the first time, had been dropped on Dartmoor by helicopter before hiking more than a mile to Crazy Well Pool. Their mission was to cross it. They changed into lightweight waterproof jackets and trousers and packed their clothes into the Bergens, which were then covered by their watertight ponchos to turn them into buoyancy aids.

Corporal Martin Wildgoose, who was leading the expedition, showed the recruits how to cross the thirty-five-meter-wide pool while lying on the rucksack and holding their rifle with one hand. Two recruits safely negotiated the crossing. Nathaniel did not. He stopped halfway, let go of his Bergen and gun, and slipped under water. The fifteen-foot-deep pool was so cold that the other recruits claimed it made their arms and legs tingle.

Nathaniel Burton drowned that day in Crazy Well Pool, the fourth Marine in thirty months to lose his life on the course, considered to be among the toughest training courses of any branch of the service in the world. After he died, his mother, Lynne Kellow, said, "Even as a young boy, all Nathaniel wanted to do was be a Royal Marine. He was absolutely focused in his desire to become one of the elite."

From the time that Edward was a small boy, exhilarated by the sound of the Royal Marine Band playing at countless official royal functions, he, like Nathaniel Burton, dreamed of becoming part of the crack Royal Marine force. Edward had formulated his dream when he was only fourteen. He met Colonel Alan Hooper at the Royal Tournament and asked him about the Marines. "He's crazy about it," confirmed Prince Andrew.

The Royal Marines (who totaled seven thousand men) pride themselves on being Britain's top fighting force, and with the exception of the paratroopers, whose reputation is equally fearsome, the Royal Marines are unrivaled in toughness—the hardest branch of the service, renowned for undertaking the most dangerous of missions.

By tradition, the Navy is where the royal sons usually serve. George V, Edward VII, Prince Charles, and Prince Andrew all served in the Navy. Neither of Edward's brothers had dared to tackle the Marines.

When Edward first went to Cambridge, he discussed his decision to join the Marines with the master of Jesus College, Sir Alan Cotterell. "He was very set on going into the Royal Marines," remembered Sir Alan. "All the other male members of the royal family had joined the forces, so I suppose it was natural that Edward should also. So at the time he really had no thoughts of a career except the Marines. I suggested another alternative, though. I suggested that he might take up a career of research in archaeology." But Edward seemed determined to challenge himself. He clearly intended to eclipse Andrew and Charles in the macho stakes by making the grade in the Marines.

Psychoanalyst Dr. Erika Padan Freeman suggests that other

deeper impulses were at work, prompting Edward to join the Marines: "Charles was going to be king, Anne was a girl and Andrew, a bully. Edward may well have joined the Marines to prove himself to his father and to please him. But Edward was sensitive, introspective, creative, and vulnerable. The services are not conducive to creativity, poetry, and vulnerability. For Edward, joining the Marines was tantamount to committing suicide."

The Royal Marines were founded on October 28, 1664, by a decree of King Charles II. Originally created as the Duke of York and Albany's Maritime Regiment of Foot, for nearly one hundred and fifty years they were called the Admiral's Regiment. In 1802, they became the Royal Marines. In 1704, the Royal Marines took part in the attack on Gibraltar. At the Battle of Trafalgar, Lord Nelson died in the arms of a Royal Marine, Sergeant Major Secker.

Initially, the Marines were formed with a view to their preventing mutiny among sailors. They evolved into a branch of the Navy—in essence, soldiers who go to sea. In the First and Second World Wars, they fought in major battles, took part in the Gallipoli landings, and in D-Day. During the Second World War, Lympstone, in Devon, was set up as a Royal Marine base. In the sixties, it was established as Britain's sole Commando Training Centre, Royal Marines.

The badge of the Royal Marine bears the word "Gibraltar," after the Marines' finest battle, topped by a crown and a lion. The badge is also emblazoned with the image of half the globe (showing Africa, Europe, and Asia—the intimation being that the U.S. Marines govern the rest of the world), an anchor, and a laurel wreath. The motto of the Marines is *Per Mare Per Terram* ("By Sea, By Land"). In 1942, The Royal Marines began wearing the green beret as part of their uniform.

In 1916, George VI, captain general of the Royal Marines, was on the bridge at the Battle of Jutland. Although the Duke of Edinburgh is the captain general of the Marine Corps, Prince Edward did not get a smooth ride in the Marines.

Far from it.

"In recruiting a Marine, you're looking for good, honest, old-fashioned common sense and the standard leadership qualities," explained Major Ewen Southby Tailyour, one of Edward's commanding officers in the Marines.

On May 16, 1982, before his first year at Cambridge, Edward started a three-day officer-assessment course at the Royal Marines Commando Training Centre, Lympstone. A spokesman for the Marines explained, "We want to give him a fair crack of the whip along with everyone else who is doing the potential officers' course. The aim of the course is actually so the candidates can look at us, but of course we look at them as well."

Edward's first day began with him crawling across a rope strung between scaffolding situated fifteen feet above ground. Next, he carried a fellow recruit five hundred yards in a lift, climbed high walls, scaled bars, balanced on ropes, and ran four and a half miles nonstop. The obstacle course was known at Lympstone as the Tarzan Assault Course. Apart from suffering a slight nosebleed, Edward acquitted himself pretty well. An eyewitness said, "He didn't seem in great difficulty, but was obviously exhausted at the end of it all. It tests every muscle in the body—but Prince Edward managed to come up smiling."

After completing the Tarzan course, Edward underwent a two-and-a-half-day assessment by the Admiralty Interview Board in Portsmouth, followed by a medical examination. He was also shown a Royal Marine training film, in which the narrator warned potential recruits, "There will be frustration, even misery. Undoubtedly there will be moments of physical exhaustion. But as a Royal Marine, you will keep going."

Edward passed the test with flying colors. In June 1983, he

joined the Royal Marine University Cadets Entry Scheme, which entailed the Marines paying his university tuition. In exchange, at the end of his three years at Cambridge, he would go through forty-five weeks of training at Lympstone before becoming a fully fledged Royal Marine.

Colonel Andy Harfield of the Marines praised him fulsomely. "He has got to where he is now on his own merits—he is a bright and determined young man, and I have every reason to believe he will make the training. Frankly, those who start on this trail find that because they are going to lead the best troops I would say in the world, they are going to put themselves out to achieve it. I am sure Prince Edward will do that. Prince Edward will be treated exactly the same as any other young officer going through the training process with him. There will be no difference in how he is addressed, what he is expected to know, how he will be treated."

In September 1983, Edward attended a two-week course at Lympstone. The course emphasized building up stamina and endurance. "Not only have the young officers got to be better than the Marines, they have got to be seen to be better," said a Marine. "For instance, Marines have eight hours to complete a thirty-mile speed march. Prince Edward and his colleagues will have only seven."

Edward was one of only three university cadet entrants in his year. The course involved getting up at six in the morning and enduring speed marches while carrying an eighty-five-pound backpack. Sometimes he was awakened at two in the morning without any prior warning and ordered onto the assault course. "We give special treatment only to the enemy," boasted recruitment officer Lieutenant Canning. "I didn't pull any punches about what he was letting himself in for." Edward more than passed muster, according to reports.

In December 1985, Edward did a second course at Lympstone, but because he had hurt his ankle playing rugby at Cambridge, was excused from undertaking the cross-country run exercise along with the forty other cadets. When his ankle healed, he was sent on a week's detachment in Belize, where he was under the command of Colonel Alan Hooper. There Edward subsisted on antimalaria tablets and iron rations.

On September 7, 1986, Edward arrived at the Lympstone training center for the grueling forty-five-week training course. Most recruits journey to Lympstone by train, traveling on the Exeter-Exmouth line. Thirty-six recruits arrived in Lympstone that day, nervous and alone. Edward arrived with Andrew Merrylees, his detective, in tow. In retrospect, the detective's presence was the first of many terrible mistakes that would cloud Edward's time in the Marines.

"It is not as if the Command Training Centre were not already guarded," observed Robin Eggar, who investigated the Marines for his book *Commando, Survival of the Fittest*, "so the introduction of private detectives simply reinforced the natural barrier between prince and paupers.

"Speculation at the time had it that the Marines thought having a real-life royal in the Royals could help ensure against the inevitable defense cuts, although to do so might mean lowering the tough standards upon which they prided themselves. The sad thing for the prince is that he never really had a chance. If they had to do it again the Corps would now insist on covering all security aspects themselves."

Matt Lodge, who was in Edward's group of recruits, emphasized to Eggar the negative effect of Edward's security team. "Every exercise we went on there was a Range Rover with two Special Branch officers half a mile behind us; it restricted the whole thing. We couldn't go on a run ashore with the lads in the same way."

Before Edward was permitted to move into his spartan bedroom, Merrylees was compelled to first inspect it. The tiny, twelve-foot-by-eight-foot cabin proved secure, especially after Merrylees changed all the locks. The other recruits watched and felt alienated from Edward. He was getting the same salary—an annual £7,391 ($12,249)—as the other recruits, and the usual six weeks yearly leave, but no matter how much Edward longed to mix with the group, his princely status could not be ignored. From that moment on, it was virtually impossible for them to regard the prince as just "one of the guys."

The creed governing Lympstone was that new recruits had to prove they had the capacity to endure extreme physical and emotional hardship. Fortunately for Edward, Gordonstoun had prepared him for some of the physical vicissitudes of Lympstone: rising at six in the morning, rock climbing, swimming through icy waters, climbing ropes that burned his hands, and crawling through dark tunnels. The contract he had signed with the Marines legally bound him to stay in the Corps for five years. "He might wish to specialize. He might wish to fly helicopters or work on amphibious craft. But it will be very tough," warned Major Tailyour.

"There will be nothing special laid on, and he will have to meet the standards of the tests of any Royal Marine officer," said his commanding officer, Major Paul Bancroft. "We are not going to demean our standards. Nor would he wish them to be demeaned. There will be no quarter given and none expected."

Major Tailyour elaborated: "All officers when they start off at the same stage as Prince Edward are young and inexperienced. And whether they are Prince Edward or John Smith from Southsea and you have passed the entry exam to become a commissioned officer, then you all start off at the same level. None of them know what is expected of them until they are trained. The training is very much aimed at the business of leadership. You can be away for ten days and come back absolutely shattered. Ten minutes later—just as you are about to have a bath—you are told to be in your full regimental mess kit for the regimental dinner.

"Edward definitely never wanted to upset people. He wasn't a great bully like I suspect his brother Andrew is. Slightly swaggering. When Andrew went onboard his first ship or second ship, the story goes, he reportedly announced to the crusty old naval captain, 'I'm Prince Andrew, but you can call me Andrew.' And the captain said, 'I am the captain, but you can call me sir.'

"Edward was very keen to be a perfectly normal run-of-the-mill Royal Marines officer throughout his training. We got on very well together. And he got on bloody well with the sergeants and the lads who initially thought, 'Cor, we've got to have this bloody prince.' And I said, 'He's not a bloody prince; he's a second lieutenant in the Royal Marines.' And he proved he was jolly fit, and that shut a lot of them up. And every morning we had to wash in a communal bucket of water, and he didn't mind in the slightest. He was good company. There is no doubt in my mind that Prince Edward would have passed his commando course."

Within the first month of the course, Edward was required to scale thirty-foot walls at breakneck speed, swing through trees as if he were Tarzan, rappel down two-hundred-foot cliffs and march thirty miles at a time in full kit. One of the biggest ordeals he underwent was to strip off and walk naked through an icy river, carrying his bag and kit above his head. When Edward and his fellow recruits reached the other side and stood shivering in front of the sergeant, he looked them up and down before sneering, "There aren't many big boys here, are there?"

Later during the course, Edward and his group were ordered to do pull-ups, fully dressed, in the ocean. One of the endurance tests involved a thirty-mile route march across Dartmoor, which had to be completed in under seven hours. After just one month in the Marines, it was reported that Edward had already been injured twice during training. He was in the midst of completing a difficult rope slide when blood began streaming out of his nose. Then he twisted his ankle badly. But that wasn't the worst of his Marine travails.

He also had to adhere to a series of strict rules. Every training officer had to make his bed to different patterns of folds every day of the week for four weeks, whiten their own sneakers, and wash their laces every night.

Edward mastered those tasks. However, as at Gordonstoun and when dealing with the media, Edward's arrogance proved to be his undoing. According to Robin Eggar, Edward antagonized his fellow Young Officers (as trainee Marines were called) by his arrogant imperiousness. "He had proved to be a bit of a prima donna on field exercises, hadn't been felt to pull his weight—the classic example of someone who wasn't that sure of himself in a command appointment, so he imposed himself by shouting and being authoritarian. When it is a YO's turn to give an O group (Orders Group), it is generally done in a low-key manner. Instead, the prince had treated them like a drill sergeant bellowing at a bunch of raw recruits."

Later that day, Eggar says, the recruits got their revenge on Edward. "They rammed mud in his ears, in his mouth, right up his nose, poured so much inside his shirt he could have been Mud Pie Man."

Major Ewen Southby Tailyour, who was Edward's commanding officer during his two-week amphibious training course on the beaches of Devon, still had a great deal of faith that Edward, unlike the thirty-five percent of new recruits who drop out of the Marines, would complete the course and win his coveted green beret.

"He got out of the car in North Devon, and he was in uniform. He saluted me and said, 'Hello, sir.' I said, 'Welcome to Five

Three Amphibious Assault Squadron Royal Marines.' And it was absolutely as it should be with a junior officer to a major.

"The training consisted of working with submarines offshore, helicopters, night paddling up rivers, faces daubed in black. We were living in a brick built hut. Spent our days in submarines, helicopters, and our nights, lifting our boats and carrying them upriver. It was pretty intense. We're not the Boy Scouts.

"Edward was on the course with two other recruits, and he was better than both of them. In my report on him afterwards, I said something to the effect that 'He is a perfectly normal young officer under training with all the problems and good points and bad points that they all have.' I said that he would make an above average Young Officer. And I particularly highlighted two things. One is that, compared to the other two recruits, Edward was particularly fit. The other was that he was particularly motivated to be a Royal Marine. Of course, he was well-read in matters of international affairs. We would go to the pub and talk about the day's news, international problems like Nigeria. Edward actually knew the leader, the leader of the opposition, the deposed head of state. He was fascinating on the subject, but without in any way dropping names or saying, 'I actually know those guys.' He enjoyed the hard work, and he enjoyed being able to relax afterwards."

Edward was playing his part to the best of his ability. But although he was going through the motions of being a model Royal Marine, his emotions towards his chosen career had undergone a radical transformation. Four years had passed since he originally made the decision to commit half a decade to the Marines. Now he realized that in doing so he had made a crucial mistake. "If I don't resign now, I will be trapped in a career I detest," he said at the time in a press interview. Later, looking back, he recalled to journalist Caroline Philips, "It was obviously a traumatic period for anybody—for everybody—and wasn't an easy decision to make.

But you have to be convinced in your own mind that what you're doing is right. I mean, whose life is it?"

"Edward fitted in with the Marines and he would have made the grade. He was a good lad, but he made too quick a decision to give it all up," says Major Southby Tailyour, who is still saddened by Edward's decision to quit. "He had all the physical ability to complete his training satisfactorily, indeed well," Colonel Ian Moore of the Commando Training Centre commented.

Edward spent Christmas with the royals, brooding about his future. On January 4, 1987, he left his family at Sandringham and drove home to Buckingham Palace alone. He was expected back at Lympstone, where he was due to take part in a grueling route march in sub-zero temperatures. He did not go. Unbeknownst to the public, Prince Philip wrote to Sir Michael Watkins, Edward's commanding officer, telling him that Edward was resigning from the Marines.

The letter was leaked to the London *Sun*, and a portion of it was reprinted in Kitty Kelley's book *The Royals*. It reveals that Prince Philip viewed the entire situation in sympathetic terms. In his letter, Prince Philip also made it plain that Edward decided of his own volition to leave the Marines. "This is naturally very disappointing, but I can't help believing that the blaze of publicity did not make things any easier for him. I think he now has to face a very difficult problem of readjustment," Prince Philip wrote.

The palace was livid that Prince Philip's private letter had been made public by the *Sun*. The Queen took the hitherto unprecedented course of initiating legal action. She issued proceedings against the *Sun* for breach of copyright. The *Sun* quickly settled, paying the Queen £25,000 ($40,750)—which was donated to charity.

In hindsight, the publication of Prince Philip's letter did not damage the royal family, but had the positive effect of elucidating Philip's attitude to Edward's resignation from the Marines. That attitude was sympathetic and kind, and its revelation did much to correct the image of Philip as a stern, thick-skinned Victorian father who had made Edward's life hell.

"The press said the duke was upset that Edward resigned. But in fact, since Edward was so miserable, the duke respected and accepted Edward's right to back out," said Lady Colin Campbell. "After all, all the royals get badly treated in the armed forces. The Prince of Wales was mercilessly bullied and the Duke of York had tough times. Edward probably thought, 'Why should I put up with this? I am never going to ascend the throne. I don't even like this sort of thing. So why don't I lead my own life and do what makes me happy?' "

Former royal correspondent Michael Cole corroborates Lady Colin Campbell's account of Prince Philip's reaction. "I believe the duke was understanding," he said, "He doesn't like Charles, and they have hardly spoken for years. Anne is his favorite. The duke counseled him rigorously regarding whether or not he should quit the Marines.

"He was doing reasonably well there. I am told that he didn't give up because it was too hard or too tough. Besides, they would never have failed him. They would have made sure he passed. It wasn't the demanding nature of the course that caused him to quit. He just didn't want to be a Marine anymore. Edward must have known there would be a big hoopla if he left the Marines. But he had made his decision. And it showed remarkable courage for him to say, 'No way, I don't want to do it.' "

On January 13, 1987, Buckingham Palace issued the following official statement: "After much consideration HRH The Prince Edward has decided to resign from the Royal Marines. An announcement about his future plans is not expected for some time. Prince Edward is leaving the Marines with great regret but has decided he does not wish to make the service his long-term career."

The uproar in Britain that greeted Edward's resignation was unprecedented. Tabloid papers heaped scorn upon him, lambasting him as a wimp. The middle-market press, however, rallied round, with Sir John Junor writing in the *Sunday Express*, "It is said that Prince Edward wept for hours after taking his decision to quit the Royal Marines. I feel like weeping for him too. If he had been an ordinary young man of middle-class parents, it would have been an awesome decision to make. . . . but no one outside his own family and friends would ever have known about it. Now the whole world knows. And even if, under pressure, he has a last-minute change of mind, it will not lessen the damage. For the rest of his life his irresolution is going to be remembered.

"Edward is no wimp," Junor continued. "The first four months of a Marine officer's training course, through which he has apparently come with flying colors, are by far the most physically arduous. No, Edward's problems are more psychological. He has merely had the good sense to question the value of a military career per se, particularly for someone in his own unique position. He has shown that he wishes to be his own man and thus to choose his own career, not have it chosen for him, not to live life merely by tradition or precedent."

Edward's strong will—the strong will manifested by him since he was a small child and which the public first observed in *Royal Family*—had asserted itself. And those who knew him well weren't the least bit surprised. "Edward gets his own way without upsetting people. But he always does get his own way," Charles Barron of Haddo House pointed out. "You could see his determination in small ways. If he wanted to end a conversation with someone, he would do it—very politely—but you could see he was doing it. He was moving on. The same thing applies to his decision to quit the Marines. It would have been easy for him to stay in. Who he was would have protected him from any difficulties he would have met with from the Marines. It must have been very difficult for him to leave the Marines, but he was determined to do it. The general public saw that as a sign of weakness, but it was just the opposite."

Romy Adlington, too, supported his decision to leave the Marines. In his darkest hour of need, he turned to her for advice. On his invitation, she went to Buckingham Palace late one night and stayed there, debating the situation with him, until three in the morning. "He phoned me because he needed somebody to be with him," she explained the next day. "He said that being home for Christmas, away from the pressures of training, had made him realize that he wasn't sure if he wanted a life in the services. He felt he had to go in because it was a kind of custom within the royal family—but it was the mental pressure he found hard to bear. Edward has been put through a terrible ordeal. And has no one to speak for him. As one of his closest friends, I want the public to know he is a normal human being who has to make an important decision. He doesn't have the same responsibility as his brothers [they are closer in the line of succession], yet he still can't go off and do what he wants. He has often asked me: 'What's it like to go for a walk alone in the park?' 'How does it feel to be able to walk into a shop without everyone staring at you?' That's all he wants to be able to do."

That wasn't quite all. First he needed to extricate himself from his legal obligation to the Marines. In sponsoring his three-year stint at Cambridge, the Marines had paid him an estimated £21,000 ($34,230). Edward was now responsible for repaying the Ministry of Defense £8,000 ($13,040) plus £650 ($1,059.50)—the full cost of his Marine uniform.

He also had to sign documents and fill in forms severing all links with the Marines, hand in his uniform to the quartermaster, collect his final wage slip, and bid farewell to the other trainees.

On January 11, he went back to the Commando Training Centre at 6:45 at night. Forty photographers were on hand to capture the prince arriving in his Rover Vitesse. He refused to make any comment. Once inside the center, Edward gathered his personal possessions and then said good-bye to his fellow Young Officers. Then his private detective whisked him off to a secret hideaway.

On the surface, at least, the Marines attempted to keep a stiff upper lip about Edward's having quit the force. The base commanding officer, Colonel Ian Moore, said, "He made the decision for very honorable reasons. He got a very good report out of his initial training. All the indications are that he had a good career ahead of him. We were surprised at the decision, but having been surprised, we now understand. It was his own decision, but we in the Royal Marines will soldier on. We respect his decision and fully understand his reasons. I speak for all the ranks of the Commando Training Centre in wishing him the very best of good fortune in the future."

Two other recruits who had joined at the same time as Edward were also quitting the Marines. One of them was Peter Fraser, a close friend of Edward's from Cambridge. The press were so intrigued by the coincidence of the two friends resigning on the same day that Fraser was forced to give a press conference to explain himself. Fraser denied that he and Edward had made a "secret pact" to resign. Instead, he defended Edward's decision: "From my observations of Prince Edward, he has the makings of becoming a Green Beret." Asked to define Edward's reason for resigning, Peter said, "I would not put it down to the physical side of Marine training. It is far more likely that his three years at university have broadened his horizons. That explanation is much nearer the mark."

A friend of Peter's elaborated even further to the *Sunday Mirror.* "They were bullied," he claimed. "Edward knew all along it was going to be incredibly tough. But what he and Peter hated was the totally unnecessary humiliation."

Edward's fellow recruit and friend, Quintus Travis, who had

tried to dissuade the prince and Fraser from quitting the Marines, categorically denied that they had been victims of bullying and abuse from senior officers. Conceding that their instructors had put them through "very hard training," Travis insisted, "Allegations of bullying by the NCOs and by the training team are completely unfounded."

But despite Travis's denials, the rumors that Edward had been bullied persisted. Yet however badly he may have been treated by the Marines, the treatment he received from the press was worse. The press had a field day when Edward resigned. Some of the more unpleasant rumors surrounding his resignation suggested that Edward was forced to leave the Marines because he was discovered having sex with another recruit. Nothing could be further from the truth. Apart from the fact that Andrew Merrylees was always with Edward throughout his time at the Marines, Robin Eggar (who spent fifteen months at Lympstone), the world's most authoritative expert on the Commando Training Centre, quotes two sources who completely negate even the faintest possibility of there being any truth in the Prince Edward gay-sex rumors. The first source, Colonel Mike Taffinder, says, "The Marines won't have anything to do with gays. Rightly or wrongly homosexuals are regarded as very nonmacho, wet handshakes and all that. . . . In my experience they are as rare as hen's teeth in the Royal Marines. The only way anyone could survive as a homosexual in this outfit would be for him to always look outside for his lovers." A Royal Marines Young Officer, Jools Ostling, said bluntly, "If we found out that one of the batch was gay, we'd kill him. And I mean that literally." Robin Eggar has summed up the entire issue: "Statistics would have us believe there must be some gay Marines, but they must be very discreet and very brave."

Edward's decision had been made. He fully accepted that he was not suited to the Marines, nor they to him. The people of

Britain were tolerant and understood his decision. A poll taken by the *Sunday Express* showed that 80.7 percent of British adults supported Edward's decision to quit the Marines.

But despite the polls, Edward did not underestimate the full impact of his decision. "I now have to live in a limbo until I rid myself of the label 'Ex-Royal Marine.'" As for resigning, "I do not regret it, but I was in a no win situation, and someone was going to come off badly in it," he said.

The aftershock of his resignation reverberated through every public event he attended. Edward was now the only member of the royal family banned from wearing a military uniform on state occasions. Even the Duke of Gloucester (a relatively minor member of the royal family), who had never served as an officer, was permitted to wear his uniform as colonel-in-chief of the Gloucestershire Regiment. But from now on, at all state occasions, like Remembrance Day—the British equivalent of Veterans Day—Edward would be dressed as a civilian, while all the other male members of the royal family looked resplendent in their glamorous military uniforms.

There was also the matter of the Royal Marine Band. Whenever a member of the royal family boards or disembarks from the Royal Yacht *Britannia*, the Royal Marine Band accompanies them. They also often play at royal weddings. One member of the Royal Marines, outraged at Edward's defection, said, "When Edward gets married, he certainly won't have us as guard of honor. Not after this."

The little boy who once worshipped the Marine band now had to face the shocking reality of adult life that actions have consequences. But before he would confront adulthood completely, Edward would return to the make-believe world he had come to love so well, the one place where he would never be regarded as a wimp.

6

A ROYAL KNOCKOUT

*E*DWARD WAS NOW UNEMPLOYED. RUMORS WERE RAM-
pant that the Queen's third son would now turn to his first love,
the theater. Actor-producer Bryan Forbes, who produced *The Rail-
way Children* and *The Slipper and the Rose* and is a close friend of
the royal family, announced that Edward would become the
patron of the National Youth Theatre. "I started the ball rolling
long before the Marines drama," Forbes asserted at the time.

Edward accepted Forbes's offer and, having established the association, spent the first few months after his Marine debacle immers-
ing himself in the National Youth Theatre. "It was obvious to me
that he was always very attracted to anything concerned with the
theater, and I dare say that, had he not been born into the royal
family, he would have pursued a much more personal stage career,"
concluded Forbes. Edward concurred, for the first time saying publicly, "I love the razzmatazz of show business. I get really absorbed
in the character I am playing on stage, and I try to be as authentic
as I possibly can be. It's a wonderful world of fantasy and make-
believe where actors can help people forget the cares and troubles
of the world and escape for a little while. I feel it is a terrific challenge to be able to entertain and captivate an audience."

On February 22, 1987, Edward was on stage again in Cambridge, where the Cambridge Youth Theatre was performing *Trafford Tanzi*, by Claire Luckham, an exuberant story of female liberation through wrestling. Edward made a surprise appearance, wearing a silver jacket and speaking with a cockney accent. He stormed down from a box, climbed into the ring, and, on the pretense of shaking hands with the stage villain, threw him over his shoulder.

The boy whom Edward threw over his shoulder, Jason Smith, an unemployed eighteen-year-old, had rehearsed for two days with the prince. "He threw me twenty times in rehearsal, and afterwards I received a nice note from him on Buckingham Palace paper saying he hoped he hadn't hurt me," recalled Jason. "As he made his entrance, the audience started cheering—and you could see something come alive in him. You know he'd love the actor's life. His smile said, 'For a moment I'm acting—and it's wonderful!' Of course, none of us had the nerve to say, 'Eddie, why don't you do it?' It is the big taboo subject. He is such a nice bloke, and it's a pity no one knows how much he is held back."

In April 1987, Edward spent two hours watching the National Youth Theatre in rehearsal for Peter Terson's play *Zigger Zagger*. One National Youth Theatre actor observed of Edward, "You can see the wistful look in his eyes. There's a yearning he's never going to satisfy because the bloody Establishment won't let him. The poor bugger is allowed to sniff the greasepaint but not wear it."

During the first six months he tried to satisfy his twin drives towards acting and doing worthwhile public service. In June, the Marchioness of Aberdeen appointed him patron of Haddo House. At the time, a spokesman for Equity, the British actor's union, said, "We are pleased to hear of Prince Edward's commitment to the Haddo House Trust. The arts seldom get the appreciation they deserve, and the endorsement of a member of the royal family can only help to correct this imbalance. If His Royal Highness is going to do professional work, we would be happy to consider his application for membership of Equity."

He enjoyed acting, but like John Kennedy Jr., who was also intensely enamored of the theater, he knew that he would never survive the unwelcome scrutiny if he became a professional actor.

Instead, true to his pattern of combining his theatrical pursuits with raising money for worthy causes, he hit on a scheme that would bring him right into the heart of the show business world.

In retrospect, it would also contribute to what some would see as the downfall of the British royal family.

The idea for *It's a Royal Knockout* was first conceived by Edward in a London wine bar. He and his friend from Cambridge, Tim Hastie-Smith, were discussing the various ways in which they could celebrate the Duke of Edinburgh Award's thirtieth anniversary, which would fall in 1986.

At first, they considered giving a charity ball. Then they rejected the idea as being too obvious. Their aim, Edward said later, "was to raise the profile of the Scheme, raise funds in new and exciting ways while having some fun at the same time."

Since 1969 *It's a Knockout* had been a much-loved British television program. It was a drawn-out slapstick contest between teams from different towns who flung themselves into competing in sophomoric tasks (throwing custard pies at one another and pranks of that ilk). In 1977, an *It's a Knockout* program was filmed in Windsor Great Park. Edward was only thirteen at the time, but the event—with its clownish jollity—made a deep impression on him.

Edward and Tim Hastie-Smith came up with the idea of a royal version of *It's a Knockout*, in which four teams in aid of specific charities were led by a member of the royal family. The plan could not have proceeded without the Queen's permission.

When it was all over, royal biographer Philip Ziegler said, "It would surely have been possible for the Queen to take a stronger line over such an ill-judged enterprise as the *It's a Royal Knockout* on television. Perhaps the full horror of this extravaganza did not become apparent until it was too late; if so, the Queen was remarkably ill-informed. Someone should have warned her what was about to happen so that she could have taken steps to stop it or at least moderate its excesses."

The Queen may have been warned about *It's a Royal Knockout*, later dubbed the most costly public-relations blunder the royal family had ever made, but her love for her youngest son ultimately outweighed all other considerations. Edward was stagestruck, and perhaps the Queen thought it would have been churlish to ban him from carrying out his cherished plan.

"It was a terrible mistake," one of the Queen's friends confided to author Ben Pimlott. "She was against it. But one of her faults is that she can't say no." "It was an awful idea," a former aide said to Ben Pimlott. "How could you not appear undignified in that set-up? But Prince Edward was determined it would happen." Press secretary Sir William Heseltine virulently opposed the royal family participating in the program, and every single other courtier agreed with him. Nonetheless, by agreeing to a compromise that none of the royal team leaders would surrender their dignity by competing in the events, Edward was able to convince his mother to give her imprimatur to the slapstick competition. The Queen followed her heart and gave Edward permission to proceed.

On May 19, 1987, Edward gave a press conference announcing *It's a Royal Knockout*. "The games aren't in fact custard pies and greasy wraps. In that sense it's slightly different from the old *It's a Knockout*, but we've deliberately kept a sense of decorum to suit the people involved. It's an atmosphere of heroism and gentility," he declared, proudly.

In actual fact, it was a combination of Laurel and Hardy, Jim Carrey, and Hell Week. However, Princess Anne agreed to captain the Red Team, representing the Save the Children Fund; Fergie captained the Blue Team, which competed on behalf of the International Year of Shelter for the Homeless; Prince Andrew captained the Green Team, representing the World Wildlife Fund, and Edward captained the Yellow Team, representing the Duke of Edinburgh Award Scheme.

Once the teams were established, Edward set about masterminding the entire event. He was only twenty-three, and full of enthusiasm for what he intended to create. With Tim Hastie-Smith and Stuart Hall, *Knockout*'s presenter, he decided that the teams should consist of celebrities from film, theater, music, sports, and television.

Edward became overall producer of the two-day event, which was to be held at Alton Towers, a six-hundred-acre British theme park in Staffordshire, one hundred fifty miles outside London. As such, he was responsible for all the major decisions. Unwisely, he decreed that the press be banned from the grounds during the event, but that they watch the entertainment on a television screen set up inside a tent. In Edward's own words, "It was decided a much more relaxed atmosphere without masses of photographers running around would be far more beneficial for all concerned." That decision, prompted by Edward's distaste for the media and by his innate arrogance, would cause Edward's image indelible damage.

It's a Royal Knockout would not only taint the public's perception of the royal family; it would also arouse within the powerful British press corps an unalloyed enmity for Prince Edward.

An independent company, Knockout Limited, was formed and headquartered in the Price Waterhouse offices, overlooking London Bridge. Edward's primary job was to convince celebrities to take part in the spectacle. Although very few celebrities, particularly the British ones, were immune to a telephonic plea from the

Queen's youngest son, Edward later described his attempts at convincing the stars to participate as being akin to fishing.

Nevertheless, he was able to persuade fifty international names to volunteer their services for the benefit of charity. Among the names Edward convinced to appear were Christopher Reeve, John Cleese, John Travolta, Jane Seymour, Tom Jones, Sheena Easton, and Kevin Kline. Part of Edward's concept was that the tournament would appear to take place in 1587, and that all the celebrities would be dressed accordingly. He said at the time, "We feel there is too much seriousness in the world. People were forgetting that they should let their hair down and have fun. The event has the active involvement of members of the royal family in a way that hasn't been done before. We're not superstars, and I hope, at the end of the competition, the royal family will come out of it much better."

The Grand Knockout Tournament (the event's official title, although in time it became truncated to *It's a Royal Knockout*) took six months to arrange. Edward had positioned himself as producer-supremo, finding the appropriate attorneys, PR agency, photographer, and, most important of all, the sponsors. He even supervised the show's costumes. "What surprised me was what a good leader he was, without being bossy," remembered official photographer Jayne Fincher.

The day before the event, the stars rehearsed their particular contests. Edward was on hand to prompt them. He attended in a T-shirt bearing the words "No, I just look like him." He was making fun of himself, a quality that was sometimes seen as being less than royal and which the press tended to use against him.

The stars, predictably, had their prima donna moments: Jane Seymour insisted that a special dress be flown in for her from America. John Travolta didn't like the lunch provided for him and, instead, sent out for a hamburger and fries. Learning that she would be dressed up as a vegetable for one of the competitions,

Sheena Easton wondered out loud, "Like, how do you measure somebody for a leek outfit?" Christopher Reeve, who flew to London on a Concorde, boarded the helicopter that was to take him to Alton, only to be fogbound at Battersea heliport.

The American celebrities were a trifle bemused by the boisterousness of the event. Actor Anthony Andrews said afterwards that he would never forget "the somewhat glazed expression on the faces of our cousins from Hollywood as they watched, white-faced, the first demonstration of the games. One could see quite clearly that it was slowly dawning on those jet-lagged brains just how silly they were about to look and just how wet they were going to get."

Afterwards, when it was all over, Reeve said, "It was fun to watch Princess Anne give over to the spirit of the day after seeming quite dubious about the whole affair; soon she, too, was putting her weight into highly charged arguments with the officials about scoring and alleged foul play. In fact all four royals behaved like any fun-loving siblings at a family picnic anywhere in the world."

The mood was established the night before at a banquet held at the Isaac Walton Hotel, during which Fergie abandoned every shred of royal decorum and pelted her husband, Prince Andrew, with mints. It was as if, after years of imprisonment, the spirited Duchess of York had been released on parole and had every intention of savoring the experience.

Edward had labored enthusiastically to make the outdoors event a success. However, the weather respects no man, not even a prince. When Edward woke up on the morning of Monday, June 15, the day of the event, he was filled with foreboding. Rain was teeming down, and as Edward surveyed the scene, he felt deeply demoralized. "I have seen rain before, but never has it cast such a gloomy cloud over a small assembly. I remember only too well standing at the window that Monday morning (at about 7:00) as the torrential rain continued unabated from the evening before.

It was literally the worst moment in my life as I surveyed the soggy scene, thinking, 'After all that hard work, what have we done to deserve this?' "

Four thousand spectators (some dressed in Elizabethan costumes) and fifty journalists were on hand for the event, as were Princess Anne, Prince Andrew, the Duchess of York, and, of course, Edward.

Before it all began, Sheena Easton prophesied, "We are all going to make fools of ourselves, every one of us, totally. And, in costumes, everyone looks as daft as we do." The royals, however, would look "dafter" than the rest. By donning Elizabethan costumes, the royals were, in effect, mocking the majesty of their past. At best, they appeared to be like small children dressing up as royalty. At worst, they were buffoons, looking ridiculous to their subjects.

After the event, Prince Philip was heard to mutter that Edward's participation in *Knockout* was "unwise and unwelcome. Why doesn't Edward let the TV people get on with it and just turn up to accept the checks? He's making us look foolish." Prince Charles, too, was dismayed by the *Knockout* spectacle and was thankful that at least he had succeeded in preventing Princess Diana from joining in.

For although Princess Anne behaved in a dignified manner—stern, composed, and calm—even when her team won the entire event, Fergie was boisterous—yelling, screaming, and disporting herself in a manner not befitting a royal princess. Andrew, her hapless husband, grinned from ear to ear, clearly ill at ease.

Years later, in her autobiography, Fergie looked back on the episode with undisguised bitterness. Describing her participation in *It's a Royal Knockout* as "my first high crime in the decorum department," Fergie went on to stress her naïveté at the time of the show. When Charles and Diana refused to take part, she had felt they were unsportsmanlike in not supporting the royal family. Later, she realized that they had, in fact, been clever in refusing.

"The show was all in good spirit, and for a good cause, but it ended as a public relations debacle. I was ready to take my share of flak for the show. I was not prepared to be cast as the villain of the piece, the pigeon numero uno, but that was exactly what happened. In the weeks to follow and for years to come, *It's a Royal Knockout* would be analyzed as my first great blunder. It seemed so unfair to me. As captain of the Blue Team, I might have mugged and cheered more freely than the rest, being such a fun-loving sort. I was still the new girl on the block—why should I be singled out as coarse and vulgar? What of Edward and Anne and Andrew, whose lead I was following? Why should I be blamed?"

Even Edward himself, dressed as a jester, looked far from royal. He was twenty-three years old and, almost single-handedly, had been the architect of an event that would raise one million pounds for charity. The tournament should have gone down in history as his personal triumph. Instead, by the end of the day, it was clear that it had been a disaster. History would look back on *It's a Royal Knockout* and hold Edward completely responsible for the fiasco.

In retrospect, however, the media attacks on the event were partially motivated by Edward's petulant behavior at the post-event press conference. He had been up since seven in the morning, it was now eight at night, and as he marched into the press tent, he obviously expected a standing ovation and hearty congratulations from all the assembled journalists. Edward had clearly not been forewarned of the media's combative mood. Assuming that he would be greeted as a conquering hero, he arrived at the press tent armed with a speech. The journalists were not in a congratulatory mood. Instead of being given the opportunity to observe the proceedings firsthand, they had been stuck in the press tent, where they were relegated to watching *Knockout* on a giant TV screen. In effect, they had been prisoners, unable to mingle with either the Hollywood stars or the British celebrities. The press had been herded into a tent like cattle, and they felt humiliated and abused by Edward, the event organizer. Moreover, given the lateness of the hour, they had missed their deadlines. From the first, Edward had proudly made it plain that *It's a Royal Knockout* was his creation. The press were now holding him responsible for the miserable day they had spent at Alton.

He was halfway through his speech when ITN reporter Joan Thirkettle jumped in and asked him if he was pleased with the way in which the event had gone. Edward had expected praise from the press. With his overweening arrogance, he was utterly unprepared for the question. Virtually speechless with shock, he finally snapped back, "I haven't finished yet!" In a querulous voice, he said defensively, "I know the captains have enjoyed themselves. I only hope you have enjoyed yourselves—have you?"

His question met with a stony and humiliating silence. Seemingly oblivious to the press's mounting irritation with him, Edward repeated, "I only hope you have enjoyed yourselves—have you?" No one answered. Instead of gracefully ending the press conference, Edward lost his temper.

"He was just like some spoiled, sulky small boy, and his little face went into a pout," said journalist Noreen Taylor. "Great! Thanks for being so bloody enthusiastic," he exploded. "What have you been doing here all day?" They had been imprisoned in a tent for fourteen hours and were all at the end of their tethers. "You may well ask," was Joan Thirkettle's acid reply. Edward—tired, dispirited, and stubborn to the end—was unwilling to give up. Dismally unaware of the cataclysmic effect his words were having on the press corps, he made matters worse by blundering on with, "Have you been watching it?" The press shuffled around in silence before one or two journalists grudgingly shouted, "Yes." By now

Edward was practically stamping his foot in frustration. "Well, what did you think of it?" he demanded. His question met with total silence. "Thanks," Edward retorted sarcastically. At that moment, by uttering that one word, replete with all of his petulance, superiority, and imperiousness, Edward virtually signed his own death warrant with the British press.

With a flourish, he pushed back his chair, hissed, "Right, that's it!" and stormed out of the room, only to be confronted by a posse of photographers waiting for him outside the tent. Completely beside himself with childish rage and disappointment, Edward stepped towards them and growled, "One of these days you people are going to have to learn some manners."

Afterwards he would defend himself, saying that the event helped charity and that the press had never exhibited much enthusiasm for the concept to begin with. But despite his brave facade, he was angry with himself for having given the press ammunition. And he knew that he had irretrievably damaged himself. That knowledge would rankle with him for a very long time.

"Eddie's problem is that he has never really recovered from his failures," said an actor friend. "He desperately wants to be like his brothers, who are both regarded as real men, but he seems to get nowhere."

Press reports of the event published the following day were scathing, attacking both the event and Edward, himself. "It was a step too far in the wrong direction. The public didn't want to see the royals in that light," says former royal correspondent Michael Cole today.

As far as Fleet Street was concerned, it was now open season on Edward. They had mocked his departure from the Marines by labeling him a wimp, and his theatrical aspirations had caused them to dub him effeminate. Driven by their ire at Edward's treatment of them during It's a Royal Knockout, the press now dipped their pens in poison and set about decimating him further. They were not altogether wrong. Lynda Lee Potter commented in the *Daily Mail* of the press having been "sneered at by a rudely offensive young man."

Edward's distrust of the press, which had been fueled during encounters such as the one he had had with the three photographers in Balmoral, now escalated dramatically. He had always been acutely aware of his own marketability and its value to the press. With the arrogance of his youth and princely status, he had judged himself able to manipulate his enemy, the media, to his advantage. At Cambridge, he had begun to charge photographers a fee. At *Knockout*, he tried to control the media by penning them. He had mishandled the media, perhaps because of a lack of advice, or because he had been given advice, but willfully chose to ignore it. Whatever the truth, the result was indisputable: through his behavior during *It's a Royal Knockout*, Edward had incited the media's hatred, and they would make him pay.

Edward did not allow the press drubbing to dampen his enthusiasm for the show. "He's so boring. God, it was 'It's a Knockout this' and 'It's a Knockout that,' all day," sniped twenty-year-old teacher Emma Lawson, who was Edward's date at a society wedding a short while after the show aired. "To be honest, he bored the pants off me and everyone else he spoke to. All he could talk about was television and how wonderful he thought this show was. He didn't seem to understand that it left almost everyone else cold. Edward was just the same even at college. He'd start a project, think it the most wonderful thing since sliced bread—and then as soon as the glamour wore off he'd lose interest. Even then he was obsessed with performing and the stage. But it would be kind to describe his performance as adequate. It was always the same—five minutes of tremendous enthusiasm, and then that was it."

Those behind the scenes continued to sing Edward's praises, with official photographer Jayne Fincher saying loyally that

Edward was "amazingly mature and bright, with ideas no matter whether they concerned costumes or picture layout. Friends accuse me of having turned crown goody-goody since my close involvement, but the prince really is extremely adept at chairing committee meetings. He was always up at six o'clock if not before, with the rest of us."

Presenter Stuart Hall defended *It's a Royal Knockout*: "Prince Edward is one of the brightest guys I have ever met. They may have looked foolish, but that was the fun of it. Fergie had a whale of a time. Fergie is a boisterous redheaded girl out for fun, and everyone just attacks her. I have great respect for them, especially Anne and Edward. What do you want the royal family to be, King George and Queen Mary, never seen and never heard, waving a hand occasionally? We are a giant theme park, and they are the main attraction."

Six hundred million viewers worldwide watched the television broadcast of the *Grand Knockout Tournament*. Much of the world enjoyed the spectacle of the British royals disporting themselves just like commoners. In America, *It's a Royal Knockout* was nominated for an ACE award. Yet although *Knockout* raised one million pounds for charity in Britain, the event was seen as having damaged the British royals irrevocably. Edward had unwittingly completed the process begun with Richard Cawston's *Royal Family*. The light was now flooding in upon the monarchy, and its magic was fast fading.

The Queen recognized what had transpired. After the *It's a Royal Knockout* fiasco, she ordered all the young royals to submit their official and social diaries to her for vetting. The Queen explained to the young royals that she wanted to ensure that there would be no more disasters like it. She firmly believed that the royal family now needed to win back the respect of the public, which she rightly judged they were in danger of losing.

Edward tried to salvage some of his dignity by having a book published about the entire experience. Entitled *Knockout: The Grand Charity Tournament—A Behind-the-Scenes Look at the Event of the Year*, with an introduction by HRH Prince Edward, the whole book may, in reality, have been written by Prince Edward. Years later, he gleefully claimed, "I wrote it all myself, but the press never caught on that I did." It was a small triumph in the face of all the humiliation that the British press had and would continue to mete out to him.

The book is enlightening, demonstrating how Edward perceives and presents himself. At one point in the book, the text says of Edward (rather pompously), "HRH was a hard taskmaster and a bit of a perfectionist. He worked hard himself and expects similar commitment from others." Later, "HRH—playing the part of a genial host (and playing it very badly he would have us believe)." The text describes Edward as "the smooth-talking prince." There is a certain amount of self-delusion in the comment that when the press saw his "No, I just look like him" T-shirt, they "enjoyed the right royal jape." His arrogance is almost painful, especially when one reads Peter McKay's words in the *Times*, written about that self-same T-shirt: "Prince Edward is so conscious of his own celebrity that he carries a derisory joke about it on his back. Self-mockery is a dangerous trick best left to experts." Whether Edward ever read McKay's barbed words is not on record, but it is clear that he was unwilling to learn any lessons from his sobering *It's a Royal Knockout* experience. Edward was about to launch his new job with a similar self-mocking ploy that would cause the media to further deride him.

7

THE PRINCE AS SHOWBOY

*T*HROUGHOUT BRITISH HISTORY, MANY A ROYAL MIS-
tress had been plucked from the theater. King Charles II and
Edward VII had both romanced actresses. In more recent times, it
was rumored that Prince Philip had had an affair with actress Pat
Kirkwood, Prince Charles had dated actress Susan George, and
Prince Andrew's girlfriend Koo Stark had even acted in a porno
film. All in all, the British public were familiar with the "Prince
and the Showgirl" scenario. Only this time, there was a new
twist—the prince was now the showboy.

After the *Knockout* debacle, on June 25, Edward was able to
take refuge in his royal duties by fulfilling a long-standing engagement to embark on an official visit to Canada. The five-day trip,
during which crowds applauded him in the street, assuaged his
sense of outrage at his post-*Knockout* press treatment. He made
speeches and presented medals on behalf of the Duke of Edinburgh Award Scheme.

The tour of Canada was deemed a public relations success by
media commentators. At the Cabequid Centre, in Truro, Canada,
Edward attended a high school graduation ceremony. Scores of
screaming girls attempted to catch his eye. Edward appeared

embarrassed but soldiered on with the ceremony. "Since quitting the Royal Marines, Edward has proved during his tour of Canada that he can play a valuable part in the 'family firm,'" the *Daily Telegraph* approvingly reported on June 29.

Distinguished former royal correspondent Michael Cole was at Buckingham Palace on the day Edward returned from Canada. "Canadian folk artists were dancing in the courtyard of Buckingham Palace. I looked up to the third floor window and saw Prince Edward standing there. I think he was watching the attractive girls dancing. There were some servants standing with him, but he looked so forlorn. I thought what a lonely man he was—as if he had nothing to do. He looked so sad," Cole recalled.

That sadness dissipated somewhat when, in July, he attended the Henley Ball, to celebrate the annual regatta, and met a nineteen-year-old Swedish blond bombshell named Ulrika Jonsson. Ulrika was escorted to the ball by Edward's friend James Baker, son of the newscaster Richard Baker, his costar at Haddo. Ulrika, the daughter of a London-based Universal Studios executive and a Swedish mother, epitomized the classic Nordic beauty, whose glamour concealed a good mind. With eight O levels and three A levels, Ulrika was beautiful and ambitious. When she first met Edward, she was employed as secretary to the boss of *TV AM* (Britain's equivalent of *Good Morning America*).

Ulrika and Edward initially met at Windsor, when James Baker drove her there to pick up Edward en route for the ball. On their arrival at Henley, photographers snapped the couple getting out of the same car. Thus was the legend of their romance born, especially after Edward and Ulrika danced together till around five in the morning. He subsequently took her to the theater, and he visited her at her London flat. Afterwards Ulrika insisted, "He's just a friend of mine. I love him dearly as a friend and see him every now and again. We always have a fun time, laughing and joking a lot."

Their romance was probably primarily a figment of the press's fevered imagination. Along the way, it enhanced the images of both Edward and Ulrika. Afterwards she protested, "All the media fuss afterwards was embarrassing. I wouldn't sacrifice my friendship with him to get some mileage or publicity for myself. If I am going to be famous, it will be for what I've done myself. Not for who I know." Despite Ulrika's assertions, her relationship with Edward boosted her career enormously. The cachet of having dated Edward and the resultant attention led to her winning a job as *TV AM*'s Weather Girl. Edward, too, received benefits from the association. Through being momentarily linked with Ulrika, Edward burnished his masculinity, which—after his resignation from the Marines—had been somewhat tarnished in the public arena.

While he was publicly linked with Ulrika, Edward was, in actual fact, involved on a more serious level with Canadian show jumping champion Gail Greenough. Four years older than Edward, Gail was a close friend of Princess Anne's husband, Mark Phillips, and of Fergie. A gutsy woman, Gail was spirited, attractive, and outgoing. They first met when she agreed to take part in *It's a Royal Knockout,* and their relationship was one of the few positive personal benefits Edward obtained from the event.

When Edward went to Canada, he and Gail met in Ontario and spent the weekend there together. And when Gail visited England a few months later, she received an invitation to Windsor and also to the high society Berkeley Square Ball, which she attended as Edward's guest.

They had a great deal in common and, without inciting too much press hysteria, managed to slip away for a two-week holiday in the chic Canadian skiing resort of Whistler. "Edward loves being with Gail and is always writing to say he cannot wait to fix up their next date," a friend confided at the time. They were seen together, dancing close on a Toronto dance floor, and although Gail denied that they were more than friends, the evidence is strong that, for a brief spell, Edward and Gail were romantically involved with one another.

The year 1987, to which Edward would always refer as "the worst year of my life," ended with the media exacting its pound of flesh in retaliation for their *Knockout* humiliation. Just before Christmas, the satirical television program *Spitting Image*, which features puppet caricatures of celebrities, included a skit in which an Edward puppet took part in a pantomime. The pantomime is a peculiarly British tradition. It is a musical version of a fairy tale, like "Cinderella," "Sleeping Beauty," or "Jack and the Beanstalk." Pantomime convention dictates that the male lead (or "principal boy") be played by a leggy woman in tights. The principal boy is the pantomime hero, there is always a villain (a wicked witch or wizard), and the light relief is provided by the pantomime "Dame,"—a man dressed up as a raddled older woman, sporting too much makeup and an ill-fitting wig.

In the Christmas 1987 episode of *Spitting Image*, the Edward puppet was dressed up as a pantomime Dame. There had, at this point, been mutterings in the press that Edward hadn't worked since leaving the Marines and that his official engagements (71 out of a potential 275) were too few. The *Spitting Image* sketch obliquely refers to this when the puppet of Edward's father, Prince Philip, demands to know why he hasn't got a proper job. The Edward puppet insists that he has, indeed, got a proper job: he is playing the pantomime Dame at the Windsor Hippodrome Theatre. Philip barks, "Four weeks poncing around as a Dame in a frock isn't a proper job for a son of mine!" They argue for a few moments. Then, in a direct parody of *It's a Royal Knockout*, they begin to fling custard pies at one another.

No matter how hard he tried, Edward would never be permitted to forget *It's a Royal Knockout*.

•   •   •

Edward began 1988 with a momentous announcement: He had accepted a job as production assistant for Andrew Lloyd Webber's Really Useful Group. The British public was stunned by the news. Edward was the first child of a reigning British monarch ever to take a paying job outside of the armed services.

His backstage job with Lloyd Webber was not his first choice of a career. His preference, he later admitted, had been to become an actor. "It might have been a job that I would have liked to have done. But it would have been totally impractical. Production is behind the scenes. It's quite another thing to be out at the front regularly," he said, thoughtfully. Asked if his reasons for not becoming an actor were prompted by a fear of looking ridiculous, Edward refused to elaborate. "A lot of reasons, and those are personal," he answered decisively.

The genesis of Edward's employment with Andrew Lloyd Webber was the Queen's sixtieth birthday celebrations, when the prince had asked Tim Rice and Andrew Lloyd Webber to compose the short musical *Cricket* especially for the event. "We really got to know him then," remembered Biddy Hayward, Lloyd Webber's thirty-four-year-old executive director. "And the idea of a full-time job sort of developed. It was a natural progression for the company to offer him a job."

Biddy was being modest. Edward's job offer arose partly from the instant rapport that she established with him. Originally Lloyd Webber's secretary, Biddy, a bright, strong-willed woman, wasn't extremely pretty, was slightly overweight, but had a winning personality. A convent schoolgirl who was brought up in Tunbridge Wells (just three miles from Pembury, where Sophie Rhys-Jones went to school), she had worked hard throughout her career. After she met Edward during the *Cricket* performance, he called her requesting *Phantom of the Opera* tickets. She obliged, and after the performance, she and Edward and *Phantom* star Michael Crawford went out to dinner together.

Dinner cemented their friendship, especially when Edward confided in Biddy that he was unhappy with his chosen career as a Marine. They stayed in touch, Biddy advised him about leaving the Marines, and when Edward expressed an interest in working in the theater, she suggested to Andrew Lloyd Webber that he employ him.

Biddy had been working for Lloyd Webber since she was twenty years old and, during their fourteen-year association, had risen to a powerful position in his organization. He listened to Biddy, evaluated the benefits and drawbacks of employing the Queen's son, and made up his mind to do so. However, two weeks before his decision was to be made public, he suddenly got cold feet and proposed to cancel the whole deal. Writer Ingrid Seward reported that Edward and Lloyd Webber met to discuss the issue. She says, "There was no natural camaraderie between Edward and Lloyd Webber." They met at Lloyd Webber's mansion, just seconds away from Buckingham Palace. According to Seward, "Andrew said, 'I have to tell you what I'm really worried about. If I have an opening and the Queen turns up, everybody is going to say that she has come because of you, not because it is some charity night.' Edward replied, 'I accept that.' Then, perhaps remembering the Queen's failure to attend his Haddo House performance in *Taming of the Shrew*, he added, 'But she would never come just because of me. She would only come because it was a charitable thing.' "

Edward succeeded in persuading Lloyd Webber to employ him. But the rest of London's theatrical community was less than thrilled to hear about Edward's new job. Jealousy of the prince flared backstage in London's West End theater district. "Most of the theater world is either laughing or kicking themselves. A lot of them would like the chance that has just been handed to Prince Edward," complained Mel Moran, a twenty-five-year-old sound operator at London's Aldwych Theatre. "Even though it is virtually

Edward, who always loved reading, at a 1969 book fair.

Edward walks behind his mother, the Queen, with one of her beloved Corgis in tow, on August 16, 1965.

Edward in the arms of his cherished nanny, Mabel Anderson.

Edward, Andrew, and their proud mother
outside Heatherdown School in 1972.

Edward and Andrew en route to Andrew's wedding
to Sarah Ferguson on July 23, 1986.

The Royal Family on the balcony of Buckingham Palace after
the Trooping the Color ceremony on June 14, 1997.

Edward suffering for his princely status while playing rugby
for Jesus College, Cambridge, in 1983.

Dreaming of a theatrical career?
The stage door prince, 1984.

Edward, the actor, on stage at Haddo House in 1986.

Edward in a kilt—the outfit that Michelle Riles
claimed so beguiled her—in August 1986.

Edward on his first day at work for Andrew Lloyd Webber,
outside the theater that housed the Really Useful Theatre Company's offices.

Edward and Diana at a reception for Commonwealth
Secretary General Chief Emeka Anyaoku in March 1993.

The Queen, the Queen Mother, and Edward
at Diana's funeral on September 6, 1997.

Sophie goes to work at RJH Public Relations
on her birthday, January 10, 1999.

Sophie with Baby Lifeline Founder
and former friend Judy Ledger, and
Chris Tarrant, Sophie's
"Capital Radio" colleague.

Sophie all set for a weekend at Buckingham Palace with Edward.

Sophie's proud parents, Mary and Christopher Rhys-Jones.

For once, the normally buoyant Sophie flounders
during a windsurfing vacation with Edward in July 1994.

Sophie, the floral princess-in-waiting,
on her last day at MacLaurin's Communications and Media.

Engaged and happy.

a messenger boy's job, it's still a chance to learn the business as an apprentice. He might never have to step backstage or go to the theater. As for picking up a hammer, he shouldn't have to touch one of those unless his office chair collapses. But he is starting with the right company. It's a bit laughable, but I suppose someone has to give the poor beggar a job."

By beginning his working life with Sir Andrew Lloyd Webber's company, Edward was, in effect, starting at the top. In the years preceding Edward's joining Andrew Lloyd Webber's company, it had produced *Cats, Starlight Express,* and *Phantom of the Opera,* the last of which Edward had reportedly seen four times. The Really Useful Group's primary function was to oversee all the worldwide productions of Lloyd Webber's musicals.

Biddy, Edward's new boss, was open and communicative to the press about her latest employee. "He's got a lot to learn, but the great thing about being a production assistant is that you learn so much you are able to work out where you want to be—and the sky's the limit. Some people end up as producers, some move into TV or films. A few show great talent as directors," said Biddy.

Announcing that the company had decided Edward could wear jeans to work, she added, "I said to him that we couldn't call him 'sir' in a busy office or backstage at a theater, and he readily agreed we should all call him 'Edward.' " The aura surrounding Edward's new job was one of democratic bonhomie, although that was temporarily shattered when a top London production manager, pondering the prospect of calling the prince "Edward," wondered, "What happens when you have to scream at him and tell him he has messed up something?"

There was very little possibility of Edward "messing up" on a large scale. "He has got a lot to learn and will have to meet a lot of people," explained Biddy Hayward. "Until he's done that, we cannot expose him to production. Later he will be liaising between technical crews, creative teams, artists—everything that goes towards making a production possible." Asked about the prince's salary, Biddy refused to divulge it: "Obviously he is not Joe Bloggs, but he is entitled to exactly the same degree of privacy when it comes to matters like that."

Andrew Lloyd Webber, then in New York for the opening of *Phantom of the Opera*, made a brief public statement regarding his new employee. "I am delighted Prince Edward is going to join the staff," he said. "I have been very impressed by his real enthusiasm for the theater and genuine desire to learn the business."

Lloyd Webber's pronouncements boded well for Edward. A note of caution was sounded, however, by Joanna Proctor, a twenty-seven-year old former production assistant for the company, into whose vacant shoes Edward would now step. "It's a frightening experience working for Andrew Lloyd Webber. He's a real slave driver because he is such a perfectionist," she said. "Andrew was a workaholic who would work twenty-four hours a day and expect you to do the same. He lived on his nerves and occasional tantrums. I was being threatened with the sack during his outbursts."

"If Edward thinks he's heard foul language in the Marines, wait till he hears Andrew," warned a Really Useful Group insider. "When Andrew is in a bad mood, no one is spared his wrath."

Before Edward began work, the press was full of reports citing the lowly nature of his job. "Production assistants are widely regarded as general dogsbodies [drudges] in theater circles," reported the *Evening Standard*, before gleefully pointing out, "He will have to run errands and help with day-to-day chores and will probably even have to make the tea."

Mindful of such reports, on his first day at work, Edward chose to turn the tea boy joke on himself. He turned up for work clutching a packet of tea bags. He may have thought that by doing so, he was mocking the press. In reality, he was actually playing into their hands by reinforcing the wimpish image they continued to project of him. Edward would be known as "tea boy" long after he left Andrew Lloyd Webber's company. The truth was that on his first day, he did not switch on the kettle at all. "He hasn't made a cup of tea all day," confirmed a Really Useful Group spokesman. "He doesn't even seem to drink tea, and the only thing he requested was an orange juice during the morning."

Edward's office was in the Palace Theatre in Cambridge Circus, familiar from John le Carré's *Smiley's People*. A lively area, Cambridge Circus is bordered by Soho—London's Forty-second Street. Full of peep shows, strip clubs, drug dens, and flats populated by prostitutes, Soho was not the usual environment for a prince of the realm.

Yet despite the tea bags and semblance of normalcy, Edward would be protected from the cruder aspects of everyday life that might upset his equilibrium. He was ferried to and from Buckingham Palace by limousine. Before he was permitted to enter the building, it was first searched by dogs trained to sniff for bombs.

Edward's day generally began at 7:45, when he was awakened at Buckingham Palace, took a shower, then had breakfast. Once a week, over breakfast, he read *The Stage*, Britain's theatrical newspaper. By nine, he left Buckingham Palace in a chauffeur-driven sedan car (usually a Rover or a Granada), accompanied by his private detective.

As always, the detective would be constantly at Edward's side. "He keeps himself busy and seems to enjoy the company," said a Really Useful insider at the time. "It was a bit weird having him around at first but now we're all used to it."

Edward's relationship with Biddy remained good. "They are a curious pair," observed one Really Useful employee. "Edward is far more imposing than he seems on TV, and Biddy is efficient rather than tough. He has the personal authority, but she knows just about everything there is to know about theater. Edward looks

the boss but recognizes that he isn't." Biddy was part mother fig-
ure, part boss, and, for the next few years, would be the most influ-
ential woman in Edward's life.

Edward quickly settled into the routine of life as a production
assistant. He and his detective normally arrived at Really Useful's offices by around nine-thirty. Edward, who shared his office
with five other staff members, started the day by sorting out the
mail, going through bills and the applications from would-be
actors, and studying press reports of current Lloyd Webber productions.

By the middle of the day, Edward had usually contacted the
agents of artists whom Lloyd Webber had decided to audition
and had conducted various discussions with producers and
members of the production team regarding casting and future
productions.

Sometimes Edward worked through lunchtime. Now and
again, he lunched at a local Chinese restaurant. More often, he
ate lunch at the Gulp! Sandwich Bar, where he grabbed a smoked
salmon with cream cheese bagel costing £1.75 ($2.85). His ever-
present detective tended to opt for something more substantial, a
giant triple layer sandwich stuffed with turkey, bacon, cheese, and
mayonnaise. According to Gulp!'s owner, James Myers, "Edward
seems very down-to-earth and quite appealing really. No one ever
recognizes him when he comes in."

In the afternoon, Edward read trade papers and magazines, and
organized contracts, flights, and accommodation for stars and technical staff. Towards the end of the day, he invariably talked to
Lloyd Webber, wherever he was in the world, briefing him on the
latest box office take of his productions.

By around seven in the evening, Edward was chauffeured back
to Buckingham Palace, along with his detective, while his coworkers chorused, "Bye, Eddie." Had they met him in the street,
though, they would not have been so informal.

Although his coworkers were allowed to address him as "Edward," it had also been decreed that if they ever met him outside the office, they would call him "sir."

In the evening, he was often to be found at the Groucho Club, a trendy haunt of such luminaries as John Cleese and Madonna. In April, he was observed at The Last Days of the Raj, an Indian restaurant in Covent Garden, where he and eight friends supped on curry.

"Edward was in low spirits when he joined us. He had taken a terrible bashing in the press and wasn't quite sure what he could do with his life," remembered Really Useful executive Brian Brolly. "But he has worked out very well. He is enthusiastic and anxious to learn as much as possible. He has become part of our team. If anything needs doing with any of our productions, whether it is *Phantom of the Opera, Starlight Express, Cats,* or this latest musical, Edward is there to muck in. He is very unassuming and doesn't wait on ceremony."

"He seems to be kept quite busy and was doing a lot of fetching and carrying," recalled Charles Hart, a lyricist working on the forthcoming Lloyd Webber production, *Aspects of Love.* "He spends much of his time on the phone organizing rehearsals so that everyone turns up at the right place and time. He offered me some tea, but I didn't have any—so I don't know how good it is! I did have some cake, though."

His co-lyricist, Don Black, echoed his sentiments: "He is very friendly and easygoing, and nothing is ever too much trouble for him. Sure he brews up cups of tea, but that's not all he does. He is caring and concerned about every aspect of his job. Mostly, it's a lot of paperwork, taking care of small details."

Aspects of Love starred British actor Michael Ball. "Well, I never went down to the pub with him, but he makes a lovely cup of tea and he's a really nice bloke. I had a laugh when people said he was a tea boy, and then he made a cuppa," wisecracked Ball about his relationship with Edward. Michael Ball's laughter would subside the following year, when *Aspects of Love* opened in New York and the rumors began.

When *Aspects of Love* had its first run-through in July 1988, Edward was listed in the program as "Edward Windsor — Production Assistant." At the same time, as agreed with Lloyd Webber at the outset, he was still fulfilling many obligatory royal engagements.

In the summer, he spent a few hours flying a twin-engined Andover at RAF Benson, in Oxfordshire. He had already gained his private pilot's license, and enjoyed flying whenever possible. In 1988, his public service work included spearheading an antidrug campaign. During the campaign, he met forty-eight-year-old Pauline Williams, whose son had died of drug abuse. The prince chatted to the bereaved mother for half an hour and pledged his help and that of the royal family.

He also spoke at the Church of Saint Martin's in the Field on London Connection Day, endeavoring to draw attention to the plight of London's fifty thousand homeless teenagers. "Talk about teenagers and people switch off," he said. "We were all teenagers at one stage, and yet we seem to wish to forget that stage of life took place."

In November 1988, he spoke at a fashion show to benefit the Worldwide Fund for Nature, in aid of whose Tropical Rainforest Program the event was staged. In 1988, he undertook one hundred sixty-six engagements, more than twice as many as the previous year. He was starting to redeem himself in the eyes of the press. "Although much of his work is linked with his interest in the theater, he has buckled down," noted royal expert Margaret Holder.

In April 1989, he traveled to Russia to support the National Youth Theatre, who were presenting T.S. Eliot's *Murder in the Cathedral* there. He flew back from Moscow early to attend the first night of *Aspects of Love*. He was eager to be part of the company, but at theatrical parties, he still felt uncomfortable. At one such party, actor Tim McInnerny came up to the prince and slapped him on the shoulder in a familiar fashion. Edward tried to look at ease but clearly was uncomfortable with the informality.

On the private front, he made the news with a series of short-lived romances. First he was romantically linked to musical comedy star Marsha Bland, from Leeds, Yorkshire. The daughter of a bus driver, Marsha was extremely diminutive, like Eleanor Weightman—"Munchkin"—before her. At four foot eleven, vivacious brunette Marsha began her career when she was only nine, in *Annie*. Musicals were her natural forte. She went on to act in *Oliver! Evita*, and, at the time of her meeting with Edward, *Cats*.

Now twenty, Marsha was seen slipping into Buckingham Palace for intimate dinners with Edward. As always, Buckingham Palace refused to comment. Edward was introduced to Marsha's parents at a London party for the cast of *Cats*, where he was also introduced to Marsha's twin brother, Michael, and little sister, Maxine. Afterwards, Marsha's father refused to say anything about the relationship. Even today, Marsha's mother, Brenda Bland, remains relatively silent on the subject and will only say, "I've seen the prince from a distance at one of the shows, but that was it, more or less. I don't know if there was a friendship. I really don't know. I've never asked Marsha, and she's never mentioned it. She's her own person."

Edward's relationship with Marsha may have been superficial, but around the same time he was involved in a more enduring love match with Rhian-Anwen Roberts, a Welsh-born Cambridge student. They had met in 1988 when Edward visited Cambridge to take part in a charity event. Anwen, as her family called her, was in her third year at Fitzwilliam College, Cambridge, where she was studying English. An insurance broker's daughter who grew up in the tiny Welsh village of Penycae, near Wrexham, Clwyd, Anwen was bright, beautiful, and popular. "I've known her all my life, and she's a lovely girl," said local pub landlady Doreen Davies.

Edward was so taken by Anwen that he invited her to Sandringham for Christmas in 1988, and he also took her to dinner at one of Princess Diana's favorite restaurants, Ziani in Chelsea, and to supper at Buckingham Palace.

But Edward's path to true love with Anwen did not prove to be smooth. During the period in which she dated Edward, she was also involved with the son of a British member of Parliament. The son, Andy Ground, had been at Cambridge with Anwen, was a swimming champion, and was not inclined to relinquish Anwen (whom her friends had nicknamed Blodwen Nipples Filofax) to Prince Edward.

Edward drowned his sorrows at Anwen's defection by romancing another actress, musical comedy star Ruthie Henshall. On March 8, 1989, just two days before Edward's twenty-fifth birthday, he dined at the Covent Garden Grill with Ruthie Henshall, Marsha Bland, and her actress friend Ria Jones. Undeterred by the presence of Marsha, Ruthie serenaded Edward with the song "You Made Me Love You."

Ruthie, a twenty-three-year-old dancer in *Cats*, and the daughter of a newspaper editor, was lively, ambitious, and the perfect diversion for Edward. She proceeded to go through Edward's familiar dating routine: first a weekend at Sandringham, where she was introduced to the Queen ("Ruthie was very excited about Sandringham and could not believe how servants were there to wait on her," revealed a friend), then there were dinners at Buckingham Palace, then Edward made the obligatory visit to her parents, and finally Ruthie issued the routine denials of a romance. "Edward is a jolly nice guy," she said. "He's a friend, and he just happens to be a royal. We have a great time together and have a mutual interest in the theater." Asked about her trysts with Edward at Buckingham Palace, Ruthie tossed her head and said, "When you have friends and you go and visit them, it's usually at their house and that's the reason I go to Buckingham Palace when I visit Prince Edward, because that's where he lives."

The British press had heard it all before and they were getting bored and irritated with the saga of Prince Edward's lukewarm romances. In their view, he had gone from "Windsor Wimp," who had fled the Marines, to "Petulant Prince," berating them after *It's a Royal Knockout*, to effete stage-door Eddie. They lusted after a more substantial story.

It would take a New York first night to bring the rumors out. And out they would come with a vengeance.

8

OUTED AND INNED

*T*HE POSSIBILITY THAT THE QUEEN'S YOUNGEST SON might be gay had been bruited about since Edward left the Marines. It escalated after he antagonized the press during *It's a Royal Knockout* and began to seep into the tabloids when he went to work in the theater.

Edward always employed cloak and dagger tactics to hide the identity of his girlfriends from the press. He was sickened by the frenzy his brothers' relationships with women had ignited and didn't want to subject any of his girlfriends to the same hysteria. At Cambridge, he told friends, "I am not going to get involved with any of that." Instead, he cultivated an air of mystery regarding his girlfriends, doing his utmost to hide their names and identities from the public.

Edward's air of mystery led to denials and subterfuge, all of which nurtured the rumors circulating in the gay community that he is gay. Those rumors included the story that he repeatedly sent Michael Ball flowers, which embarrassed the star and caused him to have a quiet word with Andrew Lloyd Webber regarding Edward. None of those rumors were ever substantiated.

The first published article to address the rumors was printed in the *Daily Mail* on April 1, 1990, when renowned society columnist Nigel Dempster wrote that "a touching friendship has developed" between the twenty-six-year-old prince and twenty-seven-year-old musical comedy star Michael Ball. "I think they were just friends," says Nigel Dempster today. Some people, however, interpreted his column as meaning Edward was gay.

Michael Ball, himself, was defensive. Ball, who lives with Cathy McGowan, a forty-six-year-old British music personality, hit back. "I couldn't believe it when I read that," he said angrily. "Edward is a production assistant with the company. We've only ever spoken five or six times and that was about work. . . . I don't know how people dream these things up."

Edward himself told journalist Georgina Howell, "If the press think I'm gay, that's great! It's a useful cover." From the vantage point of the press, it was also a good story—one that appealed to readers.

On April 8, 1990, *Aspects of Love* premiered in New York. Aware that Edward had flown in specially for the first night, the British press were out in force. Among them was a reporter named Stewart Dickson, the London *Daily Mirror's* man in New York.

At a post-show reception at the Rainbow Room, Stewart sidled over to Edward and introduced himself to him. "He was very charming," he remembers. "I asked him how he enjoyed the show, we chatted about it, then I drifted off." For a while, Stewart watched the prince from afar. Then, judging the prince to be far more affable and approachable than he had expected, Stewart went over to him again. At first, Stewart was a bit nervous and fumbled the words. "Look," he said, "I'll tell you something. In London, there are a lot of rumors that you are gay. Are you?"

For a moment, Edward was taken utterly by surprise. "I don't think he was upset or flustered," recalled Stewart. Edward quickly gathered his thoughts and said, "It's so unfair to me and my family. How would you feel if someone said you were gay? The rumors are preposterous. I am not gay, but what can I do about it? I just wish I could be left to enjoy what I do. I love the theater."

"I think he was relieved to get the denial off his chest," says Stewart. "I was quite impressed by him."

On April 10, 1990, "Queen's Son Pours His Heart Out to the *Mirror;* I'm Not Gay," screamed the London *Daily Mirror*'s headline. Given that the majority of the tabloid's four million readers had probably never even contemplated the possibility that Edward was gay, the effect of the article was to cause them to ponder the entire subject. The end result didn't particularly help Edward.

Many months after the *Mirror* story broke the editor of the *Daily Mirror*, Roy Greenslade, was invited to present the prizes at a dog show held in Wimbledon, in Southwest London. It transpired that a dog owned by Edward had been entered into the competition and that the prince was in the audience. "He sat in the front row right in front of me," remembers Greenslade. "I was afraid his dog would win and that I would have to present the prize to him. I was relieved when his dog came fourth. I wasn't about to introduce myself to Prince Edward as the man who'd outed him as straight."

After the rumors appeared, both Romy Adlington and Michelle Riles issued strong denials that Edward was gay, each drawing on her amorous adventures with him. Ruthie Henshall also came forward and made a statement: "The suggestions about him being gay are so far wide of the mark that they are laughable. He's witty, intelligent, and very masculine." Another former lover who preferred to remain anonymous stepped forward and told the newspaper *Today* that Edward "is most definitely *not* gay—I can vouch for that. He used to choose the most sensual music for our romantic nights in his room at Balmoral, and he was really good despite the fact that the room seemed half-filled with cuddly toys from his boyhood days. Unfortunately there is no bathroom adjoining his bedroom, and things went sour when I borrowed his dressing gown to slip across the corridor. He said I mustn't wear it because it had an HRH monogram on the pocket and I might bump into the Queen outside."

By issuing a denial that he was gay, Edward unwittingly put the subject of his sexuality in the public domain. As the *Mirror* put it, "Prince Edward's astonishing decision to tell the world, 'I'm not gay,' means cruel whispers about his private life can be openly discussed for the first time." Consequently, despite all attempts to dispel the rumors, they persisted.

They were raised once more in the Australian film *Priscilla, Queen of the Desert,* when the writers created a scene in which one of the transvestite characters poses the question: "Can the child of an old queen turn out all right?" "Well, look at Prince Charles," is the answer. "Yes, but there's still a question about Prince Edward," the other transvestite countered.

For a time, it was rumored that Edward was known in the gay community as "Dockyard Doris" or—in an allusion to British *Carry On* star Barbara Windsor—that he was known as "Babs."

In April 1992, during an interview filmed in Europe, gossip columnist Taki Theodoracopulos told Steve Dunleavy of a *A Current Affair,* "You have young Prince Edward, who, here in Europe, has to deny the fact that he is gay—very gay. He can't admit it because this will cause an uproar. Unlike America, this country is twenty to thirty years behind, and gay rights have not been established."

Taki ended the interview saying, "The funny thing is he'll be forced to marry and, of course, you'll have another cold marriage with lots of rumor." However, when Edward's engagement was announced, in January 1999, Taki took pains to distance himself from any such rumor.

As recently as January 1995, radio broadcaster and gay rights campaigner disc jockey Simon Fanshawe went on air and said of

Edward and Sophie Rhys-Jones, "She's meant to be his girlfriend, but we all know he's a fag." The BBC fired Fanshawe because of his comments. Asked why he made them, Fanshawe said, "It was just a joke. I have no knowledge of Prince Edward being gay."

Yet despite Fanshawe's denial, a large segment of the gay community is eager for Prince Edward to be proved gay. "He is an icon in the gay community," says a source associated with the pilot of *Glam Slam*—a quirky quiz show featuring transvestites that Ardent later produced. "Many of the crew volunteered to work on the show for hardly any money, just because they wanted the chance to meet Edward. Gays love him. And they would love a member of the royal family to be gay. When Edward heard about the gay members of the *Glam Slam* crew and how they felt about him, he stayed right away from them."

The rumors would continue until Edward took up with Sophie Rhys-Jones. Whatever the truth, Edward poured all his energies into his theatrical career and a series of brief romances.

On May 13, 1990, Edward faced the press once more, at the Royal Garden Hotel in Kensington, where he attended a brunch to celebrate the ninth anniversary of *Cats*. Andrew Lloyd Webber had just appointed Edward production administrator, giving him full responsibility for supervising all productions of *Cats* and *Starlight Express* in London and overseas. Asked what his long-term ambitions were and whether or not he wanted to be a producer, Edward protested, "Good heavens, no, I don't want to become a producer. That would be really boring. What do I want to do? I really don't know. I'm just taking it one step at a time at the moment—meeting each new challenge as it comes along."

Ironically, within weeks, a new professional challenge arose for Edward. In the beginning of June 1990, Biddy Hayward parted company with Andrew Lloyd Webber. "It was not a bitter split, just a desire to move on," said an associate. The parting was due, it was said, to Lloyd Webber's insistence on making more films than stage musicals. Biddy was fired and given severance pay of £300,000 ($489,000). On the day that she left, a colleague reported that Edward was "sad and near to tears." Two weeks later, on June 20, six members of the Really Useful Theatre Company resigned and joined forces with Hayward. Edward was one of them.

"I am particularly grateful to Andrew Lloyd Webber and the Really Useful Theatre Group for their support and encouragement over the last couple of years and especially for giving me the chance to work in the theater professionally. I hope to use this experience to progress further into production and explore new areas," Edward declared via a Buckingham Palace statement.

Edward had left because he was loyal to Biddy. John Whitney, Really Useful's managing director, telephoned Andrew Lloyd Webber in California with the news of Edward's defection. Lloyd Webber was surprised and deeply offended.

Lloyd Webber issued a statement. Underneath the bravado, the subtext spoke volumes regarding his negative feelings about the defections. "Mr. Lloyd Webber is very relaxed about it all. He does not think it is worth spending any time over. He's too busy to talk about it. These things happen in any business, and it is a good move for the people concerned, and he wishes them well," the statement said.

Lord Webber unequivocally demonstrated his feelings about Edward six months later when he married his third wife, twenty-seven-year-old Madeline Gurdon and failed to invite Edward to the wedding. Even Biddy was invited. The wedding took place in Burgh, a village in Suffolk, and was attended by Simon LeBon and Andrew Ridgely. Edward voiced his displeasure to a select few friends at having been excluded from the nuptials.

A few weeks after Biddy left Really Useful, she formed a new company, Theater Division. Delighted, Edward joined it. One of the company's first productions, *Same Old Moon*, was written by Irish playwright Geraldine Aron.

"There is always a great camaraderie in rehearsal, and it was obvious that Edward longed to be one of the gang," Geraldine Aron recalled. "Sometimes, when we'd sit around chatting, it was possible to believe he was simply an unusually polite, witty, and sweet-natured young man. But then somebody would arrive with a newspaper in which—as always—the royals were being given a roasting, and I'd be reminded that his sister-in-law was the most famous woman in the world, and normal conversation would be difficult to sustain.

"One time, we were having difficulty locating an unusual three-seater sofa for the production. Edward made me smile by saying gravely that he'd 'have a look around at home.' He has a great sense of fun. During a performance, a bed on stage began to collapse. The wooden structure split, bit by bit, with sharp little reports. The director wasn't impressed, but Edward had tears of laughter streaming down his face. The audience, who'd spent most of the performance rubbernecking at him, saw that it was okay to be amused, and the incident created a wonderful atmosphere in the theater.

"Like all male drivers, he'd rather die than ask for directions. After a rehearsal in Oxford, he and his bodyguard offered me a ride to my hotel. I desperately needed a bathroom, and when we drove past the same landmark for the third time, I said in a firm voice, 'Edward, we're lost. You MUST ask that guy in the anorak where my hotel is!' I got a stern look from the bodyguard, but Edward obeyed!"

Roger Penhale, who was company stage manager on *Same Old Moon*, had a different perspective on Edward. "I found him good fun, but a little bit inexperienced. To be honest, he was absolutely useless. He used to drive me up the wall. I used to end up sorting out my own orders."

Edward made the dreadful mistake of commissioning the wrong-sized set. It was only at the last minute, just before the play was due to open at the Globe Theatre, that he realized his error. "Someone who is supposed to be the technical administrator and doesn't even notice from the ground plan he's had for weeks that the front of the set sticks out over the front of the stage—that's unbelievable," Penhale told *Sunday People*.

The play opened in Oxford, and the media deluge began. Experiencing the impact firsthand, Penhale felt sorry for Edward. "Some of us went for a meal in a café and we were sitting around and talking. Suddenly, this guy on the table next to us turns around, slaps his business card on the table, and says he is from one of the rags and wants all the dirt and gossip. We couldn't even go to a café for a sandwich without somebody trying to find something out about Edward. Edward seemed to take all that in his stride. I think he felt it was part and parcel of being royal.

"Edward was production administrator, meaning that he organized and got the production on stage. Sometimes I felt he didn't handle it as well as somebody with more experience. There were times that I thought better decisions might have been made had he had more experience or forethought."

Another colleague was blunter in his assessment of Edward to *Sunday People*: "Biddy would always excuse him by telling us that Edward had a family business as well as the theatrical one, but that didn't make the crew feel any better. Frankly, if he didn't have time for both businesses, he should have decided which was more important and concentrated on it. There are literally thousands of people who would have given their right arm for his job, and he couldn't give it the dedication it demanded." Just before the first night of *Same Old Moon*, when the cast was working late, it was reported that Edward abruptly stopped working. "He suddenly climbed down from a ladder and announced, 'I've got to go to Windsor to have dinner with Mummy.' " His colleagues were not pleased.

Edward might eventually have won them over, but there was insufficient time. On July 12, 1991, the Theatre Division closed down, leaving debts of £600,000 ($978,000) and Edward unemployed.

Edward was still living at Buckingham Palace, sleeping in the same rooms in the northwest wing where he had always slept as a child. His bedroom walls were decorated with posters of the plays with which he was involved at Cambridge. He was still looked after by his valet, Michael Perry, who had ministered to Edward since he was a child. And when he returned home to the palace each night, his housekeeper, Miss Colebrook, made sure to leave him a cold supper, complete with mineral water and soft drinks.

He was out of work again, but his royal duties still continued, as did his sporadic flings with a variety of girlfriends. At the *Aspects of Love* first night in New York, he had met Cosima von Bulow, the twenty-three-year-old daughter of Claus von Bulow, who, in 1985, was acquitted of murdering his wife, heiress Sunny von Bulow. Sunny, the daughter of Pittsburgh gas-and-oil tycoon George Crawford, remained in an irreversible coma. Her fortune of £30 million ($48,950,000) was destined to be divided between Cosima and her brother and sister. Cosima was blonde, self-possessed, accustomed to handling press attention, and had graduated from Brown, where she majored in comparative literature. There were whispers that she would make Edward the perfect bride.

Edward invited Cosima to the Royal Tournament, and they had a few dinners together in Buckingham Palace, but the romance soon faded, as did Edward's relationship with twenty-two-year-old Anastasia Cook, a television company intern who had met Edward at a ball at Luton Hall in October 1990. "I know it's a hackneyed phrase, but they really are just good friends," said Anastasia's father, Michael Cook. Anastasia said, "It would be lovely to see him. He is a really nice boy. He really is." But the relationship was quickly over. Four years later, Anastasia married James Baker, Edward's old friend.

A more likely bride appeared in June 1991, like Edward, of royal blood and extremely eligible. Princess Martha Louise of Norway was nineteen years old and the only daughter of King Harald and Queen Sonja of Norway. The princess was in England training as a show jumper at Waterstock Training School, near Oxford. She and Edward met when the Queen invited her to Windsor. On June 10, 1991, Edward spent five hours watching her compete in a West Midlands riding contest. On July 19, Edward traveled to Norway to attend the three-day celebrations for the eighteenth birthday of Crown Prince Haakon Magnus, Martha Louise's brother.

Princess Martha did not use the occasion of her brother's birthday to escalate her relationship with Edward. Far from it. She and Edward attended a ball together, but Princess Martha spent most of the evening flirting with the dashing Crown Prince Frederik of Denmark and paid very little attention to Edward. Thus ended another of Edward's brief encounters.

Nineteen ninety-one ended on a sad note for Edward. In the middle of November, Andrew Merrylees, who was now fifty-one, retired from his post as his private detective. Andrew had been with Edward for eighteen years, and the prince had grown to respect and trust the detective as completely as if he were his own father. Andrew had accompanied Edward to Gordonstoun, had been with him at Jesus College, went through the Royal Marines with him, and followed him to Really Useful.

"It's going to be a real wrench for both of them," said a friend of Andrew's at the time. "Andrew could have left his side ages ago but has never wanted to—and the prince has always asked him to stay. Andrew is such a gentle, kindly person, and Edward trusts him implicitly and respects him enormously." His relationship with Andrew Merrylees was the most important Edward had ever known.

It would take exactly two years before he found another relationship that would eclipse it.

Through the next two years, Edward was linked with a series of eligible girls—all accomplished and beautiful. There was Astrid de Schoten Whettenhall, the daughter of a Swedish countess and a Belgian nobleman, who was twenty-two years old and lived in Brussels. She and Edward met during a cruise to celebrate the silver wedding anniversary of Norway's King Harald and Queen Sonja, the parents of his brief flame Princess Martha. For a time, Edward was captivated by Astrid. "He could not stop talking about her and told his inner circle how beautiful she was," confided a friend. "Edward was really smitten. He tried to get her to visit him at Buckingham Palace. He thought the relationship would succeed because she came from such a distinguished background. But sadly she told him that she liked him very much but only wanted to be friends."

He was also linked with Annabel Elliot, a twenty-three-year-old graduate of Durham University who had shoulder-length dark hair and large green eyes. She worked in the marketing department of London's elegant Berkeley Hotel in Knightsbridge. Like Edward's other girlfriends, she was invited to Buckingham Palace for dinner. There was, however, an element that had not been present in Edward's other dates with girls: the two of them went ten-pin bowling together. Annabel had introduced Edward to bowling, and he enjoyed it. Bowling was far removed from the kinds of aristocratic pastimes enjoyed by Princess Martha or Astrid. Slowly, but imperceptibly, Edward's taste in women was consolidating. He had tangled briefly with the aristocracy, but he was clearly happier with women from more average backgrounds.

He may well have been influenced by the spectacle of his brother Charles trying desperately to extricate himself from the consequences of having married the highly strung, unimpeachably aristocratic Princess Diana. Edward was horrified by the disintegration of his brother's once fairy-tale romance with Diana. Nevertheless, he remained cordial to his soon to be former sister-in-law. On March 8, 1993, Edward escorted Diana to a reception at Marlborough House, where Chief Emeka Anyaoku was guest of honor. Forty-eight hours before the reception, Diana had returned from Nepal, after her first solo trip since separating from Charles. "Throughout the evening, Diana demonstrated that, with her brother-in-law, she is able to put her marriage problems temporarily behind her," reported an eyewitness. "She was relaxed and radiant, in stark contrast to her gloomy appearance whenever she has been photographed recently with Prince Charles. Edward was also in top form, reducing both Diana and Chief Anyaoku to stitches with his jokes."

He was also seen out on the town with Ruthie Henshall, who was now a successful musical comedy performer and was starring in *Crazy for You*. Henshell's father squashed the romantic rumors by saying, "Prince Edward is her friend. But Ruthie is very determined to go it alone. Anyway, with the hours she works, it's practically impossible for her to have a romance with anybody . . . let alone a royal." Chances were very high that he was telling the truth.

Edward wasn't committing to Ruthie, or any other woman for that matter. By 1992, all his siblings' marriages had failed: The Duke and Duchess of York separated, Princess Anne divorced Captain Mark Phillips, and Diana and Charles were clearly heading for the same fate. Edward, ever cautious, had no intention of making the same mistake. Instead, he chose to bide his time. In the interim, he cast about for new career opportunities.

He was now nearly thirty years old with two major professional failures behind him. It was vital that his next venture be deemed a huge success.

■   ■   ■

Nineteen ninety-two marked the Queen's fortieth anniversary on the throne of England. It also turned out to be what she would later term her *"annus horribilis."* At eleven-forty A.M. on Friday, November 20, 1992, much of Windsor Castle went up in flames. Prince Andrew was on hand, helping workers tackle the blaze. The flames gutted nine principal rooms and around one hundred subsidiary rooms.

The castle where the Queen had lived as a child, where Edward had been christened, and which bore the family name, was now in part reduced to rubble. And on November 22, when Edward visited the ruins of his home, he broke down completely. "Edward walked into St. George's Hall and just took one look and his face crumpled," said a witness. "He was inconsolable. The Queen put her arms around him, told him to compose himself, and gave him a handkerchief. It could have been any mom with her son facing up to a house fire. Edward was crying his heart out, but the Queen brought him round." Edward then donned a hard hat and boarded a hydraulic platform. From one hundred twenty feet in the air, he surveyed the ruins of the state banqueting hall. "By sheer fortune, all the paintings in St. George's Hall were removed for restoration work; otherwise we'd be looking at an even greater tragedy," he said to the *Daily Mail.* "It has been a great shock. Windsor is much more of a home to me than Buckingham Palace, which is mainly made up of offices. It has far more history behind it. For me, I will never forget the sight of Brunswick Tower alight like a medieval beacon. It was desperate, just standing there watching it go up and not being able to do anything. It was the nightmare we had always dreaded."

The marriages of all his siblings were in ruins; the Windsor dynasty had fallen into disrepute. The fate of Windsor Castle was yet another symbol of the monarchy's fallibility.

■   ■   ■

The Windsor Castle fire reverberated onto Edward's life in a practical as well as an emotional fashion. The castle had not been insured for fire. The cost of restoring it was estimated to be more than $80 million. The bill was to be settled by the British taxpayer. The public was outraged at having to foot the bill for the Queen, reputedly one of the richest people in Britain. Edward sprang to his mother's defense. "I've heard these rumors that my mother has £6.5 billion," he said indignantly to the *Evening Standard*. "Absolute crap! If only she had £6.5 billion."

After the blaze, the nation radically reevaluated the Queen's financial position. In the face of bitter criticism, she volunteered to pay tax and to open up Buckingham Palace to paying visitors for two months every year. Finally—and this would impact Edward dramatically—Parliament abridged the Civil List. With one stroke of the pen, Edward's £96,000 ($156,480)-a-year allowance was eliminated. In the future, the Queen would replace it, affording Edward the identical sum. At the time, though, he was distraught at losing his income. "It was like a kick in the teeth. People say, 'Oh well, it was deserved; what did you ever do?' But you only have to look at the Court Circular records—the publicity was unbalanced," he complained afterwards to journalist Frances Hardy. "But once in this particular job, born into it, you can't get rid of it. I still do the same work. But now I have to find other ways to fund my existence."

His childhood home was partially destroyed. His career, too, was in ruins. It was time for Edward to grow up at last.

9
ENTER SOPHIE

*I*N JUNE 1993, RADIO AUTHORITIES CHAIRMAN PETER Baldwin created The Prince Edward Summer Challenge, in aid of various charities including the Duke of Edinburgh Award. The concept entailed volunteers taking on a risky challenge, which would then be broadcast by groups of radio stations around Britain. The challenge was promoted by a wily Scotsman, PR man Brian MacLaurin, head of MacLaurin Communications and Media (MCM), who hit on the idea of Prince Edward taking on one of the challenges himself.

The ancient sport of Real Tennis had always been one of Edward's abiding interests since his time at Cambridge, where he was tutored by an expert named Brian Church. Real Tennis originated in fifth century Tuscany, where it was played by monks. Today, Real Tennis is played in Britain by fewer than eight thousand people on twenty courts throughout the country.

The game is played on a roof-covered walled court. Fifty-two balls are on the court at any one time and are kept in a type of bucket from which a player serves. The balls are the same size as tennis balls and are solid, with cork in the center wrapped with thirty yards of cotton webbing that has been tied and then covered with a felt cloth sewn on by hand. Consequently the balls are harder and fifty percent heavier than those used in lawn tennis. The rackets are heavy and asymmetric. Henry VIII was a good player.

Edward grew to excel at the game. He played for Cambridge in a varsity match against Oxford and was a member of the Holyport Real Tennis Club, near Ascot, in Berkshire. Today, he plays regularly at the Royal Tennis Court at Hampton Court Palace. "He comes here a lot," says Ben Ronaldson, professional Real Tennis coach there. "The average club handicap is forty-five. The lower the number, the better. Edward's handicap is somewhere around forty, perhaps a bit under. So he's a better than average player."

Edward's prowess at the game made it a foregone conclusion that when the call came from Brian MacLaurin asking him to play Real Tennis in aid of the Duke of Edinburgh Award Scheme, he immediately agreed to take part in a twelve-hour Real Tennis marathon.

Edward's offer to participate was a kindly one, but, at the same time, the event hardly sizzled with media crackle. The resourceful MacLaurin came up with a publicity ploy to create an aura of excitement around the challenge that he hoped would attract the media; he invited British tennis champion and Sky Television sports presenter Sue Barker to appear with Edward at a photo call held at Queen's Club in London. Aware that regional radio stations would be promoting the challenge, MacLaurin arranged for T-shirts from each station to be sent to London for Sue Barker to wear during the shoot. His rationale was that if Sue was photographed in the T-shirt of a particular city's radio station, that city's local paper would publish the picture, thus maximizing publicity for the challenge.

Things did not, however, go according to plan on July 16, the day of the press conference and photo shoot. An eleventh-hour telephone call from Sky Television's head of sport, Dave Hill, banned Sue Barker from donning any T-shirt other than that bearing the "Sky" logo. Sue, who valued her well-paid job with Sky, was compelled to comply. She dropped out. Brian MacLaurin's publicity campaign for the Prince Edward Challenge was now in ruins.

Sue Barker's sudden departure from the Prince Edward Challenge cleared the stage for a new player to enter Edward's life. Twenty-eight-year-old Sophie Rhys-Jones, a voluptuous sturdy blonde, was Brian MacLaurin's assistant. An English rose buttressed by an iron will and a taste for the high life, Sophie burned with strong ambitions and an even stronger drive to win at all costs. Although it has always been said that Brian MacLaurin impulsively picked Sophie Rhys-Jones to replace Sue Barker at the press conference, there are others who claim that Sophie pushed herself forward and volunteered for the task. If she had, it would not have been surprising. Whether or not she engineered that first meeting with Edward, Sophie Rhys-Jones is an upwardly mobile middle-class girl, adept at making the most of an opportunity.

Within moments, MacLaurin whisked his vivacious PR assistant back to her apartment. She dashed inside, quickly changed, and touched up her makeup before MacLaurin drove her to the Queen's Club, where she was introduced to Prince Edward.

Sparks did not fly between them on that first meeting. Edward's heart did not skip a beat. Nor did Sophie feel suddenly faint with desire. Edward has always been shy, reserved, and tentative with women. Sophie was confident and bouncy, attractive, rather than alluring or beautiful. Later, when the press cast around for something flattering to write about Sophie, they focused on her resemblance to Princess Diana. "It's uncanny," enthused photographer Arthur Edwards, who took the notorious picture of Diana in a see-through skirt surrounded by nursery school children. "Sophie's hair, her smile, it was just like stepping back in time. But the difference is that Di was a shy young girl who always kept her head down. You can tell Sophie is a much more confident self-assured young woman."

Sophie was indeed extremely self-assured and confident and would not have thanked Edward—or anyone else for that matter—for likening her to Princess Diana. "Sophie hates being compared to Princess Diana," said a business associate who worked closely with her. "She hates it almost as much as she hates being called 'a commoner.' Sophie has always wanted to be more royal than royal."

Apart from her china blue eyes, short blonde hair, creamy English rose skin, and indomitable will, Sophie and the Princess of Wales were very different. While the Princess was over five foot ten, Sophie was more in Edward's Munchkin mold, standing five feet four inches tall. And while Diana's lineage was even more aristocratic than that of the Windsors, Sophie's was even less aristocratic than that of Sarah Ferguson, the Duchess of York.

No matter how much she may hate the characterization, Sophie Rhys-Jones is a commoner through and through.

"Sophie is an extremely ordinary girl," says *Daily Mail* society columnist Nigel Dempster. "You couldn't be more ordinary. But Sophie got Edward because, like him, she was sporty, she got on well with people, and she wanted something."

"She was just an ordinary village girl, just like my daughter was an ordinary village girl," remembered Nora Veysey, a journalist for the *Kent and Sussex Courier*, who watched Sophie grow up and still attends the same church as her father, Christopher Rhys-Jones.

Brenchley, the village where Sophie grew up, is in the heart of the county of Kent which the English fondly call the Garden of England. An elegant, yet rural area, notable for oast houses (in which hops are brewed), apple orchards, and cherry blossoms, Kent was the perfect setting for the girl who was destined to become a princess. And although she looked more like a well-muscled milkmaid than an ethereal aristocrat, Sophie's idyllic childhood was straight out of every children's storybook.

She was born in the shadow of the dreamy spires of Oxford, at the Nuffield Maternity Home on January 20, 1965, and christened Sophie Helen. Her mother, Mary, picked the name "Sophie" when she was pregnant. Mary heard a young mother calling for her daughter Sophie and turned round to see an extremely pretty little girl answer to the name. She resolved instantly that if her unborn child proved to be a daughter, she would call her Sophie. Sophie's second name was Helen, after her father's beloved sister who was killed in a tragic riding accident when she was only in her late teens.

Soon after Sophie's birth, her parents, Christopher and Mary Rhys-Jones, and her older brother, David, moved to a small village in Kent called Brenchley. Christopher Rhys-Jones (he inserted the hyphen into the family name) was born in Sarawak, Borneo. His father, Theo, was headmaster of a private school in Lympstone, Devon—ironically the same town in which Edward suffered so many humiliations while training as a Marine. Her mother, Mary, was the daughter of a bank manager and, when she met Christopher, was working as a secretary in the Chelsea district of London.

When they first married, the Rhys-Joneses moved into a modest house in the heart of Brenchley. After just a few years, they bought Homestead Farmhouse, a seventeenth-century farmhouse with four bedrooms and a thatched roof, where they still live today. The farmhouse is set back from the road amid trees, with a view of the green Kentish fields, and furnished in the classic English style reproduced with such uncanny accuracy by Ralph Lauren. The farmhouse kitchen is the hub of the Rhys-Jones home and painted yellow, with colored kitchen units. Outside in the hall, in pride of place, stands a Welsh dresser.

Life in the tightly knit community of Brenchley was safe and secure. "Sophie was a lovely little girl," enthused Rebecca Peacey, who lived next door to Sophie when she was eight. "A real chatterbox. Our door was always open, and she and her brother used to come round to play here. Sophie loved chatting to my late husband. He thought she was wonderful."

Christopher Rhys-Jones was originally an overseas representative for a firm of car manufacturers who then moved into importing and exporting tires to Hungary. The Rhys-Joneses were not wealthy—throughout Sophie's childhood, her mother worked as a secretary for a real estate company. She also took in typing at £4.50 ($7.34) an hour in order to make extra money to pay for Sophie's and David's education. Mary Rhys-Jones was an exemplary mother, creating a warm and friendly environment for her children, laughingly feeding them chocolate cookies when they behaved well.

Mary was as English as Big Ben, solid, honest, and well-meaning. It must have hurt Sophie deeply when, as a fully fledged publicist, she would hear unkind whispers from PR colleagues regarding her mother. "Sophie's mother used to do my typing," sniffed an upper-class English gentleman named Archie.

The Rhys-Joneses were determined that Sophie and David receive the best education their money could buy. They managed to send them both to Dulwich College Preparatory School—an establishment nine miles away from their home.

The school was founded in 1885 and prided itself on its academic, artistic, and sporting excellence. Children joined the school at the age of five and at thirteen, were prepared (hence the name "Preparatory") for the entrance examination to the British equivalent of high school. "We liked Sophie because she was entirely natural. She was conscientious, she worked away and threw herself into everything, and she was keen on sports. But I think it was her naturalness that we liked and encouraged," said her headmaster, Robin Peverett.

One of her best friends at Dulwich was Janie Stewart, who remembered Sophie as a well-behaved child. "She wasn't really rebellious. She would toe the line. She would never come in with her socks all wrinkled down and her cardigan half off and her hair all over the place. She always looked clean and scrubbed. The teachers liked her as well. She was pretty and bright and fun and giggled a lot, but she was never vulgar or over the top."

Even at an early age, she already shone at sports. She swam, rode bicycles, and could have been classified as the quintessential tomboy. Yet although she was perfectly capable of playing soccer with the boys, Sophie still managed to look neat, tidy, and the model pupil. Over twenty years later, Princess Diana would mock her as "Miss Goody Two Shoes," but Sophie's pristine persona was not an act concocted to impress the royal family. Even as a child, she was happy and enthusiastic, but when the chips were down she always conformed. She was not a particularly academic child and favored the arts over the sciences. Mathematics was not her strong point, but she appreciated poetry and was a graceful ballet student, managing to pass a variety of ballet examinations.

At thirteen, Sophie progressed to the £1,500 ($2,445)-a-term Kent College for Girls, in Pembury, another village not far from Brenchley. Set amid the rolling Kent landscape, overlooked by an old church and surrounded by bluebell woods, the school was imposingly beautiful. Kent College was initially founded in Folkestone, Kent, in 1886 by the Wesleyan Methodist School Association and then moved to Pembury in 1939. Despite the school's foundation, Methodism was not the prescribed religion. Instead, the school accepted girls from all denominations. The majority of the pupils were boarders, working and sleeping at the school for most of the year, except vacations. Sophie, however, was one of the school's rare day girls, going home each night and returning every morning.

Kent College was very different from Gordonstoun, the school that Edward attended at the same age. Instead of obsessively emphasizing physical challenges, sometimes to the detriment of academic achievement, Kent College stressed other facets in a child's development. The college's current headmistress, Barbara J. Crompton, quoting Helen Keller, reminded the girls that "life is either a daring adventure or nothing." At Kent College, Sophie was encouraged to study art, history, and French, take part in theater workshops, and, in general, become a well-rounded pupil.

The headmistress, Miss Margaret James, was well-known for her sensitivity and intuitive grasp of each individual pupil's character. Even today, she remembers Sophie very clearly. "I remember her parents first bringing her to the school when they thought about entering her here. They were obviously keen on education. She obviously came from a good, caring home. She wasn't the sort of highest academic high flyer in any way, but she held her own very well in what was a good year that had a high standard. She was a well-liked girl, pleasant, friendly. She was keen on sporty things like netball, and she did well in her gymnastics. She was quite good in French and was quite artistic.

"She was lively and interested in what was going on. The fact that I don't have any sort of outstanding memories of her in a sense says that she never did anything outrageous or, for that matter, exceptional. She joined in things well."

Sophie also had good manners, as Miss James recently observed after she sent Sophie a note congratulating her on her engagement. "Within a few days, I had a reply. Now, certainly, it was on her office notepaper and the central part of it had obviously been duplicated, but she had taken the trouble to address the envelope herself. And to write, "Dear Miss James," at the start, and to put a personal note on the bottom before signing the letter. So it was partly handwritten, and I thought it spoke well for Sophie that she had taken the time to put her pen in her hand and write something personal to me."

Miss James's endearing view of Sophie's Kent College years is underscored by the memories of one of her schoolmates. "Sophie was someone you could trust—someone to rely on. Sophie lived locally, so she wasn't a boarder. She had a life outside the school, and that made her very glamorous. She'd come back after the weekend and tell us about parties and boys. She was never short of a boyfriend. We'd all go green with envy. She was always right up to date on fashion and clothes. She was forever growing her hair, having it cut short, and then growing it again. In the group photos, she was egging everyone on to do sillier and sillier things. It's no wonder she netted Prince Edward. Once she set her mind on a target, it was as good as in the bag. She could always see off the competition."

Through the years, this image of Sophie as a determined young woman is one that would be echoed by many.

She met her first real boyfriend, David Kinder, during her time at Kent College. They met when she joined a theater workshop at Tonbridge Boys School, where David was rehearsing an Arthur Miller play at the time. Even in those days, Sophie gravitated towards the best catch within her orbit. Soon she was playing tennis with David on his wealthy parents' private courts on the grounds of their mansion in Chislehurst, Kent. She was fifteen years old, and David Kinder provided her with a taste of the good life. Sophie would not forget what it felt like to disport herself in a wealthy playground, and David Kinder would not forget Sophie. An ex-actor turned teacher, even today, David envies Edward his Sophie. "Sophie is a lovely girl," he said wistfully, "and Edward is a very lucky man."

Like Edward, Sophie took O levels, gaining eight in contrast to his seven. She could have stayed on at Kent College. But to the disappointment of her headmistress, Margaret James, instead of aspiring towards a university degree, when she was sixteen, Sophie left to take a two-year secretarial course at West Kent College of Further Education, in Tonbridge. Sophie had wanted to move straight to London and get a job, but for once, her father put his foot down. "We were not pushy parents, but we did not allow her to go to London until she was qualified in something," he explained. "We persuaded her to go to West Kent College, where she studied O-level law and two A levels. She also took a secretarial course."

"We had some very sophisticated sixteen- to eighteen-year-old ladies at West Kent College," remembered Marion Vellino, a lecturer there during Sophie's era. "But she was just the average sixteen- to eighteen-year-old. She was the sporty type, and when I knew her, she was the typical student in jumper and jeans."

At West Kent, where Sophie enrolled in September 1981, one of her closest friends was Jo Last. "Sophie's a great girl, she's funny, witty, smart, sweet—but not stuck-up. We were best pals for two years. Sophie is extraordinary for being ordinary, normal, and a down-to-earth decent girl. We were in the same class. She was tremendously open, warm, sweet, and funny. We poured out our hearts to each other right from the start," Jo recalled nostalgically to journalist Caroline Graham.

"We never had problems finding things to chat about endlessly—mostly our dreams for the future and, of course, boys. I had a boyfriend called Simon, and I was always going on at her about him. She would listen for hours. That's what I remember most about her—she was one of the most unselfish people I've ever known. Sophie had a few boyfriends too. But there was never anyone serious. She was incredibly pretty, with great skin, a big smile, and the same smart hairdo she has today. We first met just after Diana and Charles married. People would say how much Sophie looked like Diana."

Jo's father gave her a brown Citroën as a gift. The car was old, the sunroof didn't open and close properly, but to Jo and Sophie, "Matilda," as they christened the car, was their passport to freedom. At lunchtime, the two girls would rush out of class and dash down to the parking lot, jump into Matilda, and roar off to a local café.

"I remember picking Sophie up on the morning of our English A level. We were both sitting inside Matilda, doing some last-minute revision. Suddenly, at exactly the same time, we both looked up, grinned at each other—and threw the notes through the sunroof. We started giggling uncontrollably and were laughing as we entered the exam room. She passed with flying colors—I flunked it!" Jo recalls. Then, on a more serious note, she says, "Back then we were both pretty square. We'd have a few drinks in a pub to celebrate exams and birthdays, but were never wild party girls."

Sophie's social life—like that of most young English middle-class girls—centered around the pub. From the first, Sophie exhibited a taste for the high life, preferring champagne to beer or wine. The future princess even worked for a time as a barmaid at the Halfway House pub in Brenchley. "She was excellent behind the bar," remembers a Halfway House regular, Michael Noakes. "She was about eighteen years old at the time, very pleasant and attractive, and she always used to fill the pints up, which was unusual. She was a great girl always to have behind the bar of your local, always chatting with the customers. She always gave full measure, and I remember her as being very charming and attractive—in fact, it made me wish I was a few years younger."

In June 1983, Sophie left West Kent College and moved to London, where she intended to find a job. Her teachers, taking note of her confident, extrovert nature, had recommended that she take a job that involved her in interacting with people. Within a month of leaving West Kent, she was in London and working for the Quentin Bell PR Organization. As would be her pattern, Sophie went straight to the top, accepting a post as secretary to the managing director of the company. After six months, she switched to another job, with the Tim Arnold Sales Promotion Agency.

Her private life was divided between London, where she shared a flat with an old school friend, and Brenchley, where she returned as much as possible. Her twenty-first birthday party, held in the garden of the family home in Brenchley, was a highlight of her life in the country. Her father hired a tent to cover the garden, and under the watchful, but always indulgent eyes of her parents, Sophie threw a party worth remembering.

By dawn, her friends were strewn all over the house and garden, with one snuggled up in the dog's blanket and another one fast asleep with his headphones on and his Walkman still playing. Everyone agreed that Sophie's party had been a mammoth success.

Buoyed by her landmark birthday, Sophie plunged into a new job at Capital Radio, Britain's leading music station. There, she began in a relatively mundane job, working in the press office as assistant to press officer Jan Reid. Her work consisted mainly of doing correspondence and filing, but along the way, Sophie did what she has always done best—made friends.

Very early on in her three years at Capital, Sophie won the friendship of two of the station's most powerful figures. One was Anita Hamilton, who, when Sophie was transferred to the promotions department, became her boss. Anita, a fashionably dressed career woman, taught Sophie how to write press releases and arrange photo shoots and product launches. By the time she left Capital, Sophie had a shrewd grasp of the intricacies of PR.

She had always possessed an innate ability to charm in a low-key manner. "She's a very natural girl who has always been most aware of the people around her, whoever they are," praised her uncle, Peter Bettany. She was friendly, open, didn't flirt blatantly with men, but was happy to go drinking with them—just like one of the guys. She dressed well, if conservatively, always flashed a sunny smile, and was facile at small talk. Capital Radio's number one star, Chris Tarrant, couldn't fail to notice her.

Tarrant—now one of Britain's foremost television personalities whose show, *Do You Want to Be a Millionaire?* is today one of the country's biggest hits—was unmarried during his Capital days and was renowned for being an ace womanizer. But if Sophie was one of his conquests, Tarrant certainly has never intimated it.

Now married to a beautiful Norwegian blonde, Ingrid, he speaks of Sophie with the greatest of respect. "We were friends," he says today. Sophie and Tarrant—along with a group of Capital Radio employees, including Tarrant's co-presenter, Kara Noble—went on a trip together to Spain, from where they broadcast Chris Tarrant's *Breakfast Show.*

When they had a few hours' break, the entire team sunbathed on the beach. It was there on that beach that Sophie innocently made what might have been one of the biggest mistakes of her life. Topless sunbathing is the fashion in Spain, and Sophie was no different from the other sun-worshipping women eager to get an all-over tan. She took her top off and promptly fell asleep. Chris Tarrant tiptoed over to her, stood above her seminude body, and leered down lecherously, just in time for Kara Noble to snap a picture of the two of them.

"Sophie is lying on the beach," says the Capital Radio disc jockey known as Dr. Fox, who has seen the picture. "Tarrant has crept up and is leaning on the ground. He has his face at ground level. The shot has been taken from behind her head." Then, lest anyone get the wrong impression, he adds loyally, "She is a lively, normal girl, but Tarrant wasn't having an affair with her. That's rubbish."

Sophie was probably unaware of the picture's existence until the dreadful moment when she walked into the disc jockeys' room at Capital and found the picture of Tarrant and herself (in all her topless glory) staring down at her from the office notice board. In those days, making prima-donna demands was not yet her style, so Sophie merely smiled and did not order anyone to remove the picture. There it remained, to the amusement of all at Capital.

A close friend of Sophie's later said of the pictures from this trip (there were more, taken at a party later, of a topless Sophie with Tarrant resting his head on her bare chest), "They are sexy, not sleazy. But Sophie's terrified. The pictures have been on her mind since she met Edward, and she'd hoped they'd been lost or destroyed."

"Sophie shouldn't worry too much," countered Chris Tarrant, in an attempt to soothe Sophie's fears. "We were friends, and friends take these kinds of pictures. From what I recall, it isn't exactly X-rated stuff."

Sophie was in her early twenties, single and fancy-free. She spent the next few years living out her wildness. With Capital Radio personality Dr. Fox and other Capital friends, she traveled to the Italian ski resort of Courmayeur for a skiing vacation. Sophie loved skiing almost as much as she loved the après-ski amusements. Each night, she and her friends hit the disco floor, dancing the night away with abandon. With them was an Italian porn star, Marino Franchi, a male stripper famous for his vast endowment. Sophie was neither enthralled nor flustered by the presence of a man whom *Cosmopolitan* had labeled a "professional penis." She giggled happily with the rest of the Capital crowd when Marino did a sensuous striptease on the disco dance floor. But although she could never have been classified as a shy wilting flower, even Sophie fled in embarrassment when Marino ended up dressed only in female panties. The panties were hers. The mischievous Marino had broken into Sophie's room and stolen a pair of her panties, and was now wearing them. A red-faced Sophie took refuge in her room.

While the Italian trip with the salacious porno star might have been a touch too rich for Sophie's blood, the next Capital trip, to Florida's Disneyland, was much more to her liking. With her on the trip was Graham Dene, a Capital Radio disc jockey with whom she was friendly. After Graham met a beautiful artist named Julie Tennant in an elevator, Sophie facilitated the romance by suggesting to Graham that he and Julie pose for a photograph together. Four years later, Graham and Julie married.

During her time at Capital, Sophie found herself the romantic target of a teenager's crush. A nineteen-year-old Capital employee, James Cannon, fell wholeheartedly for her. "I was nineteen and an awkward teenager, and there was Sophie, this confident, charming, very popular and beautiful young woman," he admits. "I was completely besotted by her. I didn't have the courage to ask her out face-to-face, so I remember I bought a card and wrote a message asking if she'd like to meet up for a drink after work. I left it in her post tray, and she came up to me later in the day and thanked me, but the answer was a very firm no."

Sophie may have rejected James because of his youth, but there were whispers at Capital that she was highly impressionable, a social climber, and was only prepared to date men with status. "She was fairly enamored by titles and stuff like that, which doesn't mean much to me," said Andrew Parkinson, who went out with her briefly. "She loved to move in those circles. She was always going on about places she had been to and parties in the country. That's the kind of lifestyle she wanted. Ours was never a really serious relationship. She's lovely, very bubbly, great fun to be with. She is sparkling, a real party girl. She's a lot of fun, and she certainly enjoyed living life to the full."

Her choice of a man with whom to have her first serious adult relationship, however, gave lie to Parkinson's judgment that

Sophie only gravitated towards aristocrats. Her first intense relationship was not with an English lord, but with a run-of-the-mill businessman. His name was Jeremy Barkley, and at thirty-five, he was eleven years older than she was. "We met through my twin brother, Simon, in about 1987," Jeremy explained. "We were together for about two years. She is a fabulous girl, and we are still good friends."

Neither Sophie nor Jeremy have ever spoken out about the reasons for their relationship's end. At twenty-four, Sophie suddenly resigned from her job at Capital. "She was fed up with working at Capital and fed up with England. When the chance came to work abroad, she just took it," explained a friend. Sophie opted for a complete change of career and took a job as a representative for a skiing company, Bladon Lines.

At the end of November 1990, she attended Bladon's training course, and then signed a four-month contract to represent the company in the elegant ski resort of Crans Montana, in the Swiss Alps, where her French-speaking skills would be put to good use. "She was the kind of pretty girl all the male reps would congregate around," remembered Gareth Crump, who worked for Bladon at the same time as Sophie. "She always struck me as very capable."

She was also swiftly gaining a reputation as a party girl. "Like the rest of us, she enjoyed a party, but I only ever saw her drunk once, and that's when I photographed her rolling in the snow with one of her girlfriends," said a friend who knew her well at the time.

But Sophie didn't get carried away by the ski resort's flashy atmosphere. Amid the trendy nightclubs, stirring alpine scenery, and bustling bars, she fixed on the second great love of her life, an Australian ski instructor named Michael O'Neill. Michael was dashing, athletic, and very different from the more conventional English men with whom she had previously tangled. Sophie was young, unfettered, and had an adventurous spirit, which was further ignited by Michael's compelling tales of Australia. When the skiing ended, she succumbed to his blandishments that she return with him to Sydney.

But the romance between Sophie and Michael faltered fairly quickly. "Michael wanted to settle down, whereas Sophie was determined to go out and party," a friend revealed. They broke up soon after Sophie's arrival in Sydney. A lot of twenty-four-year-old girls, finding themselves in a similar situation, would have thrown in the towel and gone straight back to England. But not Sophie. She was proud, courageous, and was determined to make the best of her time in Australia. She moved into the flat of a platonic male friend, then took a job for an international shipping company, Jet Services. Jonathan Miller, who ran Jet Services, immediately sensed that Sophie, with her outgoing personality, would be an asset to his company and hired her as his girl Friday. Although she worked diligently for him, Jonathan read between the lines and assessed her goals as not being work-related: "I think Sophie just wanted to have a good time. She seemed a bright bubbly girl who was great fun and liked to party."

She spent an exhilarating year in Australia, indulging her love for deep-sea diving, for admiring the countryside, and for sailing. She made friends with a seventy-year-old millionaire, a former naval officer named John Young, who invited her for a long week-end's cruise on board his one-hundred-foot schooner, the *Meridien*. There were eight other young people with them on the cruise around Australia's southeast coast, including the exotically named Eon Balmain, a twenty-eight-year-old fashion designer. "Sophie's very, very, attractive — a vivacious, beautiful girl," Eon reminisced. "Her eyes captured me. She walked on board wearing shorts. Later she changed into a flimsy sarong, which she wore most of the time. That turned me on because she looked really sexy. I remember her saying she was going to let her hair down, and I thought perhaps I was on to a good thing. But all she meant was that she was going to have a few drinks, a laugh, and a dance."

Sophie retained an air of mystery throughout the cruise, refusing to talk about her private life. She and Eon sunbathed on the deck of the boat together and chatted about their mutual interests. Sophie told Eon that she was a Mick Jagger fan and had been to Stones concerts. The couple went diving, swimming, and dancing. After a wild Saturday night of drinking and dancing, Eon and Sophie ended up in the hot tub, along with another couple. As the seventy-year-old John Young poured perfumed bath oils into the tub, Sophie's reserve melted. "Our toes and limbs touched as we slid about the foam," said Eon. Then, lest he give the wrong impression, he added hastily, "But in reality it was all harmless fun."

Sophie seemed to have a lot of harmless fun before she met Edward.

By June 1991, the fun had worn thin and Sophie decided that she had experienced the best of Australia. She returned home to Brenchley just in time to celebrate her father's sixtieth birthday. She loved her father very much and wouldn't have missed his party for the world. But once the candles had been blown out and the guests had left, Sophie was forced to confront reality. She was twenty-six, unemployed, and didn't have a home of her own.

Eager to get a job as soon as possible, Sophie plied as many companies as possible with her résumé. Out of all the replies, she opted to take a job with the Cancer Relief Macmillan Fund, which provides nurses for the terminally ill. She was paid a minimal salary of £12,000 ($19,560) a year to raise money for the charity, but she believed in its work so much that, even today, she is a member of one of their committees.

Sophie was doing good works, and her life was going well. She had a brief relationship with a dentist, Tim King, who took her flying. After the relationship ended, Sophie and Tim stayed friends, and even today, he remains her dentist, which says a great deal about Sophie and the enduring affection she tends to inspire in men.

Sophie was only on a short-term contract with the Cancer Relief Macmillan Fund, but when that ended, she turned to friends from Capital to advise her on her next move. Chris Tarrant was represented by a small public relations company, MacLaurin Communications and Media, run by Scottish PR man Brian MacLaurin. An introduction was arranged. MacLaurin found Sophie charming, vivacious, and full of energy. Soon she was an account manager at the company, working on Chris Tarrant's account and doing marketing work for the children's character Thomas the Tank Engine.

She also worked on the Mobil Oil account and scored a great coup by persuading Gene Pitney to allow his song "Twenty-four Hours From Tulsa," to be played as an accompaniment to a Mobil commercial. When Pitney acquiesced and his manager telephoned to inform Sophie, she was so elated that she screamed, "Tell him I love him and I will have his babies!"

On hearing of Sophie's lighthearted offer, Pitney was highly amused. When he arrived in Britain for a concert tour, he was heard repeatedly to refer to the bubbly PR girl. But if he had any intention of taking Sophie up on her "offer," it was too late.

The year was 1993, the year in which Sophie met Edward. The party girl was about to transform herself into the determined young woman.

10

MORE ROYAL THAN THE ROYALS

*T*HE PRESS CONFERENCE AT WHICH EDWARD FIRST met Sophie was followed by the Real Tennis Challenge (a twelve-hour marathon), which took place on September 13 at Holyport, Berkshire. The canny Brian MacLaurin, sensing a degree of chemistry between Edward and Sophie, asked her to assist him during the Challenge.

As a result, Sophie was on hand to witness Ruthie Henshall sweep into the Queen's Club, with Edward by her side. A bevy of photographers snapped away at Edward and Ruthie, unaware that their relationship was long since over and that Ruthie was merely on hand to boost the charity event.

Edward played well that day against Dr. Fox, Sophie's disc jockey friend from Capital Radio. The event, too, was a success, raising £29,000 ($47,270) for charity. That would have been the end of the story, but Edward telephoned Sophie a few weeks later. On the pretext of wanting to discuss the Challenge, he invited her to play a game of Real Tennis with him and to have dinner with him at Buckingham Palace afterwards.

Sophie took a deep breath, then agreed. As she later recalled, she spent the first half of the evening darting around the tennis court "like a demented bluebottle." Edward was patient, gently guiding her on how to play Real Tennis. In an attempt to ingratiate herself with him further, she followed his instructions, then suggested that she take formal lessons in the game. As Sophie had probably secretly hoped, Edward was delighted by her enthusiasm for his favorite sport.

After the game was over, they went back to Buckingham Palace for dinner. Skilled in PR, Sophie had learned to be a brilliant listener, nodding at the right places, smiling in encouragement. Soon Edward found himself confiding in her about his childhood and his love for acting, laughing with her at his own description of his theatrical debut in *Toad of Toad Hall*. She told him about her own schoolgirl forays into amateur dramatics. They compared notes and found that despite the vast disparity in their personal circumstances, their natures were surprisingly similar. They shared the same sort of sense of humor, they both loved acting, they both were athletic and outgoing, and they both tried hard to please. As the evening progressed, Edward relaxed and started enjoying himself.

Soon he was phoning her at work on a daily basis. "He has rung her every day for the last few weeks since they fell in love," said a source close to Sophie. "When they are not together, they are on the phone," said a friend. "This is true love." Edward took to telephoning Sophie at work and leaving messages under fake names. "Gus" and "Richard" were his chosen *noms de plume*, but the amused staff at MacLaurin were not deceived. Edward's well-known voice, his regal manner, and his inborn politeness were unmistakable.

At first, the two of them acted like any conventional courting couple. They went to the movies, to the theater (they saw *Phantom of the Opera* for the umpteenth time), and to Hampton Court, where Sophie showed off her newly learned prowess at Real Tennis. Sometimes Chris Tarrant's wife, Ingrid, joined Sophie in a game, as did Barbara Powell, the London-based wife of American actor Robert Powell. They dined by candlelight at Edward's favorite Indian restaurant, sharing curry. They also spent many a night at Buckingham Palace, usually eating meals cooked by Edward's valet, but sometimes supping on simple dishes prepared by Sophie.

On the surface, their burgeoning romance was exactly like that of any other couple. However, there was one dramatic difference: Everywhere the couple went, they were accompanied by Edward's detective.

Soon the media would be part of their entourage. There was a significant difference between Edward's relationship and his previous relationships. This one seemed to be serious.

Before she undertook an astrological investigation of Edward, Sophie, and their relationship in order to discover the aspects of their personality that brought them together, internationally renowned astrologer Erin Sullivan (who is based in Tucson, Arizona) knew virtually nothing about them. After studying their individual and composite charts, she concluded, "The horoscopes of Sophie and Edward in comparison show an extraordinary amount of shared values and kinship. Very much a sibling-like relationship. Though they are vastly different in their personal daily habits and instinctive responsive natures, their variation is more complementary than irritating to them."

Sophie has a Virgo Moon, while Edward has an Aquarius Moon. Both these positions of the Moon have an emotional-distancing dynamic which allows a lot of room for the others' idiosyncrasies and also demonstrates their mutual distaste for cloying, emotionally charged, and enmeshed relationships. The Virgo Moon of Sophie is close to the planet Uranus, which is the ruling planet of Edward's Moon in Aquarius. Each of them has the capacity to compartmentalize their instinctive reactions, feelings and address them as "later," as opposed to "immediately." Since each of them has very different occupations from the other, this is probably the most important aspect in the longevity of their marriage.

Both Sophie and Edward view each other as interesting, unique, independent, and safe—wholly trustworthy in partnership. Edward's Venus in Taurus, his mother's Sun sign, does suggest that his earthy, sensual, and loving nature is bound to his mother's power and is directly linked to the duality of his soft, tender, nurturing self and his other, more cool distant, and emotionally protective self. Edward's Aquarius Moon and Taurus Venus tells us that he felt he suffered from a lack of affection and warmth in his early childhood days. So Edward has a dichotomy between the warm loving nature of Taurus, and the cool, distant nature of Aquarius. It's Edward's Venus that finds safety and nourishment with Sophie's abundance of Earth-sign planets.

The parental images in Edward's chart do not support his deepest needs, hence he will have had to find creative ways of meeting his emotional needs. Clearly, this has played a strong role in his attraction to, affection for, and selection of Sophie as his life-mate. Edward's Sun, the masculine principle in the horoscope, is in Pisces, trine to the planet Neptune. This aspect is the creative, dreamy, and highly fanciful side of Edward, which is likely where his survival instincts reside. This hopeful quality is the core of his energy and psychological fuel. The Sun also represents the father archetype, and the Sun trine Neptune symbolizes a father who is hard to grasp, a man distant but benevolent. Edward idealized his distant father, and incorporated his father's dreams as his own. Edward is more like Prince Philip than one might imagine.

He has Mercury, Mars, and Chrion in Pisces. Coming-of-age was very traumatic for him. It is very likely that he employed his Aquarius Moon to cut himself off from the emotional turmoil and split off from the pressures of his body, adopting a world of imagination and creativity. It is this sensitive and empathetic component of Edward's psyche that provides Sophie with the love and understanding she herself needs. She exemplifies the pragmatic, sensible, and un-histrionic horoscope. But she also has innate class. She is both a woman of substance as well as being socially adept.

Her Sun in Aquarius meets Edward's Moon in Aquarius. This configuration is a classic lifetime friendship. She is the stronger character and persona of the two, but that is not to say Edward is weak. He most definitely is not. He is profoundly strong-willed and has soundly established opinions and a worldview. But he is not assertive about forcing those feelings on others. He is not a fighter, but indeed, may suffer from that. I would think that Sophie, too, has found herself swallowing her own anger at times. She is more volatile than is Edward.

Sophie is primarily an earthy individual. She has four planets in Virgo, two in Capricorn, one rising in Taurus. That says she loves to be useful, loathes weakness and helplessness unless it is due to oppression or disaster. She has a lot of control over her own world, and only the select might cross over into it. Her tenth house Aquarius is her capacity for separating her private life from her public life.

This is a meeting of equals. The relationship agrees with each of them and is familiar. They have a composite Moon in Scorpio, so they will remain a mystery to the most prying stranger. They have a rather plodding aspect. The conjunction of Venus and Saturn is a key to longevity because their dreams do not exceed what they can really create. Ultimately, it is a protective and mutual friendship.

In November 1993, less than two months after their relationship first blossomed, Edward left Sophie and traveled to Swaziland on behalf of the Duke of Edinburgh Award. They missed each other desperately, running up large phone bills during the separation. Then, in the beginning of December, Edward went on another trip, this time to America, where he visited New York, Dallas, and Los Angeles.

In Los Angeles, he attended a lunch given for him by Andrew Lloyd Webber's American representative, Peter Brown. The lunch, which also signaled that Lloyd Webber had forgiven Edward for his defection from Really Useful, was given in the home of Elton John's longtime manager, John Reid. There, Edward mixed with

industry greats like Suzanne de Passe, of Motown fame, and producer Wendy Stark.

A few days later, he switched gears and visited Genesis 1, the
Los Angeles village for the homeless. There, he met homeless
activist and one-time mayoral candidate Ted Hays. Edward toured
the village, chatted animatedly with the twenty-two occupants, and
planted a Japanese flowering plum tree. He also visited the Del-
haven Community Center in La Puente, a facility for the develop-
mentally disabled.

His primary purpose in being in Los Angeles was to host the
BAFTA/LA Fourth Annual Britannia Award, a black-tie gala held
at the Beverly Hilton. Part of the ceremony entailed the presenta-
tion of the Britannia achievement award to director Martin Scors-
ese. The guests who rose in unison to applaud the veteran director
of *GoodFellas* and *Raging Bull*, included Charles Bronson, Tony
Curtis, Michelle Pfeiffer, and Brad Pitt. Surrounded by so many
Hollywood luminaries, Edward was in his element. Nonetheless,
he couldn't wait to get home to Sophie. He flew back to England.
Soon after he arrived, on December 19, the story of his romance
with Sophie was made public for the first time.

It was Andrew Morton, the author of *Diana, Her True Story*,
who broke the news that Sophie and Edward were actually living
together at Buckingham Palace. Just over five years later, on January 6, 1999, during the press conference at which they announced
their engagement, Sophie and Edward both went out of their way
to deny ever having lived together. Edward insisted, "We've never
lived together." Sophie echoed him, asserting, "Contrary to popular opinion, we've never lived together."

Yet Andrew Morton and other reporters allegedly had proof
that, during the first year of their relationship, Sophie and Edward
did just that. Morton watched as Edward's green Rover 8201 picked
Sophie up from the Edwardian villa in West Kensington where she
lived and ferried her directly to Buckingham Palace. According to

Morton, Sophie carried with her a small overnight bag, which she placed in the backseat of the car.

At Buckingham Palace, where they arrived at eight, Sophie and Edward supped by candlelight, while Edward's detective took off the rest of the night. At one in the morning, the lights were still burning in the corridor of the second-floor apartment where Edward lived. Morton did not see Sophie leave the palace all night long, until, at 8:32 in the morning, a chauffeur-driven car whisked her through the palace gates and to her job at MacLaurin's.

Aware that the relationship was about to be made public, Sophie issued a statement through Brian MacLaurin: "Prince Edward and I are good friends, and we work together. He is a private person, and so am I. I have nothing more to add."

Now that the world knew about Sophie and Edward's relationship, the harder, more calculating elements of her nature began to obliterate her lively party-girl persona. She was now high above the parapet and needed to protect herself. From now on, she would be ever watchful and on her guard.

One of her neighbors at Verger Road, where she lived, revealed that Edward was so head over heels in love with Sophie that he wasn't afraid to relinquish all reserve in front of her. "I saw Sophie come out of her flat with a man in a raincoat," the neighbor confided. "I saw them laugh and smile at each other. Then he got into the Range Rover, and when he wound down the window, she leaned in and they were kissing."

The pressures on the couple extended to Sophie's parents, who were besieged by the media. "What Edward and Sophie do is their affair," said her father, Christopher Rhys-Jones, in exasperation. Then he relented and said, "All I can say is that Sophie is a normal girl who has had a normal life." A few months later, he was persuaded to wryly admit, "We joke about the two of them marrying, as most families do when their daughter is friendly with somebody, but it's only badinage. If Sophie comes to visit, I might tease her about her young man's prospects, what sort of family he comes from, that sort of thing. That doesn't constitute a serious discussion." He unbent even further, joking, "Friends have been sending me faxes marked for the attention of Sir Christopher Rhys-Jones and Lord Rhys-Jones. Others tell me it's going to cost an arm and a leg to hire Westminster Abbey. But it really is banter at this stage."

"It is perfectly clear that Miss Rhys-Jones and even Miss Ferguson would not have been accepted in the royal family a generation ago," observed Harold Brooks-Baker of *Burke's Peerage*, "although Miss Ferguson came from a relatively rich, upper-middle-class background and that is quite a different background from Miss Rhys-Jones. Queen Victoria said it wasn't necessary for her children and grandchildren to marry other royals, but what she had in mind were people like the Battenbergs, who were not royal but had been reduced to Serene Highnesses. But there is a difference between a Serene Highness and Miss Rhys-Jones's background." There was, and Sophie knew it. She was clever and ambitious. Now that ambition and cleverness was about to pay off. Soon after Morton's revelations, Sophie received the ultimate *imprimatur*: an invitation to Windsor Castle. This was her big chance, and she would do whatever it took to succeed.

At her behest, Edward spent hours briefing her for the big day. He coached Sophie on how to address the Queen, when to stand, when to sit, when to make conversation, and when to keep silent. Following Edward's instructions, Sophie drove to the castle in her Fiat Panda and parked in a courtyard by his private apartments, which were situated on the top floor of the Queen's Tower and boasted a view of the Long Walk. After she had parked, Sophie entered the tower by Edward's own private entrance. But although the tower contains two bedrooms, Sophie had been forewarned that she would not share a bedroom with Edward. Instead, she took her suitcase to the second bedroom, where her own personal maid, Isabel, was waiting to unpack for her.

Sophie was introduced to the Queen at lunchtime. As she met Her Majesty, Sophie's curtsy was steady and her smile bright. Then she joined the Queen, Prince Philip, Edward, Princess Anne, and Commander Tim Laurence, Anne's husband, for lunch in the Oak Drawing Room. In the afternoon, she had tea with the Duchess of York, the Duke, and their two daughters, Beatrice and Eugenie.

From the beginning, the Queen warmed to Sophie. "The Queen has really enjoyed Sophie's company," said a royal source, impressed by the rapport that had been struck up between the monarch and the PR girl. "The Queen is delighted that Edward has found such an attractive girl. She has a bubbling personality and is not a bit intimidated by the presence of the royal family." She also had evolved her own private system for dealing successfully with the Queen of England. "It's just like being at school. If you think of the Queen as the headmistress, you can't go wrong," Sophie said, with some calculation.

Sophie spent Christmas vacation of 1993 with Edward and his family at Sandringham. Bought in 1862 by Edward VII, Sandringham is one of the royals' two private residences (the other being Balmoral). With the Queen and the rest of the royal family, Sophie went on a five-hour shoot on the twenty-thousand-acre estate. She had studied the protocol in advance of arriving at Sandringham and was appropriately dressed for the shoot in a waxed jacket, her blonde hair covered by a head scarf. Along with the royal party, she trudged through fields and chatted easily with the Queen. Edward was thrilled at his mother's response to Sophie. An eyewitness who observed the shoot recalled, "Edward looked very happy. He's been in a sunny mood at Sandringham, quite different from the past. He looked like a dog with two tails. He was laughing all morning. Once I saw him let out a real belly laugh. Being in love has mellowed him. Everyone is saying how much more relaxed and friendly he is."

Sophie, too, was disarmed by the family's kindness to her. In many ways, the entire experience was straight out of the most romantic of dreams. It would take time for her to adjust to the reality that her life had been forever touched by the magic of royalty. "She gave me the impression that suddenly she had been hitched up to this great, big rock 'n' rolling ride to a whole new world," offered one of her friends and colleagues, Nick Skeens. "She was in awe of her new life, but enthralled by it. I found it fascinating how she adapted to what is an incredible lifestyle, one which other people can only dream about. It's a lottery win many times over."

It was a lottery win in which Sophie had an extremely powerful ally—the Queen of England. "Sophie is an opportunist and she is doing it well," observed a famous aristocrat connected to the royal family. "My understanding is that the Queen rather likes her because she's very correct. She doesn't put a foot wrong, and she rides with the Queen. Her profile has been absolutely correct. She behaves with decorum."

By all accounts, the Queen was terrified that Sophie and Edward's relationship would meet the same fate as those of his siblings, and the Queen gave his new romance a great deal of thought. She may well have learned a lesson from Princess Diana's emotional collapse under the pressures of marrying into the family. There were those who claimed that Diana's mental state was triggered because she had neither been primed by the royals to cope with her new status, nor had she been watched over by them when she first started dating Charles. Consequently, the Queen was extremely protective of Sophie. Instead of requesting that she accompany the family to the local Sandringham parish church, as was the custom, the Queen advised her not to go with the royal party. She was determined to shield Sophie from the limelight. Her instincts were correct. When the royals arrived at the little church, twenty-five-hundred well-wishers had gathered outside, all jostling one another in the hope of getting a glimpse of Sophie.

Joan Dunne, a well-wisher from Nottinghamshire, was in the crowd that day. "I am very disappointed not to have seen Sophie," she said. "She's a real Diana lookalike—and I'd like to see Edward happy."

The public already wanted her to be their princess. Sophie would be delighted to oblige.

Edward was, indeed, ecstatically happy. Only one thing was troubling him—his old nemesis, the media. In an attempt to forestall their interest in Sophie and to prevent them from hounding her, on December 20, 1993, he wrote an open letter to the editors of Britain's leading newspapers. In the letter, he wrote, "I am taking the unusual step of writing to you directly in the hope of stopping your reporters and photographers from destroying that part of my life I am entitled to and, more importantly, Sophie's life. We are not planning to get married—we have only met each other in the last few months—but we are still good friends. I am very conscious that other members of my immediate family have been subjected to similar attention, and it has not been at all beneficial to their relationships. Therefore, please will you call an end to your harassment of both Sophie and me, and allow us to carry on our lives as normal. It is you who have the power to grant us this. Please will you consider our wishes seriously, especially as it is Christmas and the season of goodwill."

Edward had undoubtedly made his pleas to the media because he wanted to protect Sophie from their blazing flashbulbs and himself from the constant scrutiny. At the same time, it would hardly be surprising if Edward's open letter to the press had not been prompted by another factor that must have rattled him. Just six weeks before his romance with Sophie hit the headlines, eclipsing all other royal stories, he had been involved in a story that was all his own, and which he believed reflected well on him. On November 7, 1993, he announced that he was launching a new career—that of television producer. And although his announcement was quickly upstaged by the news of his relationship with Sophie, Edward was nonetheless determined that his new career win him the respect of his family, the press, and the public.

They were both set on succeeding—Edward, in his career, and the two of them, in their relationship.

Apart from his involvement in the abortive *It's a Royal Knockout*, Edward had absolutely no television production experience whatsoever. Consequently the announcement that he had formed a television production company came as a shock to Edward-watchers. His new venture went by the name of Ardent Productions, a name he chose to symbolize what he viewed as his new company's key values: "ambition, motivation, and strength." The *Oxford English Dictionary*'s standard definition of the word "ardent" is "Glowing with passion, animated by keen desire; intensely eager, zealous, fervent, fervid." "I suppose Edward called his company Ardent because he figures he's keen and enthusiastic," offered a source who worked for the company. "I've seen more enthusiasm in an insect."

From the first, the palace stacked the cards in Edward's favor. After Biddy Hayward's company, the Theater Division, for whom Edward worked, went bankrupt, Prince Philip primed a number of royal advisers to weigh in with their career suggestions for Edward. Prince Philip, himself, favored a career change for Edward and broached the possibility of accountancy. Edward was not interested. Philip then proposed that he go into management training. Again, Edward demurred. Finally, it became clear to Prince Philip and his advisers that the only business that really interested Edward was show business.

On February 17, 1992, Edward, with his father's approval, met with insurance broker and royal-family-adviser Malcolm Cockren. Cockren was on the board of various major entertainment compa-

nies and counted Walt Disney and British Lion among his broker-
age clients. Under the watchful eye of Prince Philip, Cockren proceeded to guide Edward along the path to his new career.

Coopers and Lybrand, the accountants, assembled a business
plan for Edward, and a blueprint for Ardent was formulated.
Edward would be joint managing director, along with former bar-
rister and television executive Eben Foggit. Malcolm Eldridge, a
member of the Guild of Film and Television Production Accountants, was to be company secretary and finance director. Graeme
McDonald, the former controller of BBC2, with a stellar track
record in television drama (including *All Creatures Great and
Small*) was enlisted as the company's creative executive. Malcolm
Cockren, himself, came on board as chairman.

According to sources who have worked with Ardent, Cockren's
role was to transcend that of the conventional company chairman.
"Malcolm Cockren always used to go on about how he'd had to
promise the palace that he would cover Edward and wouldn't let
the company go under and that he'd do everything in his power
not to let Edward look like he'd failed," explained a former Ardent
employee.

It was crucial that the press and public perceive that Edward's
new career was extremely successful. "To have failed in three
careers by your mid-thirties is pretty significant," noted Mark
Nicholls, former chief financial officer for Café Productions, who
worked with Ardent on a coproduction. "It would be a very difficult position for Edward if he were to find that he'd not been successful in his third career."

Ardent's chief executives—all male—had now been selected.
The company was extraordinarily well financed. Edward invested
£200,000 ($326,000) of his own money, and the other £709,419
($1,156,353) came from assorted investors. Most of those investors
were major forces in the Duke of Edinburgh Awards. "Prince
Philip convinced his cronies to rally around and back Edward,"

said a source who has worked with Edward. Such opinions may sound excessively cynical, but the widespread belief that Ardent was founded on cronyism was only buttressed when two of Ardent's investors, Tom Farmer and Graham Kirkham, were knighted by the Queen. In Britain, knighthoods are generally awarded on the recommendation of the government. Neither the Queen nor Prince Philip have any official input into the selection process. However, while both Farmer and Kirkham had both made important contributions to British industry and consequently richly deserved their knighthoods, their association with Edward and Ardent clearly did not hurt. Tom Farmer was knighted on October 9, 1997, and Graham Kirkham was knighted on February 13, 1996.

As yet, Ardent's third benefactor, Alan Jones—UK managing director of the courier company TNT, who invested £92,000 ($149,960) in Ardent—has not been knighted. A spokeswoman for Jones explained that he had made the investment personally after getting to know the prince through the Duke of Edinburgh Awards.

Tom Farmer, chairman and chief executive of Kwik-Fit, invested a similar amount in Ardent and was knighted three years later. The fifty-one-year-old millionaire had also met Edward through the award program: "I'm investing in Ardent because I think it's a good commercial business. I'm not looking for a quick return. I'm taking a five-year view." The third-named investor was Graham Kirkham, who owns the DFS furniture chain and, like the others, met the prince through the award program. Two Zurich-based investors, Ralph Luscher and Ulrich Kohli, also invested in Ardent, as did an unnamed investor whose identity was cloaked behind a Hong Kong nominee company. Rumor had it that the mysterious investor was none other than the Sultan of Brunei.

Abel Haddon, a spokesman for the prince, has denied that the sultan is one of Ardent's investors. Whatever the case, the sultan definitely was not on hand for the company's board meetings. When Ardent held a board meeting about eighteen months after its inception, one of the company's female employees challenged Edward to explain why there were no women on the board. She was horrified by his reply. "He said, 'The thing is with women that you only ever get a good two years out of them before they get pregnant. Anyway, no woman can ever earn enough money to put enough money into the company to be on the board.' "

With Ardent's finances in place, Edward set about finding suitable premises for the company. Right from the start, Edward established Ardent on a lavish scale. While the average, newly minted British independent television production company generally starts out with a skeleton staff based in a modest office, with only an answering machine taking calls, Edward launched his company with a grand flourish. His office was situated in a high-rent district in the center of London, complete with a beautiful receptionist, chic gray-and-cream decor, stylish furnishings, and expensive marble. His ambitions, too, were on a grand scale: for Ardent to become one of the top twelve independent companies by the year 2000.

"We are entering a very large and arguably oversubsidized market worth £500 million a year," said Edward to the *Daily Mail*. "But there is plenty of room for a new company with the right sort of ideas. I look forward to working full-time with my new colleagues and making Ardent Productions into a name everyone will come to recognize."

Then, perhaps aware that his offices were a trifle ostentatious, he said defensively, "I think offices are terribly important. It's where you're going to spend your days, as well as the first impression people have of the company. You don't want them to think you're working in a shoe box. We've got lots of good ideas, and the prospects for success are very good."

Edward then made a sweeping pronouncement that, to this day, still returns to haunt him: "In terms of access and understanding, I'm likely to get more cooperation. But you're not going to see a rush of royal programs from Ardent. That's not the premise at all."

Ardent's first commission, announced in March 1994, was a documentary, *The Search for the Silver Arrow*—the story of the hunt for one of the finest racing cars ever built—for the BBC2 motor show *Top Gear*. The company would be paid no more than £75,000 ($122,250) to make the documentary. It was not a particularly auspicious beginning, but it was a start.

In March, too, it was announced that Ardent had clinched a £1 million ($1.63 million) deal with Nickelodeon to make a thirteen-part series of ghost stories. Edward had hit the jackpot, but not without a little serendipity. Nickelodeon's director of programs was none other than his old friend James Baker, now married to Edward's onetime girlfriend Anastasia Cook, and also the son of newsreader Richard Baker, with whom Edward had appeared at Haddo.

Despite such strong connections, the deal eventually fell through, and Edward did not make the programs.

In the middle of April 1994, Edward and Eben Foggit flew to the south of France to attend the Marche Internationale de Films et Programs, a biannual television marketplace where broadcasters, distributors, salespeople, and independents endeavor to sell their programs.

Economy class passengers on the British Airways flight from Heathrow to Nice were amazed to find Prince Edward sitting with them. He had opted to spend £139 ($226.51) for the economy fare, rather than £572 ($923.36) for first class. "It's important for us to keep costs down," said Eben, rather self-righteously, as he and Edward snacked on chicken and ham rolls served in economy class. In Cannes, instead of staying at the Carlton, Majestic, or

Martinez, where all the top producers stay, Edward and Eben booked into a small family hotel, costing just £93 ($151.59) a night. "Edward is here to work. He wants to be called Edward Windsor. This is a working trip for us," declared Eben. "I am hoping to get as much done here as I can. I'm down here for a couple of days, and I'm trying to make the most of it," echoed Edward.

Flanked by two French Secret Service agents and two English bodyguards, Edward joined the throng of producers at the bar of the Martinez Hotel. He looked nervous and tired. He left Cannes with just one deal. After a meeting with his friend James Baker's former boss, Bruce Gyngell, now with Channel 9 in Australia, Edward made a £100,000 ($163,000) deal for Ardent to produce a documentary series on the Commonwealth. He made preliminary approaches to Nelson Mandela, but did not succeed in obtaining an interview with him.

The series was never made.

Back in London, Edward offered a classical music series to Channel 4. He arrived at the channel's offices in Horseferry Road, Westminster, accompanied by a couple of bodyguards. But after he signed in at reception, he was treated like just another producer by the channel's classical music boss, Helen Sprott.

Edward's idea was rejected for being too stuffy.

The one program (apart from *Top Gear*) that Ardent did manage to bring to the screen was the 1995 TNT Express International Real Tennis Team Trophy, broadcast in May 1995. The managing director of TNT, the sponsors of the event, was Alan Jones, one of Ardent's biggest investors. So garnering the commission was hardly difficult for Ardent. Nor was the program particularly prestigious— Real Tennis attracted a minimal audience. None of which boded well for Ardent's future or for the success of Edward's new career.

Edward valiantly attempted to cloak his failure with brave pronouncements. "We are exactly where we forecast we would be in terms of programming and expenditure," he said. "Things are going a-storm," he said. Sadly for Edward, however, it was clear that the only thing relating to Ardent that was "going a-storm" was the company's budget. There was very little support for him within the television industry.

"Edward got the backs up of everybody within the industry," said a former Ardent employee. "In the industry, pretty much everyone right at the top started off as a runner or a secretary. They've all worked their way up. Whereas, Edward came in with a big pile of cash and bought an executive-producer title. Broadcasters felt that Edward had no television experience, so why should they commission him to make a show?"

"Edward would not have a production company other than for his family connections," said Mark Nicholls. "Edward would have no place in the media other than the fact that he has a title."

It would take Edward more than determination, family connections, and the easy availability of money to succeed in television. It would take talent, vision, taste, and creativity, and Edward had yet to prove he had any.

11
THE PR PRINCESS

*W*HILE EDWARD'S PROFESSIONAL LIFE APPEARED TO be on a downward spiral, Sophie's career was skyrocketing. Her role as Edward's official girlfriend raised her profile considerably, and clients flocked to MCM in the hope of adding some of Sophie's prestige to their products or services. Her relationship with Edward was definitely an asset in attracting clients. "The most important quality a PR possesses is her connections," explained Lady Colin Campbell. "A PR doesn't have to be particularly good; she just has to be well-connected."

Aware that the palace was watching her every move and charting exactly how she conducted herself, Sophie was wary about enlisting Edward's help in promoting her clients. She did, however, make an exception in the case of Baby Lifeline, a charity whose account she worked on. Baby Lifeline was founded in 1981 by a pretty blonde nurse named Judy Ledger, who had lost three children under tragic circumstances. Her first child, Alicia, was stillborn. Her second daughter, Emma, was born prematurely, but because of inadequate hospital facilities, died a day later. Her third child, a son named Stuart, was born prematurely, suffered a brain hemorrhage, and died a day and a half later.

Although the staff at Coventry Maternity Hospital had fought long and hard to save her children's lives, Judy was keenly aware that many British hospitals lacked sufficient equipment. In Britain, more than seventy-five hundred babies die at birth each year. Judy Ledger set up Baby Lifeline in order to provide specialized training, vital technology, and clinical research, all aimed at ensuring a healthy outcome for pregnancy and birth.

Sophie began working on the Baby Lifeline account when she first arrived at MacLaurin. Her support of Baby Lifeline extended to her persuading Edward to attend one of the charity's events, a ball held in October 1995 at Weston Park, the Shropshire home of the Earl of Bradford.

Two hundred guests attended the ball, including Chris Tarrant, Ben Kingsley, Paul Daniels, and Robert and Barbara Powell. The guest of honor was Prince Edward. Together, Sophie and Edward danced to the Pasadena Roof Orchestra, a radiantly glamorous couple.

"Sophie asked Edward to come because it meant a lot to her," remembers a PR executive. "She had to be so careful not to bring Edward into things too much, but she cared about Baby Lifeline, so she did. She was lovely in those days. But she has changed herself. Nowadays she can sometimes be outrageously rude. But the real Sophie wasn't like that. She was really nice. Now she is very bigheaded."

If her new status had indeed gone to her head, it was hardly surprising. From early 1994, she and Edward ventured more and more into the limelight together. In March, Edward invited Sophie to a dinner at Buckingham Palace given for one hundred of Edward's closest friends and supporters of his Real Tennis Summer Challenge. She had repeatedly dined at the palace before, but only with Edward in his private quarters. This time it was different. Dressed in a short red cocktail dress, surrounded by one of the greatest collections of Rembrandts in the world, Sophie sat opposite Edward. "They smiled across at each other several times," said one of her fellow diners. "When the first course came, Sophie appeared nervous, but by the time we were on our fillet of beef, she was totally at home. She charmed Edward's friends."

No trace of shyness remained a few weeks later, when Sophie hosted Edward's thirtieth birthday party at London's Savoy Hotel. "Sophie took charge of the whole evening," said a guest at the party. "She organized everything from the Queen's arrival to the menu. It went like clockwork. Edward really appreciated it."

The Queen demonstrated her approval of Sophie by honoring her with her presence at the party. Edward's close friends James Baker, Anastasia Cook, Abel Haddon, and his wife, Belinda, watched delightedly as the Queen, dressed in a pink floral dress, embraced Edward. Sophie, regal in a gold bodice and black skirt with matching jacket, looked on approvingly. Her parents, however, were not among the guests. They had not been invited.

"They feel she has become a little remote," a friend confided to Geoffrey Levy and Richard Kay of the *Daily Mail*. "They may be wrong, of course. She doesn't seem to me to have changed much at all, really, but you have to understand their position. They do feel rather confused."

At the end of March, Sophie was ensconced in Balmoral with Edward. The couple stayed at Craigown Lodge, the Queen Mother's favorite house on the Deeside estate, situated a mile away from the castle. The lodge—a two-story granite house, complete with library, satellite TV, and a sauna—was cozy and romantic. Balmoral insiders claimed that Edward and Sophie were sleeping in separate rooms. *Majesty* magazine editor Ingrid Seward reported, "Edward and Sophie are deeply in love, and he is paranoid about anyone spying on them."

They vacationed together again in the summer and had a happy time on the Isle of Wight. Sophie loved the water, although all her past experiences with water sports had not been particularly felicitous. She confided to *Hello* magazine, "I learned to windsurf—but badly. My father had taught me how to sail, but I never realized that the principle of windsurfing was the same as being in a boat. The penny dropped when Edward was instructing me one day. I yelled, 'Now I understand!' and promptly fell backwards into the water." It was fortunate that she had a sense of humor regarding her water-sports disasters. During her stay on the Isle of Wight, she went water-skiing in the Solent, and promptly fell into the sea. She was rescued by the press. She was polite, even smiled at them, but she was probably not amused at the pictures of her floundering in the sea that subsequently appeared.

The sea, however, was the only place in which Sophie was floundering. According to palace courtiers, she was sailing through lessons on how to make the royal grade. It appeared that she had been readily accepted into the House of Windsor, but unlike Princess Diana or Sarah Ferguson before her, she was given ample coaching on how they expected her to fit in. She was taught to stand behind the royals when the paparazzi were on hand, to address the Queen as "ma'am," only to speak to her when first spoken to, and to wear long dresses at dinner, even on vacation, when royal men always wear black tie for dinner.

Most important of all, Sophie was rigorously drilled in security matters. In a letter marked "Private and Confidential" she was given strict instructions to be careful when speaking on the phone: "Do not use the hands-free telephone in the flat or your parents' home, or have conversations with your parents with hands-free phones, as these are easily scanned and listened to. If you are going to use a mobile phone, then purchase a digital mobile, as these are virtually impossible to eavesdrop on." She was also instructed on the etiquette of dealing with journalists stalking her: "If they turn up at your home, send them out a cup of tea. If it's Christmas, send them a cracker! But always keep your distance. Do not become familiar or on first-name terms." Sophie read the instructions and took heed.

Although Edward still hadn't proposed marriage to her, the relationship was building by the month, with one of Sophie's closest friends confiding to Geoffrey Levy and Richard Kay of the *Daily Mail*, "I have seen her look at him with absolute adoration, and when she thinks they are not being observed, she will often slip her arm around his back. Sophie does have a backbone of steel, however. When things go wrong, she lets her feelings be known in no uncertain way. She is by far the most demonstrative of the two."

Long afterwards, Sophie would define her bond with Edward to *Hello* magazine, "We laugh a lot with each other, and we have a number of interests in common. I love sport like he does, but I'm not always that good at it."

On November 22, 1995, Sophie quit working for Brian MacLaurin (who was reportedly paying her in the region of £400 [$652] a week) on a full-time basis. Instead, she took a part-time job with Hollander, another PR company. Her relationship with Brian MacLaurin would endure. Yet there were disturbing undertones. MacLaurin had known her in the days when she was merely his assistant. "Sophie is frightened of what he might do," said a source who knows them both well. "He's astute, very self-assured. Sophie doesn't trust Brian and Brian doesn't trust Sophie."

MacLaurin had been the architect of Sophie's good fortune, and she was grateful to him. Nonetheless, she was aware of his opportunistic tendencies, perhaps because she, herself, shared them. Nowadays, they still lunch together, but are wary of each other.

After Sophie left MacLaurin, she continued representing Baby Lifeline, taking on the title of national events and projects organizer. She also represented the prestigious firm of caterers Searcy's and volunteered for the Duke of Edinburgh Awards for two days a week, primarily overseeing the newsletter.

Her work with Baby Lifeline, in particular, was to receive an inordinate amount of publicity. In most instances, an impression was given by the media that Sophie worked for the charity on a volunteer basis. That wasn't the truth. She was paid a thousand pounds ($1,690) a month plus expenses to work for the charity from home one day a week.

The saga of Sophie's relationship with Baby Lifeline tells a tale about her dedication, her determination, and, ultimately, her ruthlessness.

Today in her early forties, Judy Ledger, a bright and vivacious woman, became friendly with Sophie when they first met in 1995. Sophie and Judy worked together closely, and Judy refuses to elaborate on their friendship, except to say, "Sophie was a dear friend at one stage who, although she had a very determined and strong personality, could be extremely caring at the time." Those close to Judy charted the course of her relationship with Sophie and the way in which it reflected on Sophie's character.

Sophie stayed at Judy's home in Coventry, and Judy stayed with Sophie at her London flat. At one point, while Judy and Sophie were traveling together on behalf of Baby Lifeline, Judy suffered a sudden vertigo attack. As Judy fell to the floor, Sophie was so shocked that she dissolved into floods of tears. She cried again on another occasion, while she was sitting in on a press interview Judy was giving to the *Daily Telegraph*. As Judy remembered the death of her little baby Stuart, who died of a cerebral hemorrhage, the feelings flooded back to her anew. She burst into tears at the memory. Sophie began crying as well. "She has an emotional, soft side to her," says a woman who worked with her.

At the same time, throughout her work with Baby Lifeline, Sophie never lost sight of her own goals and status. She was aware of her self-image and her ambitions. "She would talk about Edward fondly," says a source who befriended Sophie during her Baby Lifeline years. "But it is difficult to know whether she was in love with the idea of the man or with the man himself. But she was just very insecure. The problem is that she was portrayed as being royal, but she wasn't royal. She was in no-man's-land, and I think she was very insecure and nervous because she didn't know what on earth she could or couldn't do. She didn't have the palace behind her. She wasn't one of them. She comes from a middle-class background, and she has got to make a big leap into Edward's world. There's so much snobbery."

Sophie had flown close to the sun, and there were those disdainful aristocrats who longed to see her scorched. The commoner from Kent had stormed the pinnacle of British society and had won. There were those who still hoped she would be defeated. There were others, too, who used their guile in order to manipulate her to their own ends.

"Sophie is very gullible. She is not stupid, but not that astute. She would believe what she heard in the last conversation. She will listen to the last person she spoke to. And sometimes she can be terribly rude, terribly arrogant, very much 'I'm Sophie Rhys-Jones, you know who I am.' If she stopped being so hard, people would warm to her more," said a source who worked with her.

Sophie had been born with supreme self-confidence and never seemed to care what impression she made on other people. She had captivated Prince Edward and the royal family. She had no need for the friendship of anyone else.

"She doesn't suffer fools gladly, or people she perceives to be fools. PR is a very cutthroat world. Sophie would get very frustrated if somebody ever tried to cross her," said the source who worked with her.

When Judy and Sophie traveled together, they were often dogged by paparazzi. "It was very difficult for Sophie," said a source close to Judy. "Tabloid photographers would hide behind fences and try and steal shots of her. She never lost her cool. She was very good at handling it and just used to say 'hello' to them."

In August 1996, allegations were made in a national newspaper that Baby Lifeline was spending too much on office overheads and not enough on helping mothers and babies. A devastated Judy Ledger denied the allegations. Eventually the charity was cleared of all wrongdoing by the British Charity Commission. Nevertheless, Baby Lifeline suffered from the initial negative publicity and fund-raising dropped.

Soon after the commission cleared Baby Lifeline, Judy, Sophie, and Zita West (an acupuncturist and midwife friend of Sophie's) spent the weekend together at Ragdale Hall, a health farm. Judy confided to a friend the entire story of what had happened that weekend. "Judy said that Sophie was in a strange, pensive mood all through the weekend," said the friend. "Judy's fortieth birthday was imminent, and Sophie had promised to attend her celebration dinner. She abruptly informed Judy, 'I am afraid I am not going to be able to make your fortieth. Edward and I are going on holiday.'

"According to Judy, Sophie's tension level rose perceptibly as the weekend progressed," said Judy's friend. "Judy was accustomed to Sophie eating, drinking beer, and having fun. But on this particular weekend, she had the air of a schoolteacher, continually lecturing Judy and Zita regarding their eating habits. She was troubled, on edge, and her tension manifested itself when a waitress accidentally dropped a butter knife. Sophie screamed, 'Oh— get it off my shirt! It's all over my shirt!' The waitress was so upset that she went home in tears.

"As the weekend wound down, it seemed increasingly clear that Sophie wanted to communicate something important to Judy. She started to talk to her, but when Zita walked into the room, Judy told me Sophie stopped in mid-sentence."

The next day, Sophie resigned from Baby Lifeline. Judy's response to Sophie's defection was reported in the *Sunday Mirror:* "We had a fearful row. Sophie kept saying we should close down, but there was no way I would agree. When I told her I'd be carrying on as normal, she went hysterical. She kept saying, 'What about me? What about me?' "

Judy later denied the report, insisting, "There was no row between Sophie and me, and she is still an extremely good friend of mine." But although Judy's loyalty to Sophie is commendable, Judy's friend tells quite another story, one that illustrates the dark side of Sophie. "Sophie couldn't deal with the bad publicity Baby Lifeline received. Judy told me she approached her and said, 'Why don't we have a press conference in London? Everybody will come because it's me. Then you will make a speech and cry a little bit. You are a genuine lady and a kind lady, and that will come through. Then you will announce that you are going to have to give up the charity.'

"Judy was beside herself. She burst into tears. She had dedicated fifteen years to the charity and wasn't about to give it up because of bad publicity. Sophie snapped at her, 'Oh, don't be ridiculous. For goodness sake, what about me? Have you ever thought about my position in all this? You can start up another charity in a few years time and call it something else.' Judy told me she was up all night crying. She didn't want to resign, otherwise she would have looked as guilty as hell. Sophie rang Judy at eight in the morning and asked her what she was going to do. Judy told her that there was no way she was resigning. Sophie's response was, 'Right, then I resign.' And that was it. Sophie could have done so much for the charity, but instead, she distanced herself."

A PR associate of Sophie's and Judy's, commenting on the Baby Lifeline contretemps, observed, "Sophie has got three dangerous qualities. She is not very intelligent, but is very bigheaded and very proud. Had she merely distanced herself from Baby Lifeline, that in itself would have been bad enough. And her attitude [and perhaps you can understand it because she probably had some pressure from the courtiers at the palace] was, "Save yourself, Sophie, and let them drown."

According to Judy's friend, Judy tried to talk to Sophie once more in early 1999. "Judy told me that she telephoned Sophie's office to verify some details surrounding an event which Sophie had arranged for Baby Lifeline at the Hurlingham Club," Judy's friend recalled. "Sophie's personal assistant answered. Judy introduced herself, then, very politely, said, 'Look, I'm terribly sorry to bother you, but could you just ask Sophie about the Hurlingham Club event and the crèche she arranged for us? I just need to check a detail.' Judy waited for what seemed ages. Then the personal assistant came back and said, 'Sophie is on the phone at the moment, just hold on.' Judy held on.

"Then the personal assistant came back and said, 'Sophie can't remember the Hurlingham Club event.' Incredulous, Judy said. 'Sorry?' 'She's looking . . . She's smiling . . . She's very amused,' said the personal assistant. Sophie must have been sitting right there, refusing to come to the phone and talk to Judy, and Judy knew it. Humiliated, she had one more try, 'Can you ask her again? She organized a crèche for children at Hurlingham.' Judy held her breath and waited. After a moment or two, the personal assistant came back to the phone, 'Sorry,' she said, 'Sophie is looking very puzzled.' Judy told me that she waited for her to continue, but the personal assistant just said good-bye to her."

Sophie never came to the phone to talk to her old friend.

In 1997, Sophie set up her own PR company, in partnership with Murray Harkin. From the first, Harkin had great respect for Sophie. "She's loyal, discreet, and professional. She can be serious and mature, but she's also a lot of fun," he praised. "When she does not agree with something she's not afraid to say so. She has amazing strength of character." Sophie holds fifty-four percent of the company's shares. Today, RJH (Rhys-Jones Harkin) Public Relations, as the company is named, has contracts worth more than £724,000 ($1,180,120). Those contracts include the Comite Colbert, which is composed of seventy-five French retailers of luxury goods, including Hermès, Christian Dior, Louis Vuitton, and Givenchy. Another client is Boodle and Dunthorne, a top London jewelry store, and the Lanesborough Hotel. RJH also represents a breast cancer charity, Haven Trust. According to *Punch* magazine, the charity is paying RJH over £60,000 ($91,800). Other public relations firms had offered their services pro bono, but the charity had opted for RJH, aware of the power of Sophie's name.

Again, her link to Edward was of immeasurable help in gaining her accounts. Other PR professionals were not afraid to express their displeasure at Sophie's edge over them. At the time of Sophie's engagement, Tanya Hughes, managing director of M & C Saatchi Promotions, sniffed, "Her impending royalty will no doubt boost her upmarket client list, but I don't think mainstream clients will find her celebrity appealing. Mainstream clients need a mainstream approach." Jane Boardman, managing director of Ketchum Life, agreed and commented, "The engagement will do an awful lot in certain circles. The question is can she do a better job for her clients and will it open doors to new clients. I think the answer is yes, but only for a particular type of client."

Thomas Goode, a Mayfair luxury goods store, was the perfect type of client to benefit from Sophie's royal connections. The path through which she secured the contract to represent Thomas Goode (where she would ultimately lodge her wedding list) is a classic example both of the way in which she operates and the manifold advantages of her exalted position.

Thomas Goode's owner, Rumi Vergi, a canny Kenyan-Asian

businessman, had built up a prestigious client list, which included Prince Charles, Elton John, and the Sultan of Brunei.

However, Vergi had further goals. His dream was to transform Thomas Goode into a household name, which he could then franchise with stores in Rome, Paris, and other cities. With that goal in mind, he resolved to increase the store's profile. He consulted a leading public relations executive, asking for guidance. The executive made a study of the company and realized that it catered primarily to an older clientele.

"He advised Rumi Vergi to get in with the younger set," said one of the executive's employees. "Then he said, 'You could do worse than find a role or nonexecutive directorship for Sophie Rhys-Jones. Because if she ever marries Edward, it would be a feather in your cap.' "

Subsequently, Sophie, who was then in the process of setting up RJH, was contacted by Vergi regarding her representing Thomas Goode. A few days later, she and Vergi and the public relations executive lunched together. Shortly after that, Vergi appointed Sophie to do the PR for Thomas Goode. The account was extremely lucrative (reportedly in the region of £80,000 [$130,400]), and Sophie continues to service it today. According to his employee, Sophie's only thanks to the executive who had made it all possible was a short note. The next time she saw him at a party, she ignored him completely.

To some, it appeared that Sophie's arrogance was beginning to rival that of Prince Edward. To others, it was proof that they were perfectly matched.

Sophie's brilliant PR career has engendered a great deal of jealousy within the PR world. "Sophie is a mediocre PR," carped a competitor. Others, outside the business, disagree. "Sophie is very affable," noted writer Noreen Taylor. "I've seen her at a book launch, and she was your caring PR."

Most PR executives are cautious about obtaining personal publicity for themselves, nor do they want to be quoted on record regarding one another. However, James Campbell, chairman of Campbell's Television and Media Group, who worked with Sophie on a PR project for a few months and has lunched with her on several occasions, is an exception. Unafraid of going on record about her, he says, "I quite admire Sophie. She would make a good secret agent: whilst blending into the background, she is very determined, she knows what she wants, and she gets it. She coped well on the sidelines of court life for five years—a tricky situation which she handled successfully. We all like to know where we stand, so it was quite natural that up until Prince Edward proposed marriage, Sophie was somewhat unsettled, in the twilight zone. She was clearly intimidated by the palace and understandably nervous and apprehensive of whom she could trust. She will do well in the House of Windsor, and after five years she must be prepared for the role. I do hope, though, that she will avoid 'red carpet fever.' "

Campbell's hope that Sophie will avoid becoming intoxicated by her status is praiseworthy. However, there are others in public relations who, from the very first, have felt that Sophie is arrogant and self-important. "Sophie is very hard," said a PR colleague. "There are an awful lot of people who are keeping their heads down at the moment, who cannot stand the ground she walks on. But she is marrying Edward and will never rock the boat, because she is just so thrilled at having captured Edward. This fairly ordinary little girl is going to become the Duchess of Cambridge."

"Sophie's been so clever. She's got the Queen and the Duke of Edinburgh eating out of her hand," said another PR colleague who has worked and socialized with Sophie. "They just think the world of her. But if she were to turn nasty, she would make Diana literally look like a saint. If you think Diana was duplicitous, this girl could have taught her. She's a very tough woman. She'll tread over whoever to get where she wants. She picks you up, and when you are of no use to her, she slings you down. All her friends now are Edward's friends—although most of them can't stand her. She has dropped all her old friends. For some time now, she has suddenly started to behave more royal than the royals. She has got incredibly grand and almost expects that when she walks into a room, everybody stands up. Everyone is trying to keep a straight face, because there is little Sophie, the PR girl. You wonder if she has gone completely crazy.

"At first, I felt sorry for her because Edward wasn't around a lot. She said, 'I just sit home at night.' I invited her to a club opening, and she was just as nervous as a kitten, worrying if there were photographers around. She really didn't want to say anything to anybody."

Sophie's ability to manipulate was clearly a match for Edward's. She was shrewd, street smart, and had Edward under her sway.

"She's very determined, very dynamic," said her PR colleague. "Edward struck me as being very much under Sophie's thumb. She is the dominant one in the partnership. We were at a party, and she wanted to chat with me about something. She was with Edward, but left him standing against the wall. She stood and had a conversation with me for five minutes. And literally, he was three feet behind her. He stood there like a little boy against the wall while Sophie finished chatting away to me. Then she went back to Edward.

"But I don't think she is actually bright enough to understand all the risks inherent in marrying Edward. I asked her point blank if she understood what she was letting herself in for. She laughed and said, 'Oh, I think so. Oh, God, I hope so.' I think she wants the status and the position and she'll do anything to get it. She will do exactly what she's told. She'll conform completely.

"Sophie loves the attention that goes with being with Edward. She's there for what she can get out of it and what it means. She went out with me one evening and kept saying, 'Oh, are people looking at me? Are people looking at me?' "

She was Edward's girlfriend, and soon to be his wife. They *were* looking at her, and from now on, they always would be.

12

THE PRINCE AND THE PRODUCER

*I*N EARLY 1995, IT WAS ANNOUNCED THAT EDWARD'S production company, Ardent, had lost £450,000 ($739,500). "If we made that kind of loss, we would be out of business," said Alan Wright, head of productions at the British television company Talisman. "It is an exceptionally large amount of money to lose in your first year," echoed another producer, Graham Benson of Blue Heaven Productions. Up to early 1995, Ardent had managed to get just four hours of programming on air. "Edward's production company is unlike any I've ever come across," said Mark Nicholls, who worked with Edward on a coproduction and has also worked in the financial sector of the media for fifteen years. "It is unusual to have such a well-capitalized business where the shareholders are prepared to put up with such tremendous losses without chopping the management."

"It was weird because the less luck Edward had, the worse the company was doing, the more ego-driven he became," said a former Ardent employee. "So instead of saying to himself, 'God, it's not going right. I've got to do something about it. I've got to take advice,' he became almost obsessed with not allowing anyone near and not allowing anyone to know that Ardent was failing."

No matter how much Edward attempted to deny the truth, it was clear that far from conquering British television, Ardent appeared to have been resoundingly trounced in the TV stakes and was now languishing in distress. And then, as in the best of tales, a knight in shining armor miraculously appeared, and instantly transformed Edward Windsor from struggling producer into respected television presenter and Ardent into a television production company replete with status.

Edward's and Ardent's reputations were transformed by Desmond Wilcox, the legendary British television producer-presenter and the Man Alive Group chairman. Desmond and his partner and co-chairman, Michael Latham, originally conceived the idea for *Edward on Edward* and selected Edward Windsor to investigate and report on his great-uncle the Duke of Windsor. Desmond Wilcox and Mike Latham were to salvage the reputation of Edward's ailing company. Desmond, in particular, was an unlikely instrument of Edward's fate.

While Edward was born a prince of the realm, petted and cosseted by staff and family, received a private school education and attended university, Desmond's life and career couldn't have been more different. The son of an architect who fought in the Second World War, Desmond and his two brothers were raised during the war by their mother. Already a rebel, after a grammar school education, he ran away to sea at fifteen to serve first on a square-rigger and then in the Merchant Navy. An injury forced his resignation, and he went on to become a tabloid journalist. With his instinct for recognizing, investigating, and reporting a story, his rise was meteoric. After nine years as a London *Daily Mirror* foreign correspondent, including a stint at the United Nations in New York, he moved on to British television, where he interviewed then first lady Jacqueline Kennedy—among others. He also pioneered news and current affairs programs similar to *60 Minutes*. By 1972, he was head of BBC General Features, with a staff of two hundred fifty and an extremely high profile. Flamboyant, shrewd, outspoken, with considerable charm, Desmond was an iconoclast who evoked both admiration and controversy.

After he left the BBC, Desmond, with his own company, produced and narrated countless award-winning documentaries, many of which were shown in America. Christine Carter, who worked for him as associate producer on *Edward on Edward*, said, "Desmond's reputation is a shining light. He is hugely respected. He is an Ed Murrow or Walter Cronkite. In person, he is very dominating. Desmond is larger than life."

At the time of his first meeting with Edward, Desmond was in his early sixties, twice Edward's age, with a reputation for professional excellence, for alternating charisma with cantankerousness, and for not suffering fools at all gladly. By now, after thirty-seven years in television, Desmond had employed virtually everyone of note in British television, from David Frost to his own wife, Esther Rantzen, the doyenne of British television talk show hostesses. His reputation would have daunted anyone with far more television experience than Edward Windsor.

However, Edward was not about to be intimidated by anyone at the top of his field. Young as he was, Edward had already been through fire and survived. Contrary to reports, Edward has never been intimidated by Prince Philip, nor has he been cowed by his temper, his caustic remarks, or his swaggering personality. Edward was—and is—self-confident in the face of powerful older men. He took that confidence into his first meeting with the formidable Desmond Wilcox.

The prince and the producer first met at Ardent's headquarters in Charlotte Street, London. Desmond was accompanied by the equally formidable Mike Latham. Soft-spoken and self-effacing, Mike Latham is one of British television's most experienced writers and producers, whose most recent production for the Discovery Channel, *Connections*, with James Burke, is shown in America. In social situations, Mike plays the straight man while Desmond dazzles with anecdotes. But once the tales have been told and the charm has worked its spell, Mike and Desmond, in the words of another television producer, "are great operators."

Desmond had the rights to film the Windsor villa in Paris, where the Duke and Duchess of Windsor spent their twilight years and which had been bought and restored by Egyptian millionaire Mohamed Al Fayed. As yet Desmond hadn't found a presenter exciting enough for the television companies. Then Mike Latham was asked by Edward's joint managing director, Eben Foggit, if he could help Edward "get off the ground." So the idea of *Edward on Edward* was born.

The four of them—Edward, Eben, Mike, and Desmond—had lunch at an Italian restaurant close to Ardent's office. Initially, Edward projected himself as shy and insecure. "Edward regarded us a bit like a frightened rabbit caught in headlights, unsure of what we might do to him. He was very friendly, but very cautious because he has been immensely bruised and pursued by the media," recalled Desmond.

After a few minutes of pleasantries, it became clear that Edward, far from being frightened of Desmond and Mike, had, in fact, come fully armed to tangle with the big league. "He and Eben Foggit played a kind of double act," said Desmond. "It was quite intriguing to watch—an embassy type of protocol in which the headings and agenda they'd clearly arranged between them were introduced by Eben. Then Edward joined in as though it was the first time the subject had been discussed. Eben said, 'I know Edward wants me to ask if Ardent Productions can have some kind of mention in the credits.' "

The request was breathtakingly bold. The Man Alive Group was inventing and producing the documentary and proposed to hire Edward as presenter and associate producer (senior researcher), but Ardent was *not* producing the documentary.

Nonetheless, aware of the value of Edward's participation, Desmond and Mike agreed to give Ardent the credit "in association with."

Almost any other small independent producer might have been delighted with the concession. But Edward Windsor, much as he would assert to the contrary, was not just any producer. His next request was even more startling. Voiced on his behalf by Eben, it was that Edward, who had no writing experience except for the book he wrote in New Zealand as a teenager and the *It's a Royal Knockout* book, be given a "written by" credit. Both Desmond and Mike were seasoned writers with impressive track records, but they agreed to give Edward the writer's credit.

The prince had won the first round.

Along the way, Edward led Mike and Desmond to believe that a primary part of his contribution to the program would be to facilitate exclusive and unprecedented access to the Royal Library at Windsor Castle, which housed hundreds of documents relevant to the Duke of Windsor and his abdication. Edward assured the producers that he would provide them with all the hitherto unpublished archival material. The deal was struck. The Man Alive Group would produce *Edward on Edward*, Edward Windsor would be presenter and also be credited as associate producer, Ardent would get an "in association with" credit, and Edward would also get a writer's credit.

The last two credits were Mike and Desmond's gift to Edward. They were convinced he would reciprocate.

Once Desmond and Michael sold the idea of *Edward on Edward* to Meridian Television, one of Britain's major companies for network broadcasting, they turned their attention to Edward's role as presenter of the two-part series. Desmond's wife, Esther Rantzen, who had thirty years' experience as a major television star, agreed to teach Edward how to present well on television.

Man Alive hired a camera and crew for a day, complete with Autocue (a TelePrompTer), and Esther met Edward at Man Alive's office in Acton, West London. There, Esther spent three hours teaching Edward the tricks of television presenting. She taught the prince not to fiddle with his cuff links or his watch, and how to take charge of the Autocue and not be led by it, and to realize that it will adapt to the presenter's speed. She taught him not to stop at the end of each line and not to stare at the line, but to glance away, or over the Autocue. Most important, she taught him how to look up and behave naturally.

"Edward was a very quick learner and a natural," says Esther Rantzen. "Not all the royal family are natural performers. Edward is. He is confident and very direct with the camera. He did very well. He really enjoys performing."

Yet despite Esther's efforts and praise of Edward, there are those who worked on *Edward on Edward* who claim that he resented taking instruction from her on how to read an Autocue. Nor was he particularly willing to learn from Desmond's vast experience as a presenter-producer. "He never asked me for any advice about his television career," said Desmond. "But if he had, I would have told him to start at the bottom. He wouldn't have had to stay there for very long, because he was bright and educated. I would have told him to repress his royal image and behave as "Mr. Smith," and learn research, camera techniques, and direction. The handicap for him was that he started at the top. He became managing director of an independent television production company without two days of previous television production experience."

From the first, Edward claimed that he wanted to be treated like just another member of the production team. He asked everyone to call him "Edward." Desmond and the rest of the team obliged. Only Robin Bextor, the tall, boyishly handsome director whom Desmond and Mike had hired, continued to call him

"Prince Edward." "Robin was determined from the start that he would 'bond' with Edward," says a confidential source close to Bextor. "He wanted Edward to offer him work after *Edward on Edward* was finished and went out of his way to please him."

Desmond, however, had no such agenda. "He treated Edward with respect, but he didn't treat him like royalty," says associate producer Christine Carter. "He treated him like an associate producer. He told him what to do, which was fair enough. Edward came into the business saying he wanted to be a producer, so he had to learn."

Before filming began, Edward was asked to supply the relevant archival material. "It became harder and harder to get some of the documents," said Desmond. "It was a bit like drawing teeth." Another production source said, "We were supposed to have got all the stuff out of the royal archives free and Edward had promised it, but in the end the royal archives charged for everything and it cost twenty thousand pounds. Edward often promises more than he can deliver."

Filming began on June 6, 1995, in Paris. Desmond, Mike, and Edward had already been there together on a short research trip. This time, Robin, Desmond, Mike, and Martin Sole, the production assistant, stayed together in a flat on Rue Arsenne Houssaye, which was owned by Mohamed Al Fayed.

During the previous research trip, Al Fayed had invited Edward to stay in the hotel's Duke of Windsor Suite as his guest. Today, the price of one night in the suite is Fr32,000 ($5,120)—a price not only dictated by the spaciousness of the suite, but by the tragic and romantic history that it evokes. It was here, on the first floor of the Ritz, overlooking the Place Vendôme, that the duke and duchess often stayed after a glamorous soiree at the hotel. The suite is composed of three rooms—two bedrooms and a sitting room. The centerpiece is the "Wallis" blue bedroom, decorated in the duchess's favorite color. The red, beige, and salmon sitting room is graced by two portraits of the duke and duchess. It was a setting fit for a prince.

On this, his second trip to Paris with the team, Edward was naturally eager to stay at the Ritz again. His eagerness was understandable.

Founded in 1898, the Paris Ritz is one of the world's most celebrated luxury hotels. Synonymous with elegance and opulence, the hotel has a history redolent of glamour, eroticism, and excess. With its twenty-four-hour room service and twenty-two palatial suites, the Ritz was an oasis for heroes and for villains. A week after the Germans marched into Paris, Field Marshal Goering moved into the Imperial Suite, only recently Winston Churchill's Paris base. There, Goering spent most of his time high on morphine, parading around in women's clothing, and swinging a solid gold, diamond-studded marshal's baton, which had been fashioned exclusively for him by Cartier.

Proust considered the Paris Ritz his second home. Coco Chanel was ensconced there during the Second World War. As a young struggling writer, Ernest Hemingway saved every penny so that he could afford a weekly drink at the Ritz. When he finally made his fortune, he spent most of his days there, and the Ritz named their bar after him. Charlie Chaplin, Marlene Dietrich, Humphrey Bogart, Lauren Bacall, and Barbara Hutton (who generally arrived there with seventy trunks in tow), all adored the Ritz.

Above all, the Ritz was a magnet for royalty. The Czar of Russia stayed there. So did the Shah of Persia. Prince Edward's own great-great-grandfather, Edward VII, dallied with his most-favored mistresses at the Ritz. It was no wonder that Prince Edward considered it his due that he be a guest of the Ritz's management.

Mohamed Al Fayed, who bought the Ritz in 1979 for $30 million and then proceeded to spend another $100 million renovating it, knew how to entertain his illustrious guests. The hotel's cellar contains thirty thousand bottles of priceless brandies dating back to

1812, wines from 1897 (including the celebrated vintage years of 1928, 1929, 1947, 1953, 1955, and 1961). In 1991, the value of the Ritz's cellar was estimated to be in excess of $1 million.

When Edward checked into the Duke of Windsor Suite, he found that the fourteen-foot bar boasted priceless bottles of vintage champagne, Russian vodka, brandy, and cognac, all provided by Al Fayed, the quintessentially generous host. A gesture for a prince. No television producer would ever expect or receive such treatment.

However, the opulence of the Ritz was set into sharp relief for Edward the following day, when he began filming at the Louis XVI villa on the outskirts of the Bois de Boulogne where the Windsors had spent much of their exile. At the end of the morning, to everyone's dismay, it was discovered that there was no time to go out for lunch. Instead, one of the crew was dispatched to buy baguettes, ham, and cheese, which were duly set out buffet style.

Seeing the spread, Edward seemed at a loss for what to do next. He hesitated for a moment or two. Then he edged closer to the cameraman and began following his lead. "You could see him," said production assistant Martin Sole, "watching and thinking, 'He's getting a baguette. Okay, I'll get a baguette too. He's putting some butter on it. Okay, I'll do the same. He's putting ham and cheese on it together. Okay, I'll do the same.' I got the impression that it was possibly the first time Edward had ever made his own sandwich."

Edward may have been the presenter of *Edward on Edward*, but he was not expected to do the interviews. Interviewing had always been Desmond's forte, and he was justifiably famous in Britain for his skills. In this case, Desmond's voice was to be cut from the documentary in postproduction, leaving just the answers on film. He would have extracted his usual gems from the interviewees. Based on his reputation and expertise, everyone assumed that as always Desmond would be doing all the interviews for *Edward on Edward*. But just as Dr. Jean Thin, the Duke of Windsor's doctor, arrived for his interview, Edward strode confidently up to the set and demanded to know when he could start interviewing. Even Desmond was speechless. He paused, considered the options, then suggested he sit on the floor next to Edward (who remained in the shot) and feed him the questions.

"Edward said he wanted to do the interviews, so I wrote lots of questions and he had his own questions as well," said Desmond. "He wasn't without initiative or thoughts."

Edward was hijacking the production and attempting to make it his own.

Initially just presenter and associate producer, he was now interviewer, and his company might be seen, in a reversal of its true position, to be producing the documentary, in association with the Man Alive Group. He had also taken to rewriting the scripts. It was suspected that he might have been showing them to the Queen or her senior advisers for their approval and even censorship. A palace spokesman later acknowledged to the London *Daily Telegraph* that Edward had kept the royal family informed of his progress. No one could have blamed Edward too much if that had been true. He was, after all, involved in the making of a documentary on a member of the royal family, albeit a black sheep.

"I got the impression from Edward that the royal family had no love for the Duke of Windsor and nor did he," said Desmond.

However, when the documentary was finally broadcast and Edward publicized it, like the true professional he was gradually becoming, he made suitably glowing public statements about his great-uncle. "If I met him in the street, I think he would be someone that I would like very much," Edward said. "I think he had enormous charm, charisma, and humor, whereas I might have had more difficulty trying to like Wallis. He seemed to me to be a man who had an enormous zest for life. He loved people, he was very good with people, and he was obviously a very good host. He seemed to live life to the full."

Privately, though, Edward expressed other views to Desmond. "He once said to me, 'The man was a thief.' He didn't elaborate on that greatly, but there was considerable evidence that he had taken into exile things that didn't belong to him: oil paintings, furniture, clothing, hospitality," said Desmond.

Edward, too, had assumed that he could take Al Fayed's hospitality for granted on this, his second stay in Paris. However, after a week, when the team finished filming and Edward checked out of the Ritz, Desmond was presented with a bill for Edward's stay. At the time, Desmond was not amused. Today, however, he is relatively philosophical about the stratospheric fee for the prince's suite: "Although the bill was horrendous, much more than the budget could take, I think the hotel was quite right to charge. And perhaps that is the price of having a royal presenter, who, although he may be a presenter on the road, would rather be a prince when it comes to pajama time."

More sequences were filmed in the south of France, Spain, Portugal, Ireland, and at Windsor Castle. By that time, Edward had begun to win the respect of the crew. "He was a confident, good presenter," said Steve Gruen, the cameraman. Martin Sole, too, was impressed by his interpersonal skills: "He has an amazing recollection for names. I haven't worked with him for three years, but I am sure if I bumped into him, he would remember my name. But I don't think he is ever going to be one of the gang."

Christine Carter, the associate producer who worked with Edward closely throughout the summer and autumn of 1995, as well as when the documentary was premiered the following year, developed a warm relationship with Edward. A researcher on another program went to her home and witnessed her receiving a

telephone call from Edward. The nature of the call was evident—
Edward was in a quandary regarding possible venues for a party he
was planning to throw. He was asking Christine's advice. She was
then in her early forties, and Edward spoke to her as if she were his
mother. And Christine appeared to respond. "I think she felt sorry
for him going home alone to the palace every night, with no one
to praise him for his accomplishments," said the researcher. "I
think she felt he needed a mother."

Later, Christine was to say, "Edward was getting into a business
where people were jealous of him, everyone wanted him to fail;
where people said things about him like, 'It took me fifteen years
to be a producer. Why should he be a producer?' To the industry,
he was a prince and not a producer. But he has worked steadily to
earn their respect."

At times, though, Edward still flexed his princely muscles. On
one Friday morning, Edward expressed surprise that the filming
was scheduled to continue after lunch. "Don't people go to house
parties at weekends?" he asked bemusedly. Another time, when he
was delayed at an evening viewing at Man Alive, Edward suddenly
discovered that he was late for a dinner party held in the London
suburb of Croydon. At his behest, three policemen on motorbikes
arrived and escorted him through all the red traffic lights. "It was
an abuse of privilege," said a confidential source who was there
that evening. "Although Edward was efficient and charming, he
behaved like a royal who was pretending to be part of a team. He
still wanted to be the prince."

If Edward ("Call me Ed—I am just one of the team") was feeling that insufficient homage was being paid to his royal status, he
was mollified after July 9, 1995, when he flew to New York, where
he received a princely welcome replete with adoration. His first
interview, on July 11, was at Harry Winston with archivist Laurence
Kraches, who was instantly beguiled by Edward: "He was far more

genuine than I thought he would be. He was a very real person. He is not a cold fish. He had a nice, interesting personality. He sent me a nice letter thanking me for my help, and the following season after the taping, I got a Christmas card from him. About a year later, I met him in a restaurant. I went over to him, and he recognized me immediately and said, 'Hello, Laurence, how are you? It's good to see you. How have you been?' He is extremely kind."

That same day, he also interviewed Mme Gisèle Masson, at La Grenouille, a Manhattan restaurant the Windsors frequented. He had lunch at the restaurant with Mme Masson. "He requested the same menu that we always served to the Duke of Windsor," said Mme Masson. "The duke always enjoyed very simple food, but well prepared. We had poached bass en fumé with cucumber and a little bit of cream. Then we had the duke's favorite ice cream, rum and raisin. The prince had a lot of enthusiasm, and he's eager to learn. He asked me how come all the chefs are mostly men. I told him that when a woman cooks, she cooks for herself, but a man cooks for everybody. He agreed with me. He had the same incredible quiet elegance that the Duke of Windsor had. There was a total refinement about Prince Edward."

Mme Masson also got to see the prince's sense of humor. After the technician clipped a microphone onto Mme Masson's dress, he heard a little beep. She remembers, "He said he couldn't understand why a beep was coming through the microphone. And I shouted, 'Oh, it is my pacemaker!' The prince thought it was very funny."

One morning, Edward was due to do a camera statement from a boat in New York Harbor, with the Statue of Liberty in the background. Edward, his police protection officer, and Christine Carter took a taxi to the docks. Along the way, the cabdriver collided with a biker. According to Christine Carter, the biker "was resplendent in skintight black-and-pink Lycra, with a menacing helmet and goggles, and screamed through the driver's open window, "'You f—— dickhead.'" A shouting match ensued between the cabdriver and the biker. Edward's policeman and Christine exchanged nervous glances, but Edward remained unperturbed. "Coolly, Edward passed me a sheet of manuscript. 'This is the piece to camera I've written for today, Chris,' he said. 'What do you think?' " remembers Christine.

She liked and respected Edward and commented, "I felt that Edward was at his happiest when he was working as a member of the crew, being judged as a professional whose input was valued. We worked long days, but he never faltered and courteously entertained the interviewees when technical snags meant long waits in between shots."

On July 12, the team traveled to Long Island, where Edward interviewed Alexander Slater, a die-hard royalist with whom the Windsors often stayed. The day was hot and, on Mrs. Slater's suggestion, Edward removed his jacket. "He wanted to know where his uncle stayed in the house," said Alexander Slater. "He is awfully attractive, awfully pleasant, certainly not snobbish in any way, shape, or form. He had us all at ease immediately."

From the Slaters', the team traveled to Old Westbury, Long Island, where Edward interviewed the widow of Winston Guest, C. Z. Guest, one of America's great beauties, who first met the Windsors in 1950. Edward reminded her of his uncle, and she was charmed by him. Her daughter, former debutante of the year Cornelia Guest (who was once linked to Sylvester Stallone) was at her mother's house during the interview.

Christine Carter, in a quote approved by Prince Edward, later told the following story for attribution in this book: "One Windsor friend arranged lunch prior to her interview, and her beautiful blonde daughter was seated next to Edward. During the day there were hints in the air about him being invited back to go riding with her. Over drinks that night, the film director pointed out, 'If she had pushed her daughter further at you, she would have been in your lap!' Joining in the laughter, Edward said that he had noticed for years that on official visits he was frequently introduced to the available young daughters of his hosts."

Edward appeared to be immune to Cornelia's fabled charms. She, however, was definitely captivated by Edward. "I think he's lovely," Cornelia said. "It is wonderful for someone who is as young as he is to be so fascinated with his family and with the past. The Duke of Windsor was my godfather, and he was very nice and respectful towards me. Prince Edward was the same way. We talked about my horses. He understands that being nice gets you a long way in life. I think he is very handsome, very articulate, and has a lot of guts," she said.

Edward exhibited his so-called guts when he returned to England and tangled with Mike and Desmond during the editing of *Edward on Edward*. "Although Edward demanded and was given the writing credit, in reality, it was Mike Latham who wrote the script and the commentary," said Desmond. "When we were trying to subedit the commentary, Edward kept taking it away with him overnight, altering it, and coming back. Mike and I, without any sense of ego, felt that Edward's version was dull. We would try and pep it up again. Finally, Mary McAnally, the managing director of Meridian, came in on one of those long sessions and was entirely fierce."

Without mincing her words, McAnally informed Edward that he was fortunate to be working with two of the most experienced documentary makers in the industry. She suggested that he kindly shut up and work, because Desmond and Mike were acting in Edward's best interests. Desmond remembers the prince's response: "To do him great credit, Edward said, 'Yes, I do know.' He never lost his temper. He never became an egomaniac or a diva." Desmond has one final observation of working with Edward:

"He has the most highly polished shoes of any man I've ever seen, and he's immaculately trained in manners."

On November 15, 1995, the *Guardian* reported that "with a great fanfare, Ardent yesterday unveiled its most ambitious project yet." The newspaper went on to mock the prince turned producer: "Why has Prince Edward been chosen to produce and present such a documentary? He is neither a historian nor a journalist; as far as one can tell, his only qualification for the job is that he happens to have the same Christian name as his subject.

"Still, it is most generous of ITV to offer work to members of the royal family, many of whom would be otherwise unemployable. Perhaps the whole gruesome clan should form a production company—the Really Useless Group—and start preparing a few sequels: *Andrew on Andrew,* in which the Duke of York chooses his favorite melodies from the musicals of Andrew Lloyd Webber; and *Queen on Queen,* a personal tribute by the monarch to the late Freddie Mercury."

Edward's ego might have been bruised by the liberal newspaper's sarcasm, but ITV, livid at the premature and unwelcome publicity for *Edward on Edward,* blamed the prince for talking to the press. Urged by ITV to write to Edward accordingly, Desmond complied, asking Edward to refrain from independently publicizing the project and to be clear and truthful about its genesis. An outraged Edward replied on November 16, demanding an apology. None was forthcoming.

Edward on Edward was broadcast on the ITV network on April 23, 1996. "Love has worked wonders for the Queen's more sensitive son," wrote Judy Wade in the London *Sun.* "As he tells the story of his great-uncle King Edward VIII, he is a confident performer. There is no sign of the miserable bloke who abandoned a manly career in the Royal Marines. If the applause that greeted him at a recent press preview of *Edward on Edward* is any indication, at last his TV company, Ardent, has a hit."

"The program, written and presented by the prince and *produced by his own company, Ardent* [italics added], is naturally going to be controversial," observed the London Sunday *Times*. Desmond later said, "It was unfair, but natural, that the press would think Ardent had made it. We had expected that Edward would rather vigorously (and fairly) emphasize that it was a Man Alive Group production and that Ardent were glad to be associated with it."

Through the years since *Edward on Edward* was first broadcast, the media has persisted in dubbing Ardent as the documentary's sole producer. All Edward needed to do in order to rectify that false impression was to write a simple letter to a national newspaper correcting the misconception. According to the published record, he did not.

Edward did give credit to the Man Alive Group on a minor occasion for having conceived and produced *Edward on Edward*. On April 29, 1996, at a small gathering held at the Automobile Club in Paris, he conceded, "Two men came to me and they gave me a wonderful opportunity, and I want to thank them for it." He named Mike and Desmond, but his comments were not reported in the press.

A year later, *Edward on Edward* was responsible for a dramatic transformation in Ardent's hitherto lackluster fortunes. "Thanks to *Edward on Edward*, CBS paid Ardent £2.5 million [$4,075,000] for a series of documentaries on American dynasties like the Kennedys, the Gettys, and the Fondas. Part of the deal was that Edward produced and presented," reported Stuart Millar in the *Guardian*. "We were very impressed with the quality of the eight programs to date by Ardent and broadcast internationally, especially *Edward on Edward*, which Edward also hosted," confirmed CBS executive Rob Dalton. And on January 15, 1997, the *Daily Express* reported, "Edward, still in America finalizing the project, is ecstatic at the coup which has rescued his production company, Ardent, from financial ruin. The decisive factor, I understand, was *Edward on Edward,* his documentary about the Duke of Windsor. The Americans were very struck by his ease and maturity as a presenter."

For all intents and purposes, Edward has never set the record straight regarding the fact that the Man Alive Group and not Ardent produced *Edward on Edward.* Nor, apparently, has he ever given credit to Esther Rantzen for teaching him to present. Quite the reverse. In fact, in July 1998, when Topaz Amoore of the *Sunday Express* asked Edward for the secret of his natural presenting style, he replied, "I have had no formal training. You look at that awful black hole staring at you. You just picture a face; picture someone slumped in their chair, and you tell them a story, just as if you were sitting at home. That's how I do it."

"Edward definitely stole the lion's share of credit from the Man Alive Group, Desmond Wilcox, and Mike Latham," said a British television industry insider. But if Desmond and Mike were surprised, perhaps they shouldn't have been. After all, they were dealing with a prince of the realm, whose family rules England by divine right. And by stealing much of the credit for *Edward on Edward,* Prince Edward was merely exercising droit du seigneur— the right of the ruler to take whatever strikes his fancy.

But had either Desmond or Mike witnessed the following incident, they might, perhaps, have been more fully prepared for what was to come.

Whenever the royal family travels by plane, their luggage is not loaded through the normal airport luggage system. Instead, it is carried onto the plane by officials. On one occasion, when Edward flew back from Paris with the production team, his luggage was lifted onto the plane by a member of the party. Everyone heard the loud clink of bottles in Edward's suitcase. He had not arrived in

Paris with bottles, but his suite at the Ritz had boasted vintage bottles of champagne, Russian vodka, brandy, and cognac, courtesy of Mohamed Al Fayed. Apparently the temptation to benefit from Al Fayed's largesse had clearly been too great for Edward to withstand. It was impossible not to conclude that Edward had taken the bottles with him from the Ritz. Seeing the look of amazement on everyone's faces, Edward smiled conspiratorially and said, "Who would leave them behind?"

At that moment, Edward Windsor's genes were in ascendance. His great-grandmother Queen Mary had been labeled by historians as "a country house kleptomaniac." It was said of her that she was to fine art what the Vikings were to Britain: she looted and pillaged wherever she went. She would stay in people's houses, express a fancy for an object, a piece of furniture, or a carpet, and expect it to be sent to her at the palace. She was highly displeased if people didn't take the hint. A distinguished art dealer was in an antique shop in London's Bond Street when an assistant ran in and said, "Quick, Queen Mary is coming down the street." The owner promptly removed anything of value off the walls and took it out of the room. Queen Mary glided into the store, looked around, then left. The art dealer said, "Some of my colleagues in the street have gone bankrupt because of what Queen Mary took from them."

Edward has inherited his great-grandmother's tendencies. He took exactly what he wanted from two of the most celebrated and experienced television executives in the business. And then he moved on. *Edward on Edward* will always be known to the general public solely as an Ardent production. Although Edward's princely maneuvers may have won him a lucrative CBS contract, British television insiders know the truth.

As a result of those maneuvers and countless others similar ones, Edward will never win the respect from his peers that he so deeply craves.

13

VERY ARDENT

*E*DWARD ON *EDWARD* WOULD BRING EDWARD WINDSOR great success in America. But on the home front, Ardent was not making great progress. However, in October 1995, Ardent won a big commission to produce a comedy-drama about Britain's House of Commons entitled *Annie's Bar*. The head of Channel 4, Michael Grade, signed Ardent up to make the ten-part £2 million series. Heartened by the coup, Edward promptly voted himself a twenty percent pay raise, bringing his salary up to £114,125 ($186,004) a year.

One of the show's advisers included political insider Derek Draper. He recalled, "I remember noting that Edward surrounded himself with idiots. The people who were supposedly running his TV company were quite clearly not up to the job. Blatantly not up to it. I was new to television, but when I met these people and heard them speak, I could tell they were incompetent. I thought I must be wrong, but as weeks went by, I was proven right by the complete, appalling standard of the program. But also everyone I knew who did know what they were talking about—like people from Channel 4 and experienced directors whom Ardent brought in—said they couldn't believe he was working with people like

Eben Foggit, whose ludicrous lack of talent was only overshadowed by his ludicrous name. That basically made me question Edward's judgment. It seems to me that if you were Prince Edward and wanted to be set up in television, you wouldn't be short of people who were good."

Draper was stunned by the incompetence he witnessed, but he nevertheless had favorable things to say about Edward personally. "The second thing that struck me about Prince Edward is that he was a nice man. He didn't have airs and graces. At the after-show party—which was a very sad affair because everyone knew that was that—in a horrible tacky little bar, Edward came and chatted to people and was quite nice."

Annie's Bar was a resounding flop canceled after just one season. Malcolm Cockren, Ardent's chairman, quickly stepped in to run damage control. "It was a mistake," he told the *Guardian* afterwards. "It could have been a huge success for Ardent. Channel 4 found a spot, but they decided to bring the whole thing forward by something like three to six months. To tell you the truth we weren't ready for it, but we were a new company and we wanted to help Channel 4."

Peter Ansorge, the Channel 4 executive who originally commissioned Ardent to produce *Annie's Bar*, loyally absolved Ardent from all blame: "*Annie's Bar* won't be remembered as one of my greatest achievements with Channel 4, but that's because we plunged into it. Our problem was not with the company but that we had bitten off more than we could chew. The criticism of Edward is terribly unfair. He had surrounded himself with good people. It wasn't that different from dealing with any other independent. Edward didn't have a huge involvement, so he was in the background. He was very encouraging. He definitely has taste and judgment and those are invaluable."

Ansorge went on to marvel at Ardent's resources: "They

appeared very well resourced compared to other independents. You did get the feeling that if they needed anything, say another researcher, they would have the funds to bring that person in. They also had a very talented drama department. Edward was backing a very original idea, but it's a competitive world. Not every development comes to fruition. That's the nature of the business."

After *Annie's Bar* failed, Edward turned to his family for inspiration. He cast around and came up with the concept of making a £3.5 million ($5,705,000) eight-episode drama based on the life of his grandmother Queen Elizabeth, the Queen Mother. Written by scriptwriter Julian Bond, the drama series covered the years from 1932 to 1953 and the coronation of Elizabeth II. Early reports in the London Sunday *Times* by media critic Nicolas Hellen, stated that Edward had sought and won approval from the palace for his project, but "is keeping his distance." It was difficult for observers to believe Ardent's assertions that Edward would relinquish all control of the project based on his grandmother's life. "For him to argue that it is nothing to do with him just won't wash," said a leading constitutional historian, adding, "Nobody is going to believe it, even if it is true. It is a question of whether it is a good thing for a member of the royal family to give his imprimatur on delicate topics of this kind."

In the past, Edward had said adamantly, "I don't want to trade on that association any more than I intend trading on my title," but the success of *Edward on Edward* had convinced him otherwise. So after his Queen Mother series was rejected, he turned to yet another royal subject, *Crown and Country*, a six-part program about the royal family's associations with the south of England.

During the making of the series, he granted a number of interviews to the media.

"I've been living a schizophrenic existence for a long time, so it's nothing unusual for me," he told journalist Caroline Philips. "I would never describe myself as quite ordinary or normal. But I don't see myself as removed from the mass of people. I feel I am part of it. I walk down the street, I use the roads like everybody else, go into shops and move around town, hopefully without causing any interference to anybody else."

In an interview with the Sunday *Times*, he showed himself to still be sensitive to criticism that the Ardent offices were far too plush for an independent television company, "We could have gone into a small garret and paid extremely low rent," he argued. "But I don't think I would have been allowed to do it from a security point of view. Yes, there is always going to be the sniping. If I fail, it is because of who I am; if I succeed, it is because of who I am. I am in a no-win situation, so you might just as well get on with it."

In April 1997 Edward attempted to "get on with it" by following up on Christine Carter's proposal that he make a documentary, *The Sport of Kings*, on international horse racing. In the hope of getting financing for the project, he flew to Dubai during the Dubai World Cup. His efforts failed, and he returned to London, disappointed.

Mark Nicholls, who worked with Edward in developing the project, was dismayed by his next move. Edward was approached by two Irishmen. They proposed setting up a company and applying to the Irish government for a grant to make *The Sport of Kings* under section 35 of the Finance Act. Section 35 was set up by the Irish government to encourage filming in Ireland. If 75 percent of a film was made in Ireland, 60 percent of the budget would be provided by the Irish government. The initial sum of money would be £1.2 million ($1,956,000), with the remaining £8 million ($13,040,000) to be raised through the stock market.

The Irish men who met with Edward proposed that they take 60 percent of the deal and Edward 40 percent. In effect, they were intending to use Edward's name to raise money from the Irish government.

Edward's desperation to succeed had led him to be reckless. With the exception of *Edward on Edward*, Edward had a trail of failures behind him. He was stubborn and willful. That combination could have proved to be his undoing.

Mark Nicholls was appalled: "I was called to a meeting by him. Given his position, Edward should never have even entered the realms of possibility of having a meeting with these people," Nicholls said, "and yet he very seriously pursued them. There is absolutely no way that a member of the British royal family could apply for an Irish tax subsidy. I found myself in the position of having to say, 'Look, Edward, given your position, you cannot deal with people like that.' He is terribly naïve. It would have been ludicrous for him to have done it. The deal was not made, yet he continued to talk to these people for ages. It is evident that he had a very sheltered upbringing.

"It doesn't take an awful lot of imagination to work out what the *Sunday Times* or the *Irish Independent* would have made out of the story if they had discovered that a member of the English royal family was exploiting their government subsidies for profit.

"Of course, the Irish financing would have been stopped," Nicholls concluded, "because I know from friends that everything Edward does gets vetted by the palace. Ardent was a highly unprofessional company with which to work, and rather depressingly so. Of course, it was courted by some individuals who liked having a link with Edward."

"Edward was very dull," says senior researcher Tara Cole, who devised the program *Glam Slam*. Tara was employed by Ardent.

Tara worked for Ardent for two years, during which she developed *Glam Slam* for the company. *Glam Slam*, a camp quiz show, featured two transvestite hostesses and starred risqué comedienne Jenny Eclair. The show features a scene in which Jenny Eclair implores the audience to join her in a tribute to "high heels,

G-strings, and push-up bras." More embarrassing (and perhaps another example of Edward's naïveté in letting the program go forward) was a scene in which Eclair cracks that the Queen's handbag sometimes contains "a bumper bag of glow-in-the-dark condoms."

Tara Cole was heard to warn Edward about the show's cutting-edge irreverent humor. "She kept saying, 'It's very camp. Are you happy to be associated with this?' " says a source who heard the conversation. "Edward was kind of, 'Oh, yes, it's wonderful.' He knew we had drag queens in it and it was quite sort of saucy and over-the-top. Then he and Eben both decided they wanted to be executive producers. But we couldn't see them for dust. Edward was just busy walking around saying, 'I am an executive producer.' "

A pilot was made of the show. "Can Edward be the king of glitter and showbiz? Will the prince be the king of Saturday night?" wondered Channel 4's senior commissioning editor, Seamus Cassidy, before answering his own question with, "I don't think so," and rejecting the program.

"The problem was that basically nobody wanted to touch anything that was from Ardent," said a source associated with *Glam Slam.* "Edward got the backs up of everybody within the industry. There was no way anyone was going to give any money to Ardent, because Edward had no experience."

Since *Edward on Edward,* Edward had perfected the art of hogging a credit on all productions that he presented. His tactics, more fitting for a show business mogul than a British prince, shocked the *Glam Slam* source who observed, "The deal Ardent invariably does—so that they can say they produced something—is that if Edward is asked to present a program, Ardent is put down as coproducer. He's conning people. I remember saying, 'God, that's such a scam that you're doing that.' Whenever I see a producer credit for Edward, I suspect that the truth is he isn't actually producing the program at all, but is presenting it."

"He did all that, 'Call me Edward,' stuff, but he is not good on emotion. The mother of a friend of mine who worked at Ardent was dying of cancer. Edward just stuck his head in the sand."

Edward's former employee at Ardent believes that Edward's arrogance and lack of skill at dealing fairly at all times with his employees can be attributed to his upbringing. "He's always been pampered; he's always had a detective there with him. He is obviously very used to having people waiting on him. Tea had to be brought to him at three every afternoon. That was typically Edward. He would try, and miss every time. If he was really trying to be one of us and not have people wait on him, he would have made his own tea and let somebody else clear it away. That's how everyone else behaved. We were all very much sort of servants. He knew how to treat people, in that he'd been brought up with valets and things like that, but not in any kind of personal way."

The employee's comments echo those of Lady Cotterell, who, when observing Edward at Cambridge many years before, noticed that he was far more comfortable dealing with servants than with other people.

"He doesn't know what to say," his former employee elaborated. "He walks off in the middle of conversations. But that is what all the royals do. When they have to meet the great unwashed public, they always keep moving. When Harry and William faced everybody after Diana died, Charles and the detective chivied them along to keep them moving. Obviously in that kind of a situation, they could get stuck. But when you are in an office, it is all very safe."

Despite his attempts to be one of the crowd, Edward was clearly uncomfortable functioning in a work environment and dealing with people who weren't necessarily always subservient to him.

"He wasn't really good at having his own opinions," the former employee continued. "If you asked him a direct question, he rarely knew what to say. He just laughs and walks away very, very quickly. That's his trick. His own opinions are those of a man in his seventies, usually his father's. Other than that, he has no opinions of his own. He just regurgitates everybody else's information. I had stories and things that I'd told him which were suddenly being repeated back to me from other people. He used it as his material."

As ever, he had no problems in appropriating something that belonged to someone else. At times, however, his former employee still felt sorry for him: "He was very easily influenced. There is a very immature side to him. He made his office open plan because the Duke of Edinburgh Award offices were open plan, so Edward wanted that too."

He tried to be part of a team, but rarely succeeded. His former employee recalled, "I remember standing at the bus stop in the freezing cold one night. Suddenly, all the traffic was cordoned off. Police motorbikes roared along the street. And there was Edward in his Bentley or whatever they have. He was on his way to a premiere. Supposedly, he had avoided all that, and he had said he didn't want any of that. It was very odd having just left him at the office to see him just whiz past. It is another life."

Now and again, Sophie visited Edward in the office. "She wasn't around an awful lot," remembered the former Ardent employee. "She didn't like any of us. She didn't seem to like it at all that we were calling him, 'Edward.' She has fallen in love with the princess idea and everything that goes along with it. We weren't really playing along with that. It was clear that she wanted us to call him 'sir.' The Ardent staff were invited to a ball at the Grosvenor House Hotel. Beforehand, we were briefed not to call Edward 'Edward' whenever Sophie was around. We were told that when she was within earshot, we were to call him 'sir.' She's very dull, very snooty, very stuck-up."

■　■　■

While Edward was endeavoring to consolidate his company, he put all plans to marry Sophie on hold. She still had the Queen's support, with Her Majesty telling close friends, "Sophie is easy, uncomplicated, and intelligent. She doesn't stand out in a crowd. She's good for Ed." Although Sophie still maintained her own small flat (where she had placed a silver-framed picture of Edward by the side of her bed), she spent most of her time at Buckingham Palace. Reports alleged that she and Edward generally spent the night together in Sophie's room there, but he always crept back to his own room by six in the morning, when his valet brought him his customary cup of tea.

According to a palace insider, Sophie had not charmed the staff: "They find her aloof, and she never tips. She already thinks of herself as rather grand, and she isn't enormously popular there."

"It is an unusual situation," observed Harold Brooks-Baker in 1995. "They are living at Buckingham Palace and acting as if they are married, but the prince appears unwilling to commit himself."

He was not yet ready to make a formal marriage proposal, but was prepared to spend all his free time with Sophie. She and Edward spent ten days cruising around Scotland's Western Isles on the Royal Yacht *Britannia* in August 1995. The Queen and Prince Philip accompanied them, another indication of the esteem in which Sophie was held.

In February 1996, Edward and Sophie went away on their first foreign trip together. They flew to Switzerland, where they stayed in the exclusive ski resort of St. Moritz. Dominated by the elegant Palace Hotel, playground of Christina Onassis, playboy Gunther Sachs, Queen Saroya, and assorted European jet-setters, St. Moritz was a fairy-tale setting for Sophie and the prince.

Back in London, Sophie's high life continued apace. She attended a society party in March at the top jewelers, Asprey. Gone were the conservative outfits of yore, replaced by ample cleavage. Edward was not with her that night, which only fueled rumors further that their marriage would never happen. Friends of the couple sprang to Sophie and Edward's defense, with Edward's old Cambridge friend the Reverend Tim Hastie-Smith, now chaplain at Stowe School, declaring, "Everyone hopes they'll get married, but we are all conscious they will do what they want. They are playing their cards close to their chest. They are so happy."

"Edward feels vulnerable," explained a close friend. "It makes him petulant sometimes. He knows that everyone is waiting, and it weighs on him heavily. Look what happened to Charles when his father told him, 'Get on with it.' He married Diana."

From the first, Sophie had been acutely aware of the Diana syndrome. She professed to hate comparisons between herself and the Princess of Wales. "I think she aped her unconsciously," said a PR colleague who observed her during many events.

"Sophie wouldn't thank you for likening her to Diana," said Lady Colin Campbell. "Diana was considered by the royal family to be a Judas. Diana was the person who, due to her various emotional and mental illnesses, has done more to undermine the monarchy than Wallis Simpson. No one who is royal would wish to be likened to Diana."

"Sophie hated Diana because the royal family did. She was more zealous than the zealots," said a PR colleague, echoing the widely held feeling that Sophie wanted to be more royal than the royals.

Sophie's wickedly accurate imitations of Diana, complete with her classic "Shy Di" smile, reflected the venom she felt for the Princess of Wales.

The two women assiduously avoided one another. However, on a rare occasion, the Queen held a tea party at Windsor Castle for her grandsons William and Harry, Diana, Edward, and Sophie. Royal protocol dictates that a commoner is not permitted to speak when a senior royal is conducting a conversation. During tea,

Diana ignored Sophie completely. Yet whenever Sophie started a sentence, Diana began talking, forcing Sophie to break off what she was saying, as royal etiquette dictated. Finally, unable to cope with Diana's treatment any longer, Sophie requested permission from the Queen that she be allowed to leave the tea party. The Queen, who above all wants her family to coexist in peace and harmony, knew that as far as Sophie and Diana were concerned, there was no hope of this. They were both strong-willed women with remarkable destinies.

Despite their mutual enmity, Diana and Sophie had one thing in common: extraordinary determination. Diana once grudgingly alluded to Sophie's laser-beam focus. "Sophie will get Edward in the end," Diana said. "No matter how long it takes, she'll get him."

In November 1997, Edward met with another professional failure, when his proposal to televise a live concert at the Royal Festival Hall marking the Queen and Prince Philip's golden wedding celebrations was rejected by the BBC. The concert, featuring Dame Judi Dench and Cleo Laine, among others, was to be attended by King Juan Carlos of Spain, King Harald of Norway, King Carl Gustav of Sweden, and Queen Margrethe of Denmark. But instead of opting for Edward filming the event, the BBC decided instead to film a two-hour broadcast from Westminster Abbey and a program featuring interviews with couples around Britain who were married in the same year as the Queen. Edward was not afraid to express his disappointment to Bill Frost of the *Times*. "It's a shame," he said. "This is a unique event, and television companies around the world would have been very interested in buying it."

His documentary on the restoration of Windsor Castle was also rejected by all the British television companies. Officials acting on behalf of the Queen had given Edward's company free use of four years' worth of television footage that had been filmed at their expense. "It is not true to say that Edward gets any special access or favors by virtue of being the Queen's youngest son," Buckingham Palace asserted against all evidence.

Selling the project was probably not made easy by the ambivalence of Edward's position in the media.

"All the television programs Edward makes are a gross exploitation of his position," said Roy Greenslade, media critic of the *Guardian*. "He uses his royal connections all the time. He lives off his connections. Everyone does, but he said he wouldn't. He is a hypocrite. Like the rest of the hangers-on—Princess Michael, etcetera—he lives off the family. It comes with the Windsor territory. Edward is a bit of a nonentity. The third son of a Queen isn't somebody who is going to set the world on fire. He's lived down to his promise."

"Far from being the vehicle that allowed the prince to find a proper role for himself in life, Ardent looked worryingly like a vanity publishing operation," wrote Jim White in the *Independent.*

The British media establishment may not have been set on fire by Edward, but he continued to make television programs, with the help of director Robin Bextor, his friend and associate. Bextor had directed Edward in *Edward on Edward* and had made a marked impression on the prince. "Robin once told me that he was quite happy to make the royal family's home movies," a source who worked with him revealed.

Bextor went on to direct Edward in *Crown and Country*, which was broadcast on British television in July 1998 and met with a mediocre reception from critics. "Prince Edward, who really is a TV presenter, should be one of those instantly forgettable reporters lumbered with mind-numbingly pointless stories on *Newsroom Southeast*," Lucy Etherington wrote in the *Evening Standard*. "Only he's Prince Edward, so he gets a whole series to himself charting the history of England and how important his ancestors have been in shaping it. Very dull."

Edward fought back in a variety of press interviews. He spiced up the interviews with anecdotes, telling an endearing story about the filming of *Crown and Country*: Prince Andrew, he said, came to see him on location. "A bystander turned to me in great excitement and said, 'Guess who I've just seen.' He didn't have a clue who I was." Robin Bextor obligingly chipped in and contributed an anecdote designed to implement the image of Edward, the people's producer. According to Robin, while they were filming a scene in which knights on horses galloped through fields, a driver started revving up his van. The noise of the engine was deafening. Robin yelled, "Will someone shut that van up?" Someone did. It was only later, Robin said, that he discovered it was Edward who tapped on the van window and asked the driver, "D'you mind turning that down, mate? It's just that you're spoiling our shot."

Away from the set, Edward did all he could to reinforce his democratic image. During filming, he and the team had lunch two days running at the Wheelwright, a restaurant in Chatham, Kent. "The PA [personal assistant] reserved a table and told me that they would be paying cash," said the chef, Barry Turtle. "When they came in for lunch, I saw Prince Edward sitting at the table with fifteen other people. He'd obviously come incognito. We kept the service very low key, because he obviously didn't want any fuss. We left him alone, and respected the fact that he just came in. We did ask if the next day we could present our visitor's book to him for his signature. He said yes and did. He had our £4.70 [$7.66] special of fish and chips, followed by whiskey bread-and-butter pudding. It was obvious that he just wanted to get on with his business and be natural and normal about it, which is great."

Edward was informal and friendly to James Robinson, assistant to photographer Steve Poole, who photographed him for the *Daily Mail's Weekend Magazine*. It was James's first day working for Steve. James remembered, "I'm at the bottom of the ladder, but Edward was very nice to me, which was quite unusual. I was actually terribly nervous, but he put me at ease. He was very nice, with lots of eye contact. I really noticed he made an effort with me. He asked me questions about what I'd done in the past. He was quite open, talking about the Windsor fire and how upset his family was by it."

Steve Poole recalled, "It was James's first job, and I was quite worried about how he would get on, but he probably has more in common with Prince Edward than I do, in terms of education. James has been to university and speaks with a well-brought-up English accent, whereas I'm working class, left school at fifteen with no qualifications. We are from completely opposite ends of the spectrum. But Prince Edward was very relaxed, easy to talk to, and down-to-earth."

At the end of June 1998, Eben Foggit, Edward's codirector, mentor, and business partner for the past five years, resigned from Ardent to form his own company. Despite Edward's concerted media campaign to promote *Crown and Country*, it was clear that the company had not taken the British television world by storm. America, however, was quite another story, proving that, as the saying goes, no one is a prophet in his own country.

Aware that his major market was across the Atlantic, Edward focused on selling programs to America. In January 1997, Edward traveled to the NATPE conference in New Orleans, where he scored by signing his £2.5 million CBS contract to make documentaries on leading American dynasties like the Gettys and Kennedys.

In February 1998, Edward took a two-day trip to Hollywood, where his agent, Sam Haskell, was West Coast head of television for the William Morris Agency. Haskell and his wife, Mary, threw a dinner for Edward at their Encino home, and invited Brooke Shields, Martin Short, Walt Disney Television president David Neuman, William Morris chairman Norman Brokaw, 20th Century-Fox Television president Sandy Grushow, and USA Network's entertainment president Ron Perth.

Edward was in his element. He loved doing business in America, he said, because Americans treated his royalty as irrelevant. "In Britain if you've got a title, then you also don't have any brains," he said. "So there's no point in talking about anything else. We just have a hang-up about titles."

In contrast, Americans were comfortable with Edward, treating him as one of the guys. "I've known him for a year because I've been working with him," confided actor Corbin Bernsen, who was developing a project with Ardent. "I ran up and said, 'Hey, Edward,' and I didn't realize there was a kind of a receiving line. A small social faux pas."

Unlike their British counterparts, the guests that night were enthralled by Edward. "Great television is about having a great point of view, and he's got one," enthused Disney TV executive David Neuman. Brooke Shields, who came without her then husband Andre Agassi, was seated next to Edward. "I told Andre, 'Do you realize that because you're not coming I'm sitting next to the prince?'" Agassi retorted that he wasn't particularly concerned because she was coming home to him.

Edward had found his audience in America, with Americans lending a sympathetic ear to anything he cared to say. He was a television producer, but he was also acutely aware of his role as ambassador for the British royal family. In the aftermath of Princess Diana's death, his festering hatred of the British press had intensified. He took the opportunity of lashing out at their treatment of his nephews William and Harry after the tragedy. "They are doing remarkably well under the circumstances, although I think people forget that they do actually read newspapers, so that these people who go on about conspiracy theories . . . What are they doing to these boys? It's nobody's business, really."

In September 1998, Edward made yet another attempt to conquer British television. This time, his vehicle was a drama, *The Inspector Pitt Mysteries*. Again, he peppered the media with heartwarming anecdotes, including one by the drama's star, Eoin McCarthy. In all likelihood, McCarthy wouldn't have told the following story without Edward's tacit consent: "We went to dinner at a posh restaurant and came to the mutual understanding that both our parents didn't like what we did for a living. When I told my own father I was becoming an actor at the age of twenty-seven, he said to me, 'Jesus, you'll be unemployed for the rest of your life!' And the prince said that his parents told him more or less the same thing."

In October 1998, Edward returned once more to royal subjects when he sold a three-hour drama documentary to the Learning Channel, *Tales From the Tower*, a history of the Tower of London.

In November, Edward announced that he and Robin Bextor were making a documentary on the Rolling Stones's early years, for a three-part series entitled *Legends*. Again, America was the impetus behind the series, with the Learning Channel commissioning the series. "Ardent is known for its historical and royal programs over here," Robin Bextor explained. "But we have got involved in three or four different types of programs in the U.S. We are going more into entertainment."

14

ENGAGED AT LAST

$\mathcal{I}$N JULY 1998, EDWARD LEASED BAGSHOT PARK IN Surrey from his mother. Prince Andrew had reportedly considered leasing the house and opening a golfing school there with golfer Nick Faldo, but had changed his mind. Bagshot was now available to Edward. He agreed to pay his mother £50,000 ($81,000) a year to rent the one-hundred-twenty-year-old house, which was set among eighty-eight acres of land. A mile-long tree-lined drive, offering views of Windsor on one side and the Surrey hills on the other, lead up to the house with its Portland stone and red-brick Gothic facade, wrought-iron gates, and oak-paneled interiors. In addition to its nine en suite bedrooms, five reception rooms, and three staff apartments, the crowning glories of the house included a chimneypiece in the smoking room designed by Sir Edward Lutyens and an Indian Room and corridor.

Today worth between £8 million and £10 million ($13 million to $16 million), the original building was used as a hunting center by monarchs dating as far back as King James I. The present-day mansion was built by Queen Victoria in 1877, as a wedding present for her third son, Prince Arthur, the Duke of Connaught, and his wife, Princess Louise Marguerite.

The Duke of Connaught, who was catered to by sixty servants, lived in the house until he died there in 1942 at the age of ninety-one. During the Second World War, Bagshot Park became a wing of the Military Staff College. In 1947, Bagshot was briefly considered as a home for the then Princess Elizabeth, who ultimately decided to move to Windlesham Moor. Since then, Bagshot became the Army Chaplain Training Centre. In 1996, due to defense cuts, the Army moved out, leaving the house empty and primed for a new tenant.

Edward commissioned architect Stephen Batchelor, of the London practice Bower Langlands and Batchelor, to carry out renovations on Bagshot and proceeded to invest £2 million ($3 million) in rebuilding and redecorating his new home. Although he would retain his private apartment and office at Buckingham Palace, Bagshot was now, for all intents and purposes, his home.

When queried in October 1998 about whether his move to Bagshot signaled that an engagement was imminent, Edward was contemptuous as always of the media. His hatred and distrust of the press continued to rival that of any beleaguered Hollywood star. Consequently, he was consistently determined to manipulate the media as much as he could by denying that an engagement was in the cards. He said firmly, "I have enough on my plate." His denial that he was on the verge of getting engaged was disingenuous. In August 1998, one colleague claimed to have helped Edward pick out Sophie's ring, a round center stone of 2.05 carats flanked by two heart-shaped gems and set in white gold, from Asprey and Garrard.

Finally, during the first week in January 1999, when all the accredited royal reporters—who, in Edward's view, had traditionally subjected him to excessive harassment—were out of England covering Prince Charles's skiing trip to the Swiss resort Klosters, Edward took the momentous step of announcing his engagement.

Buckingham Palace announced Edward's engagement on

Wednesday, January 6, 1999, at ten in the morning. The announcement read, "The Queen and the Duke of Edinburgh are delighted to announce the engagement of their younger son, Prince Edward, to Miss Sophie Rhys-Jones. The couple sought the permission of their respective parents between Christmas and New Year. Both families were thrilled at the news."

It had taken Edward five years to propose to Sophie. The facts regarding where and when he proposed to her are shrouded in contradictions. Journalist Charles Rae alleges that Edward proposed to Sophie at the £500 ($815)-a-night Pink Beach Cottage in Bermuda, just before Christmas. However, journalist Fiona Barton, in the *Mail on Sunday*, reported that Edward proposed to Sophie on Windermere Island in the Bahamas. Edward refuses to confirm either story. The timing of his proposal, too, is in question. Given that Robin Bextor knew about the engagement on December 16 (and that the engagement ring was allegedly purchased in August), and that the royal family was told "between Christmas and New Year," it is difficult to pinpoint accurately the exact date on which Edward proposed to Sophie.

The announcement was the perfect photo opportunity, one clearly orchestrated by seasoned publicist Sophie Rhys-Jones. The dialogue, too, was perfect, perhaps even scripted in advance by a media-savvy writer. The British weather, too, was idyllic, warm, and pleasant for January. Sophie, radiant in a gray Tomas Starzweski suit, smiled her glittering smile, while Edward held her hand, gazing at her in rapt admiration.

"I managed to take her completely by surprise," he said of his proposal. Sophie's now-famous response was, "Yes. Yes, please." "It was very staged," says Nigel Dempster. "All this rubbish about Sophie being surprised that Edward proposed to her. She has been princess-in-waiting for two years. I think she knew about the engagement a long time before it was announced. It was not spontaneous." Sophie and Edward were not unnerved by the press's often intrusive questions. If they hadn't rehearsed their answers in advance—and many media watchers judged that they had—it was highly possible that they had, at least, predicted most of the questions ahead of time.

Asked why he had waited so long to propose, Edward said, "It is impossible for anyone else to understand why, but I don't think it would have been right before, and I don't think Sophie would have said yes. Hopefully, by the fact that she did say yes, I must have got the timing right."

Then, for the benefit of the photographers, Edward kissed Sophie's cheek gently. It was not a performance overflowing with passion, but one that far surpassed Charles's during the press conference announcing his engagement to Diana.

At that moment on the day of Edward's engagement to Sophie, it was impossible not to remember the other day, eighteen years before, or to forget Charles, Diana, and the promise of happily ever after. When Charles was asked whether he and his fiancée were in love, he had replied, "Yes. Whatever 'in love' means." An honest reply, but not one that appealed to most romantics.

Edward, however, canny and perhaps prepared by his PR fiancée, had an answer ready. Asked if he was prepared for marriage, he said, "If I'm not ready for it now . . ." He laughed, then finished with, "it's too late, so yes. You have to be the best of friends." Then, in a lower voice, he said, "It also helps that we happen to love each other."

His last words were drowned out by a reporter firing another question at him. Edward repeated his answer, almost as if by rote: "As I said, you know, we are the very best of friends, and that's essential. And it also helps that we happen to love each other very much. And it's great, so we are very happy at the moment and long may it continue."

He was prepared, too, when the press threw at him the unpleasant question of whether the failure of his siblings' marriages had put pressure on him. He even managed a laugh and cracked, "Oh, somebody had to bring that up, didn't they? More pressure? I don't know. I think if anybody's going to get married, I hope that they think they are going to get it right."

Sophie nodded in agreement. At times, observers agreed, she exhibited a startling resemblance to Diana, all those years ago in 1981. But the similarity was only superficial. Diana had been nineteen then, shy and unconfident, whereas Sophie was thirty-four, confident, and unafraid to display her self-confidence to the world. Asked how she felt about joining the royal family, she said, "It is slightly nerve-racking in many ways. But I am ready for it now, and I am fully aware of the responsibilities and commitments."

They stood there, Sophie and Edward, their arms entwined, and dealt with all questions in a cool and composed manner. Asked if she was prepared to cope with the pressures of the media, Sophie considered the question for a second, then said, "Perhaps I am slightly better geared up to second-guess what might happen."

Sophie had waited five years to marry Edward, and this was her moment of triumph. "Sophie had to overcome the reserve that the royal family would have felt about her," says an aristocrat who knows the royal family well. "She was on probation because they wanted to be sure that what they saw they got. She was accepted to a point. Finally the royal family decided she wasn't the latest in a line of adventuresses who wanted to marry a prince for the rank and position, like Diana had done.

"She had to endure the pressures of publicity, the constraints of royalty, before she was even considered for the role. Given that five years have now passed since she first met Edward, she could never fall back on the excuse, 'Oh, I didn't know what the pressures were; I couldn't cope; it was everybody's fault but mine.' If she hadn't coped, she wouldn't have been allowed to marry Edward. The royal family tested Sophie through time, and she stood the test of time."

Body language expert Susan Quilliam studied both Edward and Sophie during their engagement press conference and concluded that their marriage has a better chance of enduring than had Fergie and Andrew's or Charles and Diana's: "They were clearly working as a team. When one ran out of something to say or hesitated, the other chipped in to keep the interview running smoothly. They exhibited the body language of best friends rather than lovers. That's not surprising after five years together. There is love, but it is that second stage of love that develops over time."

Time is on their side, and Sophie and Edward both know it. They are still young, rich, healthy, with every advantage the world has to offer. Sophie is neither Princess Diana nor Sarah Ferguson. Not an aristocrat or a fashion icon, not reckless or unconventional, she may prove to be the saving of the royal family. And Edward, the first royal to try to simultaneously be a prince and an ordinary person, and to have it all, could, by his very difference, ultimately enhance the image of the monarchy.

And if marriage does succeed in changing the sometimes petulant prince, perhaps he and his bride will once more infuse the British royal family with a genuine magic, one that will reverberate into the twenty-first century.

Source Notes

INTRODUCTION

Re: Edward claiming producer credits when his major role was that of presenter, from interviews with Mark Nicholls and a former Ardent employee. Background on Sophie's relationship with Diana, from Lady Colin Campbell. Quotes on the relationship, from a friend of Diana's.

Ardent debts, from Ardent's Annual Return, which is on record at Companies House in London.

Article consulted: "Royal Staff Boycott Wedding Whip-round for Edward and Sophie," by Fiona Barton, the *Mail on Sunday*, May 2, 1999.

CHAPTER 1

Interviewees include: Sir David Attenborough, Robert Lacey, Roy Greenslade, Jim Bennett, Nigel Dempster, confidential source who observed the contretemps with the three photographers at Balmoral.

Documentary viewed: *Royal Family*, BBC/ITN, 1969.

Articles consulted include: *News of the World*, April 5, 1964; *News of the World*, April 21, 1968; *Daily Mail*, October 5, 1968; *Daily Telegraph*, January 16, 1969.

CHAPTER 2

Interviewees include: Harold Brooks-Baker, Michael Cole, Paul Arengo Jones (the International Award's secretary general for the Duke of Edinburgh

Award), Lady Colin Campbell, and author interview for *US* magazine with Prince Charles's valet, Stephen Barry.

Documentary viewed: *Gordonstoun at Fifty*, BBC TV.

Articles consulted include: *Sun*, July 17, 1971; *Sun*, December 3, 1971; *Sun*, August 2, 1973; *Daily Telegraph*, September 24, 1973; *Daily Mirror*, December 18, 1974; the *Evening Standard*, October 18, 1994; the *News of the World*, September 13, 1987; the *Evening News*, August 28, 1980; the *Daily Mail*, November 14, 1989, by Rodney Tyler.

CHAPTER 3

Interviewees include: Gina Oates and Anne Adlington.

Re: Michelle Riles. Michelle Riles professed to be writing a book about her alleged liaison with Prince Edward. But after the palace issued an injunction, she did not. Nor has she appeared to benefit from the revelation that she took Prince Edward's virginity. Her sister, Gina Oates, revealed in an interview for this book that her sister, who is now in her mid-thirties, is still working as a chambermaid in London. She lives with her brother at times and moves around a lot. She has not married.

Articles consulted include: the *People*, February 18, 1998; the *Sun*, March 10, 1982; the *Daily Mail*, November 29, 1983; *Sunday Express*, July 10, 1983; *Daily Express*, March 10, 1983; the *Sun*, September 15, 1982; *News of the World*, by Clive Goodman; *Sunday Mirror* feature by Tim Wilcox, March 28, 1993; *Sunday Mirror*, July 29, 1990.

CHAPTER 4

Interviewees include: Sir Alan Cotterell, former Master of Jesus College; Lady Cotterell; Claudette Bryanston-Cross, the Cambridge Youth Theatre; Paul Daniels; Charles Barron, artistic director, Haddo House; a guest who was at Haddo to witness Edward's performance in *The Taming of the Shrew*; Rose Tobias Shaw; Sir Tim Rice; Richard Baker, his costar at Haddo, shared his memories of Prince Edward.

Re: Edward winning a place at Cambridge despite his low grades. During my interview with Sir Alan Cotterell, he intimated that admission to Cambridge is a two-way street and that when deciding whether or not to admit a particular student, the college based its decision not solely on what the college could do for the student but what the student could do for the college. In Edward's case, his contribution to the college, in terms of prestige and notoriety, was unimpeachably positive.

The Jesus College prospectus was consulted.

Articles consulted include: *Daily Telegraph*, November 16, 1982; *Daily Mail*, August 16, 1983; *Sunday Times*, October 9, 1983; *Daily Telegraph*, October 3, 1983; *Mail on Sunday*, March 4, 1984; *Daily Telegraph*, April 7, 1984; *Stop Press*, November 11, 1983; *Daily Mirror*, August 31, 1984; *Daily Express*, March 29, 1985; *Times*, April 3, 1986; *Today*, June 28, 1986.

CHAPTER 5

Interviewees include: Sir Alan Cotterell, Charles Barron, Lieutenant Colonel Ewen Southby Tailyour, Michael Cole, Lady Colin Campbell, and Brigadier Robert Tailyour.

Articles consulted include: *Daily Mail*, March 31, 1999; the *Times*, June 28, 1983; the *Sun*, December 29, 1984; Caroline Philips interview, *Today*, January 13, 1987; *Daily Express*, January 21, 1987; *Daily Telegraph*, April 2, 1987; "Tough Life for a Prince," *Express and Echo*, August 8, 1986; the *Western Morning News*, May 20, 1982.

CHAPTER 6

Interviewees include: Michael Cole, Noreen Taylor, James Whitaker; Bryan Forbes shared his memories of Prince Edward with the author.

It's a Royal Knockout program was viewed, as was the *Introductory Video* to *It's a Royal Knockout*.

Articles consulted include: *Daily Express*, February 3, 1987; *Daily Mail*, February 1987; *Mail on Sunday*, April 5, 1987; *Daily Telegraph*, May 20, 1987; *Daily Telegraph*, June 29, 1987; *Sunday Mirror*, October 31, 1987; November 18, 1987.

CHAPTER 7

Interviewees include: John Whitney, former managing director of Really Useful Theatre; Michael Cole; Brenda Bland.

Articles consulted include: *Daily Telegraph*, November 5, 1987; *Sunday Mirror*, October 31, 1995; by Tim Wilcox, *Today*, June 26, 1989; *Daily Mail*, January 19, 1988; *Daily Telegraph*, 1988; *Sunday Mirror*, January 24, 1988; the *Times*, February 19, 1988; *Today*, February 25, 1988; *Daily Express*, July 21, 1988; *Today*, February 20, 1989.

CHAPTER 8

Interviewees include: Roy Greenslade, Simon Fanshawe, Stewart Dickson, Nigel Dempster, Roger Penhale; Lady Colin Campbell; confidential source in British theater world, Geraldine Aaron shared her memories of Prince Edward with me.

Re: Edward being gay. A royal insider told the author that she had heard, in great detail, about Edward's heterosexual lovemaking from a girlfriend who had been to bed with him. Nonetheless, gossip about Edward's alleged homosexuality continued to be repeated to me—none of it remotely substantiable.

Articles consulted include: *Evening Standard*, January 22, 1990; *Daily Mail*, May 14, 1990; Sunday *Times*, June 24, 1990; *Today*, July 20, 1990; "The Lonely Prince and Friends," by Paul Palmer, *Daily Mail*, October 30, 1989; *Daily Mail*, June 21, 1990; *People*, October 27, 1991; *Weekend* magazine interview by Frances Hardy, *Daily Mail*, November 15, 1997.

CHAPTER 9

Interviewees include: Nigel Dempster, Nora Veysey, Miss Margaret James, Robin Peverett, Mary Cavalero, the Reverend Trevor Vickery, confidential source who has worked with Sophie in public relations, Ben Ronaldson.

The brochures for Dulwich Preparatory School and Kent College were consulted.

Articles consulted include: the *Daily Mail*, by Edward Verity, November 8,

1993; Caroline Philips, *News of the World*, December 26, 1993; *News of the World*, December 19, 1993; by Andrew Morton; *Mail on Sunday*, December 5, 1993, by Louette Harding, interview with Jo Last by Caroline Graham, feature by Rebecca Hardy and Edward Verity, March 19, 1994: The *Sun*, August 26, 1995; *Punch* by Garth Gibbs and Sean Smith, *Sunday Mirror* Special by David Rowe.

CHAPTER 10

Interviewees include: Harold Brooks-Baker, Mark Nicholls, Lady Colin Campbell, confidential source associated with MacLaurin's company, and confidential source who worked for Ardent.

Also consulted, press release from Dale C. Olson and Associates, December 10, 1993.

Articles consulted include: *Mail on Sunday*, November 7, 1993; *Daily Mail*, November 8, by Edward Verity; the *Daily Express*, April 29, 1994; April 19, 1994, The *Times*, by Louise McElvogue; the *Yorkshire Post*, February 9, 1994; *Today*, April 26, 1994; the *Guardian*, May 27, 1994; the *Daily Telegraph*, December 21, 1993; the *Daily Mail*, December 20, 1993; the *Los Angeles Times*, December 11, 1993; *Mail on Sunday*, December 5, 1993, by Louette Harding; *Sunday Independent*, February 6, 1994, the Caroline Philips interview.

CHAPTER 11

James Campbell shared his recollections of Sophie with me in a letter. Judy Ledger also gave me exclusive quotes in a letter on her relationship with Sophie.

Baby Lifeline press release.

Donations to Baby Lifeline can be sent to Baby Lifeline, Empathy Enterprise Building, Bramston Crescent, Tile Hill Lane, Tile Hill, Coventry, CV4 9SW, England (telephone: 01203 422135/ fax: 01203 422136).

Articles consulted include: the *Birmingham Post*, November 18, 1996; the *Warwick Courier*, November 22, 1996; *Sunday Mirror*, by Andrew Golden, "The Palace is Blamed As Sophie Storms Out on Charity," November 1996;

Wolverhampton Express and Star, February 1994; the *Sunday Express*, March 6, 1994; *Daily Express*, March 17, 1994; *Daily Express*, March 28, 1994; the *Mirror*, April 29, 1994; *Women's Wear Daily*.

CHAPTER 12

Interviewees include: Steve Gruen, Desmond Wilcox, Esther Rantzen, Phillipe Goubert, Mark Andre Relave, Christine Carter, Martin Sole, two confidential sources who worked closely with Edward. Interviews done in New York: Cornelia Guest, Laurence Kraches; Mme Masson, Alexander Slater.

Programs viewed: Man Alive Group documentaries *Putting on the Ritz*, and *Edward and Mrs. Simpson—Going, Going Gone*, and *Edward on Edward*, Parts 1 and 11.

Articles consulted include: *Today*, July 14, 1995; *Daily Mail*, April 23, 1996; Topaz Amoore's interview with Prince Edward, *Sunday Express*, July 1998; Judy Wade, the *Sun*, April 23, 1996; Robert Hardman, *Daily Telegraph*, April 6, 1996.

CHAPTER 13

Interviewees include: Mark Nicholls, Derek Draper, Steve Poole, James Robinson, Nigel Dempster, and confidential source who was employed by Ardent for a substantial period.

Video viewed: *Glam Slam* pilot.

Articles consulted include: the *Observer*, September 3, 1995; the *Guardian*, January 11, 1996; the *Times*, January 20, 1996; the *Sunday Times*, August 11, 1996; the *Sun*, June 29, 1996, by Andrew Morton; the *Sunday Times*, October 27, 1996; *Hello*, December 7, 1996; *Daily Mail*, December 12, 1996; *Daily Express*, April 4, 1997; the *Times*, *Weekend*, *Daily Express*, January 15, 1997, November 1, 1997, by Bill Frost; "The Producer Formerly Known as Prince" by Jim White, the *Independent*; "Out and About in the Edwardian Age," by Irene Lacher, *Los Angeles Times*, March 1, 1998.

CHAPTER 14

Interviewees include: Lady Colin Campbell, Roy Greenslade, Robert Lacey, and Harold Brooks-Baker.

Re: Advance knowledge of the engagement from Robin Bextor. Robin Bextor and I sat next to one another at a Christmas party held at Michel's Restaurant in Chiswick, London, on December 14, 1998. Bextor was charming and the conversation centered around *Legends*, the upcoming Ardent production on Mick Jagger. We talked again on the telephone in January 1999. In that conversation, we arranged to have lunch on February 11 at Quo Vadis restaurant in Soho. In the course of that conversation, Robin revealed, "When we met at the Christmas party, I already knew about the engagement."

Articles consulted include: the *Guardian*, January 7, 1999, by Julie Burchill; the *Daily Mirror*, June 7, 1999; the *Daily Express*, by Anthony Holden; the *Daily Mirror*, by James Whitaker; the *Mail on Sunday*, by Fiona Barton, January 10, 1999; the Sunday *Times*, January 10, 1999; the *Sunday Telegraph*, by Vicki Woods, January 10, 1999; *Hello*, January 16, 1999; *Daily Telegraph*, by Julia Robson and Sandra Barwick, January 7, 1999; the *Evening Standard*, January 7, 1999.

Bibliography

ALLISON, Ronald and Sarah Ridell. *The Royal Encyclopaedia*. Macmillan, 1991.

AUSTEN, Jane. *Pride and Prejudice*. Penguin Books.

BAGEHOT, Walter. *The English Constitution*. Rpt. Chapman and Hall, 1993.

BARRY, Stephen. *Royal Service: My Twelve Years as Valet to Prince Charles*. Macmillan, 1983.

BARRY, Stephen. *Royal Secrets*. 1985.

BRADFORD, Sarah. *Elizabeth*. Riverhead Books, 1996.

CAMPBELL, Lady Colin. *Diana in Private: The Princess Nobody Knows*. Smith Gryphon, 1992.

CAMPBELL, Lady Colin. *Royal Marriages*. Smith Gryphon, 1993.

CRAWFORD, Marion. *The Little Princesses*. Duckworth, 1993.

DEMPSTER, Nigel. *HRH The Princess Margaret, A Life Unfulfilled*. Quartet, 1991.

DEMPSTER, Nigel, and Peter Evans. *Behind Palace Doors*. Orion, 1993.

DIMBLEBY, Jonathon. *The Prince of Wales*. Warner Books, 1995.

DUFF, David. *Queen Mary*. Collins, 1985.

EDGAR, Donald. *The Queen's Children*. Hamlyn, 1979.

EDWARDS, Anne. *Matriarch: Queen Mary and the House of Windsor*. Hodder and Stoughton, 1984.

EGGAR, Robin. *Commando Survival of the Fittest*. John Murray, 1994.

FOSTER, Nigel. *The Making of a Marine Commando*.

FRIEDMAN, Dennis. *Inheritance: A Psychological History of the Royal Family*. Sidgwick and Jackson, 1988.

GARNER, Valerie, and Jayne Fincher. *"My young Friends—": The Queen's Young Family*. Weidenfeld and Nicholson, 1989.

GIBBS, Garth, and Sean Smith. *Sophie's Kiss*. Blake, 1997.

HARRIS, Kenneth. *The Queen*. Weidenfeld and Nicholson, 1994.

HOLDEN, Charles. *A Biography*. Bantam Press, 1998.

HRH The Prince Edward, *Knockout: The Grand Charity Tournament*. Collins, 1987.

JAMES, Paul. *Anne: The Working Princess*. Piatkus, 1987.

JAMES, Paul. *Prince Edward: A Life in the Spotlight*. Piatkus, 1992.

JAY, Antony. *Elizabeth R: The Role of the Monarchy Today*. BBC Books, 1992.

KELLEY, Kitty. *The Royals*. Warner Books, 1997.

KORTESIS, Vasso. *The Duchess of York Uncensored*. Blake, 1996.

LACEY, Robert. *Majesty*. Hutchinson, 1977.

LONGFORD, Elizabeth. *Elizabeth R*. Weidenfeld and Nicholson, 1983.

MARTIN, Ralph. *Charles and Diana*. Grafton, 1986.

McNIGHT, Gerald. *Andrew Lloyd Webber: A Biography*. Granada, 1984.

MORTON, Andrew. *Diana—Her True Story in Her Own Words*. Michael O'Mara Books, 1997.

Oxford English Dictionary, 2nd ed., vol. 1. Clarendon Press, Oxford, 1989.

PARKER, John. *Prince Philip: His Secret Life, 1991*.

PEARSON, John. *The Selling of the Royal Family*. Simon & Schuster, 1986.

PIMLOTT, Ben. *The Queen*. HarperCollins, 1996.

A Royal Wedding: Prince Edward and Sophie. Dennis Publications.

RUSSELL, Peter. *Butler Royal*. Hutchinson, 1982.

SEWARD, Ingrid. *Prince Edward*. Century, 1995.

SEWARD, Ingrid. *Royal Children*. HarperCollins, 1993.

WALSH, Michael. *Andrew Lloyd Webber*. Viking, 1989.

WILSON, A. N. *The Rise and Fall of the House of Windsor*. Isis, 1993.

YORK, Sarah, Duchess of, with Jeff Coplon. *My Story*. Simon & Schuster, 1996.

Acknowledgments

First and foremost, I am extremely grateful to Cassandra Wilcox for her impeccable research, stellar interviewing, and diligence in working on every aspect of the book.

Debra Kasler's secretarial work was greatly appreciated.

During rare interludes between researching, interviewing, and writing, the Phillimore Club in Kensington—where Sarah Perrett was my enthusiastic personal trainer and owner Andrea Dennis offered friendly encouragement—provided an oasis of tranquillity.

Many thanks to Ann Chubb, Jackie Modlinger, and Sandy Williams for their styling advice.

Jo Hansford in Mount Street, Mayfair, where my hair was colored by Sarah Jane O'Brien and cut by Graham Hamps, was a serene and stylish haven.

Thanks, too, to Vanya Jankovic at Harvey Nichols for her beauty treatments and Neve Mooney for her hairstyles.

Throughout the research and writing of the book, my life, both professional and personal, was immeasurably enhanced by my conversations with Dr. Erika Padan Freeman, whose wisdom, insights, and brilliance are unparalleled.

I am very grateful to Alexander Smithline for his advice and skill in guiding the book during the early stages.

I should like to thank my literary agent, David Vigliano, for his counsel, enthusiasm, and encouragement.

Jameson Maskey and Alice Henfrey of the *Express* were wonderful in providing pictures for the book. At Pocket Books, endless thanks to Emily Bestler, Donna Ruvituso, Donna O'Neill, Linda Dingler, Joann Foster, Twisne Fan, Lisa Feuer, Henry Krawitz, Laura Mullen, Pam Duevel, Felice Javit, Laura Hardman, and the unflappable Amanda Ayers.

Above all, my deepest thanks goes to my creative and supportive editor, Mitchell Ivers of Pocket Books, whose foresight and talent have made this book possible.

INDEX

About the Author

WENDY LEIGH began her journalistic career at BBC Television in London. She is the author of several biographies, including *Arnold: The Unauthorized Biography of Arnold Schwarzenegger*, *Liza: Born a Star*, and *Prince Charming: The JFK, Jr., Story*. She has contributed to a wide variety of publications, including the *London Sunday Times*, the *London Daily Telegraph*, the *Daily Mail*, the *Mail on Sunday*, *People*, *Elle*, *Ladies' Home Journal*, *McCall's*, *Marie Claire*, *US*, *British GQ*, and *Cosmopolitan*. She currently lives in London, and is an associate producer for the Man Alive Group, which co-produced *Edward on Edward* with Prince Edward. Ms. Leigh has appeared on *Entertainment Tonight*, *Geraldo*, CNBC, CNN, the E! Channel, and the A&E *Biography* series.